Identity, Social Class and Learning in the 'Bottom' Reading Group is an eloquent and beautifully written account of the negative impact of ability grouping. It brings to life the voices of a largely unheard group, revealing the damage inflicted on children, as well as providing practical, research-informed ways of making teaching and learning fairer.
Prof. Diane Reay, *University of Cambridge, UK*

A fascinating and important book about disrupting reading hierarchies. Through it, Jess Anderson details children's perspectives on being in the 'bottom reading group', considers how ability-grouped reading reproduces social inequalities, and offers layered evidence that mixed ability grouping affords more scope and hope for young readers. A valuable read for all educators.
Prof. Teresa Cremin, *The Open University, UK*

IDENTITY, SOCIAL CLASS AND LEARNING IN THE 'BOTTOM' READING GROUP

The common practice of ability-grouped reading in UK schools, often termed *guided reading*, influences children's sense of identity, feelings and progress as readers. Drawing on a rich ethnographic study of three primary classrooms, this book reopens a critical inquiry into ability-grouped reading that has been quiet since the 1990s, when guided reading in literacy education became established practice in the UK and the US.

Through the lens of children's agency in accommodating, resisting and at times transforming such reading pedagogy, the book shows how readers are shaped by ability-grouped reading and by the more egalitarian reading pedagogies introduced in the study. Children's individual and collective experiences are brought to life through extended narratives that attend as closely to gesture, posture, visage, silences and prosody of speech as to spoken words.

The book ends with a provocation: how literacy pedagogy might change if reflexive noticing and dismantling of hierarchies become the compass of pedagogical change. This demands attention to structural inequalities around race, gender and class and a turn towards deep listening to children. As well as being a valuable read for scholars of the sociology of childhood and education, it should appeal to anyone concerned with making education more equitable, including teachers, school leaders, parents, carers and policymakers.

Jess Anderson is a post-doctoral fellow in the Faculty of Social Sciences at the University of Stirling. A primary teacher and teacher educator for many years, she brings a practitioner lens as well as theoretical and research perspectives to issues of social equity and inequity in primary school literacies.

Routledge Advances in Critical Diversities

Routledge Advances in Critical Diversities provides an exciting new publishing space to critically consider practices, meanings and understandings of "diversity", inequality and identity across time and place. The book series will have a particular focus on developing an extended conceptualization of diversity and division which incorporates dimensions of political, social, economic and cultural, as well as the bodily and intimate, to consider how diversity is lived-in, inhabited, mobilised and refused.

Series Editors:
Yvette Taylor, *University of Strathclyde, UK*
Sally Hines, *University of Sheffield, UK*
For book proposals please contact the series editors or Emily Briggs in Routledge at Emily.Briggs@tandf.co.uk

Situated Mixedness
Understanding Migration-Related Intimate Diversity in Belgium
Edited by Asuncion Fresnoza-Flot

Intersex, Variations of Sex Characteristics, DSD
Critical Approaches
Surya Monro, Adeline Berry, Morgan Carpenter, Daniela Crocetti, and Sean Saifa Wall

Identity, Social Class and Learning in the 'Bottom' Reading Group
Jess Anderson

For more information go to https://www.routledge.com/Routledge-Advances-in-Critical-Diversities/book-series/RACD

IDENTITY, SOCIAL CLASS AND LEARNING IN THE 'BOTTOM' READING GROUP

Jess Anderson

LONDON AND NEW YORK

Designed cover image: *Reading Imagines the World* by Lua Watt Tang

First published 2025
by Routledge
4 Park Square, Milton Park, Abingdon, Oxon OX14 4RN

and by Routledge
605 Third Avenue, New York, NY 10158

Routledge is an imprint of the Taylor & Francis Group, an informa business

© 2025 Jess Anderson

The right of Jess Anderson to be identified as author of this work has been asserted in accordance with sections 77 and 78 of the Copyright, Designs and Patents Act 1988.

All rights reserved. No part of this book may be reprinted or reproduced or utilised in any form or by any electronic, mechanical, or other means, now known or hereafter invented, including photocopying and recording, or in any information storage or retrieval system, without permission in writing from the publishers.

Trademark notice: Product or corporate names may be trademarks or registered trademarks, and are used only for identification and explanation without intent to infringe.

British Library Cataloguing-in-Publication Data
A catalogue record for this book is available from the British Library

Library of Congress Cataloging-in-Publication Data
Names: Anderson, Jess, author.
Title: Identity, social class and learning in the 'bottom' reading group / Jess Anderson.
Description: Abingdon, Oxon; New York, NY: Routledge, 2025. |
Series: Routledge advances in critical diversities |
Includes bibliographical references and index.
Identifiers: LCCN 2024046605 (print) | LCCN 2024046606 (ebook) |
ISBN 9781032785660 (hardback) | ISBN 9781032785677 (paperback) |
ISBN 9781003488514 (ebook)
Subjects: LCSH: Ability grouping in education–Great Britain. |
School children–Great Britain. | Reading–Great Britain.
Classification: LCC LB3061 .A45 2025 (print) | LCC LB3061 (ebook) |
DDC 371.2/540941–dc23/eng/20241127
LC record available at https://lccn.loc.gov/2024046605
LC ebook record available at https://lccn.loc.gov/2024046606

ISBN: 978-1-032-78566-0 (hbk)
ISBN: 978-1-032-78567-7 (pbk)
ISBN: 978-1-003-48851-4 (ebk)

DOI: 10.4324/9781003488514

Typeset in Sabon
by Deanta Global Publishing Services, Chennai, India

CONTENTS

List of Figures   x
List of Table   xi
Acknowledgements   xii

1   Ability-Grouped Reading   1
    Picture This 1
    The Research Project 4
    Two World Events 6
    Stories 8
    A Personal Reflection 11
    Reading Development, Literacy, Emotion and Identity 14
    Outline of the Book 15
    Notes 17
    References 19

2   Sociopolitical and Emotional Landscapes of
    Ability-Grouped Reading   22
    Introduction 22
    Social Class and Educational Research 23
    Capital Assets, Social Class and Children in the Study 27
    Guided Reading and Literacy Capital 28
    Ability Grouping across Age Phases and Subjects 32
    Emotion, Affect and Ability Grouping 35

Conclusion 39
Notes 40
References 41

3   A Feeling for Reading   47
    Introduction 47
    Enthusiastic Lovers of Stories 48
    Books in the Matrix of Children's Lives 53
    Reading Can Also Be a Wee Bit Nerve-Wracking 58
    Conclusion 64
    Notes 65
    References 65

4   Social Positioning in Hierarchical Reading Groups   68
    Introduction 68
    Appreciation for Ability-Grouped Reading 69
    "It's like Football Top 5": Elite Positioning in the 'Top'
        Reading Group 75
    Accommodation and Resistance to Positioning as a
        Struggling Reader 82
    Conclusion 88
    Notes 90
    References 91

5   How Class Matters in Classroom Reading Hierarchies   93
    Introduction 93
    Holding Readers in Place 94
    Not Down to Luck: Placement and Relationship in
        Hierarchical Reading Groups 99
    Family Habits and Reading Group Placement 102
    Conclusion 109
    Notes 111
    References 112

6   Print Reading Difficulties and Ability-Grouped Reading   115
    Introduction 115
    A Double Bind? Navigating Print Challenges in the
        'Bottom' Reading Group 117
    A Close Encounter with Print Reading Difficulties 121
    Developmental Dyslexia: Affordances and Limitations 124

*Affective Shifts, Cultural Resonance and Dissonance in
    Reader Experiences 126*
Symbolic Violence and the Tyranny of Print Literacy 130
Conclusion 134
Notes 135
References 136

7   Disrupting School-Based Reading Hierarchies   139
    Introduction 139
    Mixed-Attainment Reading 140
    Wee Books, Chapter Books and Who's the Top Reader 149
    A Radical Decentring of Print 153
    Conclusion 158
    Notes 159
    References 160

8   Conclusions   163
    Introduction 163
    Theoretical and Epistemological Influences 164
    *The 'Bottom' Reading Group: A Place of Learning,
        Sanctuary and Stigma 165*
    *Social Inequality and Discrimination through Ability-
        Grouped Reading 167*
    Disrupting Hierarchy in School-Based Reading 169
    Final Thoughts: Limits, Dissemination and Further Work 173
    Note 174
    References 174

*Appendix 1: Explanation and Example of a
                Running Reading Record*   177
*Appendix 2: Reading café picturebook selection centring
                and celebrating the lives of Children and
                Families of Colour*   180
Index   181

FIGURES

3.1	Self-portrait by Jamie	49
3.2	Self-portrait by Puzzle	51
3.3	Self-portrait by Millie	54
3.4	Self-portrait by Jeffy	56
3.5	Self-portrait by Lucia Jasmine	59
3.6	Self-portrait by Puffy	63
4.1	Self-portrait by Tom	70
4.2	Words made by Puffy with magnetic letters	73
4.3	Self-portrait by Bingo	75
4.4	Self-portrait by Kayla	78
5.1	Self-portraits by Bella May and Jack	105
5.2	Self-portrait by Lola	107
6.1	Self-portrait by Alf	119
7.1	Field sketch of Puzzle reading	142
7.2	Field sketch of George reading	143
7.3	Dog Man themed car built by Puzzle and Stella	148
9.1	Running reading record conducted with Jamie, Fairfield, Kelvin, 1 of 3	178
9.2	Running reading record conducted with Jamie, Fairfield, Kelvin, 2 of 3	179
9.3	Running reading record conducted with Jamie, Fairfield, Kelvin, 3 of 3	179

TABLE

2.1   Educational advantage in ability-grouped reading   31

ACKNOWLEDGEMENTS

The Vietnamese Buddhist monk and peace activist, Thích Nhất Hạnh, encouraged contemplation of all the natural elements and labour invested in bringing food to our table. When I contemplate this, I begin to appreciate our interconnectedness with other living beings and with the earth. Likewise, the inception, development and completion of this book has involved innumerable acts of generosity, love and support.

First and foremost, my thanks go to the brilliant, beautiful, funny, smart and sensitive children of the study who shared their lives, thoughts, fears and enthusiasms with me. My life is forever enriched from knowing you. And equally to the teachers and head teachers who welcomed me into their classrooms, shared my enthusiasm for the project, their invaluable expertise and who cared so passionately about those same children.

My life took a fortuitous turn in my early twenties, without which there would have been not the remotest possibility of undertaking the project, of which this book is a product. I give heartfelt thanks to all the people, past and present, who have accompanied me in this turn, sustained me and helped restore me to sanity and peace of mind. As my mum often says, things could have worked out so differently. But they would also have been very different without her love and that of my dad, and their passionate belief that education can be liberatory. When the opportunity presented itself to write this book I took it, for the learning it promised (and delivered).

Thanks to all at Routledge for your faith in the book. In particular, thanks to Lakshita Joshi for guiding me through the process of submission, to the reviewers and series editors, Yvette Taylor and Sally Hines. A special thanks to Lua Watt Tang for drawing the best book cover I could ever hope for, a cover that says so much about the wonderful places reading in all its forms can take us. Thanks to Gordon Hay too for the photographic work involved in the cover image.

Thanks also to the Economic and Social Research Council and to Renfrewshire Council, who co-funded the project upon which the book is based. Thanks in particular to Julie Paterson for your enthusiasm and belief in the project, and for your invaluable insider knowledge and wisdom.

I often reflect on the feedback I have received from Yvette Taylor, Virginie Thériault, Cara Blaisdell, Maddie Breeze, Navan Govender, Sarah Wilson and Zinnia Mevawalla. I have always appreciated it, but it was only when I got deeper into revising each chapter that I realised just how incisive and transforming your feedback has been.

Writing the book has incurred some pretty intense emotional labour, but this has been met in equal part with wisdom and kindness that transforms the fear into faith and curiosity, thanks to Farida Mutawalli, Nic Power, Elaine Murdie, Ajahn Candasiri, Ajahn Succito and my friends. Wisdom has also come from my community anti-racism group and library. A special thanks to Sapna Agarwal for your knowledge, insight, heart and fantastic children's book recommendations.

I would not like to imagine having to write without my writing pals, who let me know over and over again that the challenges I face are shared. Thank you to Seabo Morobolo for your courage, perseverance and emotional honesty. Thanks to all at the Saturday morning writing group and everyone at York (SZWG). Thanks to Jayne Artis and our weekly stints at the Mitchell Library, with refreshment, both spiritual and earthly, at the Ottoman Coffee House. And to Sidonie Ecochard, for our early conversations that helped demystify the writing of Bourdieu. Thanks also to Rukhsar Hussain, Becky Gardiner, Sue McGonigle and Corinne Angier for reading chapters from the book and giving such helpful feedback. Thanks also to my teacher friend, Penny Browning, who has a fierce love for all her pupils and was so keen to try out the ideas in the book because she had a hunch they might help.

And thanks to you, my John Gordon, proof-reader extraordinaire, endless discusser of the ideas in this book, my dear earth-born companion and fellow mortal.

1
ABILITY-GROUPED READING

Picture This

The classroom is empty, and my observation notebook lies pristine and awkward on my lap. It is my first day of fieldwork in Avon[1] infant class at St Jude's, a small Roman Catholic primary school, situated in the more densely populated post-industrial central area of Scotland. It's early morning and the teacher has gone to collect the children from their parents, grandparents and carers in the playground. I hear children's voices calling out to each other, getting louder as they make their way into school and along the corridor, the odd adult voice above this, feet stamping. As the children enter the classroom, some seem surprised to see me, their eyes widening. One boy comes over and says, "Something's changed for me," and shows me a wobbly tooth. The children drink from their water bottles and put their bags in a big bright-red plastic container. One of the boys, who I will come to know as George, heads over and asks what I am making notes about. Another asks if I am teaching them today and I say no, that I'm here to hang out and see what they're up to. The teacher asks the children to stand, face the altar and they begin to recite a familiar prayer. I make a note to learn this prayer, so that I can join in and show respect for this daily act of worship at St Jude's.

Prayer complete, chairs scrape back and the children sit down at their desks. The children had previously chosen a pseudonym for the study and the teacher now walks around, calling for quiet, and pins their name/pseudonym badges on their jumpers to help me get to know them. Some pseudonyms recall favourite activities and precious relationships, like 'Chewbacca' who watches Star Wars with his dad and 'Puzzle' who chose part of her online gaming name as a pseudonym. The first activity of the day is independent

DOI: 10.4324/9781003488514-1

reading, and children collect their book or other reading material from their individual trays. George does not have a book and heads over to the book corner, where he spots a magazine. "There's a newspaper here, what's it doing here?" he asks, the words inflected with a note of outrage. "Maybe someone thought it would be good to read," responds the teacher. "Can I read this?" asks George, in a tone I hear as mild incredulity.

While the children read independently, the teacher calls the first reading group, the "Julia Donaldsons" to read with her, a group she describes as the "second top group". When she asks the children who wrote the book, two boys say the author's name in unison. "Jinx!" laughs Kieran, pointing his finger at Horris. The children are then asked to follow along the text with their "magic finger" as each child takes a turn to read a page aloud. The next group up is the 'top' group, the "Oliver Jeffers". "Fiction or non-fiction?" asks the teacher. A chorus of "non-fiction" chimes out. "Because it's real," says Sienna. In a tone that suggests they find it cute, some of the girls say, "Oh, baby crocodile." Tilly, who is not in the 'top' group, has wandered over to have a look. "Show Tilly the picture," instructs the teacher. "Awww," says Tilly, looking at the book.

Meanwhile, George, who has been watching as I make observation notes, comes over again to ask what I am writing in my notebook. He mentions the Pixies, pointing to children wearing Pixie cards around their neck who seem to be wandering around helping other children. I asked George if he could tell me about the Pixies. "They are the bosses," he tells me. "If you don't know what to do you ask them," he explains, "and if someone hurts you, you tell a Pixie and they say, 'don't hurt him'. You only go to the teacher in an emergency." Examples of emergencies, according to George, include fire, hearing a bad word and sticking up the middle finger. I ask him how you get to be a Pixie. "You get to be a Pixie if you're good," he explains, "you get to be a second teacher." He tells me to write this down, and I do.

I begin the book with this classroom scene, composed from fieldnotes, for two reasons. Firstly, it acts as a door opening for the reader into the playful, agentic, but also constraining, world of children's reading in the infant classroom. Secondly, I begin with the scene to highlight themes of identity and positioning around children's reading that I observed in the fieldwork at St Jude's and also at Fairfield, a nearby school, which are developed in the book. The first of these themes concerns the often inadvertent creation or reinforcement of social hierarchy that produces insiders and outsiders in classroom reading culture. The reading groups, named after popular children's authors, were organised around children's perceived level of print fluency. Despite their non-hierarchical names, they were frequently referred to as the top, middle and bottom groups.[2]

Hierarchy is signalled too by the Pixies. Although imagined as a practical means of supporting children with reading, the unintentional message conveyed is eloquently articulated by George. They are "the bosses" and "second teachers", both roles that carry authority within society to control and sanction others' behaviour. They are also, as George explains, chosen from the "good children". Since the Pixies were exclusively chosen from the 'top' reading group, how are children in the 'middle' and 'bottom' groups to interpret this, when the characteristic of "good" is ascribed only to those other than themselves? There is also the hint in this scene (explored more extensively in the book) of how different types of texts, and that of the printed word itself, come to be imbued with different levels of prestige and validity. This can be heard in George's initial indignation that a magazine should be found in the book corner. Yet, the choosing of pseudonyms also reveals children's emotional connection with other text types, such as film and computer games, and in this I imagine the children pushing back against the tyranny of the printed word in their worlds.

Lastly, it is interesting to pause on the gender norms, enacted within classroom reading, which are illustrated in the scene. There is the attraction of cute babies, albeit crocodiles, for girls in the reading group and for Tilly who moved across the classroom to have a look. The leading role that George assumes within the scene speaks again to gender normativity, as a boy who immediately called my attention as a knower and explainer. Always, we must ask ourselves as researchers, whose voices we are missing while others press forward. What is not visible within the scene, but is a central concern of this book, is the push and pull of social class, of race and ethnicity in children's experience of reading. Class and race were rarely spoken aloud in the study but rather signalled over and over in the ways children were positioned as readers within hierarchical reading groups and other forms of classroom reading.

The book offers children's perspectives on being in the 'bottom' reading group, within classed, gendered and raced relationships of power. It also tells the story of shifting pedagogically to mixed-attainment reading instruction and opens out to a meditation on the nature of reading itself. The term *mixed attainment* refers to contexts that allow children with different skills, knowledge and understandings to work together. The study, its motivations, methods, context and participants, is introduced in the next section, *The Research Project*. Following this is *Two World Events*, in which global occurrences are discussed that changed the shape of the study from the initial project design and prompted reflection on my interactions with the children. *Telling Stories of Children's Reading* introduces the concept of story in the research and how this is utilised in the book. All histories are classed and raced, and in *A Personal Reflection*, I articulate how my positionality has both illuminated and occluded understanding and interpretation in the study. Finally, given that pedagogies of reading development are highly contested, I offer an overview of theories of reading employed in the book in the section, *Reading Development, Literacy, Emotion and Identity*. My intention is to provide theoretical background on what will be meant by the term *reading*, as well as introducing what I assume supports children's reading development. The chapter will close with *An Outline of the Book*.

The Research Project

I first became interested in researching children's experience in the 'bottom' reading group when, as a literacy researcher, I encountered a way of teaching reading using mixed-attainment groupings.[3] Prior to this research post I had been a primary teacher and teacher educator for many years. On hearing the new method, an uncomfortable memory arose from my teaching years, of refusing a refugee parent's request to move her son from the lowest-positioned group where she feared he was falling further behind in learning to read in English. Despite my commitment to mixed-attainment learning, I, like many teachers, had never found a viable way out of these fixed reading groups because of the need to match children with a level of text they can decipher without meaning breaking down and frustration arising (Bodman & Franklin, 2014; Clay, 1993). And so many of us have relied on hierarchical reading groups even when philosophically opposed to those hierarchies, because we simply couldn't see a way to teach less fluent readers otherwise.

The study upon which this book is based took place in Avon infant class (previously introduced) and in two other classrooms: Clyde, also at St Jude's and Kelvin in Fairfield Primary nearby. The children were between the ages of 6 and 9. Pupils at St Jude's came mostly from the large estate that surrounds the school, which has a mixture of private and social housing. The area, a suburb of a small town, has a row of convenience shops and a train station. I identified all children as White[4] and mostly of Scottish heritage. Two children in the study were Polish and spoke Polish as their first language. Using Savage's (2015) Bourdieusian conceptualisation of class, which is explained in Chapter 2, the majority could be situated in the hazy middle between working and lower middle classes. A small minority were either traditionally middle class or economically poor. Fairfield, situated in the large town near St Jude's, serves an area with one of the highest instances of economic poverty in Scotland[5] and this was reflected in the economic composition of the school's population. There were lower numbers of families in the hazy middle compared with St Jude's, and fewer traditionally middle-class families. There were three Children of Colour in the study at Fairfield, each of Pakistani heritage. Two spoke Urdu as a first language and one English as a first language, though his parents were Sindhi speakers. Most of the children were White and of Scottish heritage. One White child had Slovakian heritage and spoke Slovak as a first language. In terms of gender, 22 girls and 40 boys participated in the study. No children said they identified as non-binary or as a gender different to the one assigned at birth. In Clyde, there were almost three times more boys than girls. I was told this by one of the girls who when asked what that was like said, "*You know,* nightmare!" Her words reflected frequent comments by staff that perceived the boys as harder to manage, less compliant and more boisterous.

The study was ethnographic, which means I hung out, observed, listened, talked and kept field notes of classroom life one day each week over the course of two years.[6] Such ethnographic immersion allows reading and readers to be observed relationally and understood in the situated natural, emotional and interconnected ways they develop (Calderón López & Thériault, 2017; Dunn, 2004). Ethnography has the potential to create space for children's affective, social and intellectual experience to matter most in research inquiry (Street, 2002). Because of generational power dynamics within schools and wider society, children's perspectives are more likely to emerge when adults immerse in children's world, tuning into what Christensen (2004) calls their "cultures of communication".

Four research methods were employed in the ethnography: observation, audio-taped facilitated conversations, reading with children and the intervention of mixed-attainment reading.[7] I observed classroom life generally, but my focus was on reading events. These reading events included: ability-grouped and mixed-attainment reading with the teacher, children reading together or alone through choice or teacher direction, incidental chats about reading, teachers reading and discussing texts with the whole class and picturebook-focused reading cafes. I observed how children felt or appeared to feel about reading and about themselves as readers. Patterns of sociability around reading were noted, how children positioned themselves and were positioned by others. What happened pedagogically in different reading groups was also a focus of inquiry. I was interested in how class, race and gender were lived in these reading encounters. When mixed-attainment reading instruction was introduced the observation focus was on how its introduction affected existing hierarchies around reading, reader identities, feelings about reading and the changes and challenges it prompted.

As well as being in the classroom, I engaged in audio-taped facilitated conversation[8] with individual children and small groups that generally lasted around 40 minutes. The term *facilitated conversations* comes from childhood researchers such as Christensen (2004) who emphasise the need to loosen one's research agenda enough to allow conversations to develop from children's points of reference. At times, I realised in hindsight that some questions I asked were soaked in middle-class assumptions that centred intergenerational (book) reading. This centring might have delegitimised other aspects of children's literacy lives. Yet despite these limitations, much of our conversation *was* free flowing and led enthusiastically by the children. In this way, there was more time spent gossiping, and talking about friendship, football, computer games, worries and home life than talking directly about reading. Through this I got a sense of the weight, space and shifting position that reading took up in their complex inner and outer/social lives.

The third research method, reading with the children, combined research skills with pedagogical knowledge of reading to gain insights into children as readers. When reading with children, I was interested in how they engaged with and talked about books. I observed what happened when they read, both affectively (in body, gesture, words and facial expression) and in the strategies they used to decipher print and illustrations. Children chose whether to read to me, us read together or me read to them. Some children, for example, did not like being observed stumbling on a word and chose not to read to me. I also spent a day at Fairfield conducting running reading records with the children, which showed how closely children's reading book, and thus their reading group, matched their level of print fluency. Through this assessment I identified children who were misplaced in their reading group. How social class and ethnicity mattered in these misallocations is discussed in Chapter 5 (for an example and details of how running reading records work, see Appendix 1).

Finally, in terms of methods, mixed-attainment reading instruction was introduced as an intervention at St Jude's, but not Fairfield. Its introduction had been delayed at Fairfield and, unfortunately, was planned for the week schools closed because of the COVID-19 pandemic in 2020, making its introduction unviable. For the intervention, I worked with the teachers at St Jude's to develop a pedagogical understanding of a mixed-attainment approach to reading development, as follows. In brief, the children (reading different books) are brought together in random groups, discuss, for example, what they would do if stuck on a word, read aloud to themselves while the teacher moves round, coaching them individually and then they come together again to work out unfamiliar words in each other's books.

Two World Events

For a few weeks before schools closed in efforts to limit the spread of the coronavirus it felt like I and the teachers were trying to outrun a sandstorm, hoping to conclude the fieldwork before the storm engulfed and derailed the project. The surrealness of that moment is captured in this fieldnote from St Jude's Clyde class:

> The children come into class ... from his bag Jeffy produces a taut red balloon and a colourful packet of hand wipes. He tells Will and Jay the hand wipes are to wipe his hands. Within five minutes I have heard the word, "coronavirus" six times.

Two weeks later, Scottish schools closed and the exploration into mixed-attainment reading that had begun a month earlier at St Jude's came to an abrupt pause. It was a strange time. I felt as if I had abandoned my participants; my night-time dreams were vivid. There were days when I woke to find Chicken Licken had taken up residence inside me. Chicken Licken, a character from a European children's folk tale, runs frantically from one animal to another warning them that the sky is falling in.

As the consumerist fabric of society quietened, cafés and bars boarded up, and the skies emptied of planes, society was locked down. In the oddness of this moment, I sought ground in reading fictional narratives. One of my preparation-for-lock-down purchases was not a large pile of toilet rolls (as reportedly it was for many) but the very fat new book by Hilary Mantell (2020), *The Mirror and the Light*. I felt a settling, that I would be in good company in the lockdown with Hilary Mantel, Thomas Cromwell, his kith and kin. This being the third of a trilogy, I was excited to live again in the evening light among the orchards of Austin Friars.

Reading first worked this settling magic and welcome transportation, when as a child I found myself climbing up *The Magic Faraway Tree*, in the prolific hands of the children's author, Enid Blyton(1943). Oblivious to her racial stereotyping and my real-life exclusion from the cosy middle-class worlds she created, I found myself at home in the fictional Land of Do-As-You-Please and Topsy-Turvy. It offered relief from the boredom, and sometimes tension, of my childhood home. Later, in tumultuous teenage years, I found escape and solace in the wild heaths and market towns of Thomas Hardy's Wessex. I vicariously lived through characters such as Bathsheba, Tess and Eustacia.

It is unsurprising then that my first thought on the shock of school closure was to find ways to read to my child participants. I imagined how lockdown might unsettle them, curtail freedoms and connection, as well as exacerbate social inequalities. I read, and recorded, a chapter a day to post in the children's online learning community, starting with the delightfully silly *Ottoline and the Yellow Cat*, by Chris Riddell (2010). My preference for reading emotionally complex fiction with children was temporarily replaced by a desire for unrealistic simplicity and guaranteed happy endings. In the virtual learning hubs, which had been hastily set up by schools, the children could also communicate with me, write or post video responses to the story. In these virtual ways, the fieldwork continued from March until the July summer break.

When schools reopened in August 2020, mixed-attainment reading continued at St Jude's. Since, at this point, schools only allowed entry to adults essential to the running of the school, I continued to research mixed-attainment reading through monthly virtual conversations with the two study teachers who practised it. It would be later again (May 2021) before I could return to school for a six-week period, by which time I was able to observe mixed-attainment reading as an established practice and to engage in individual and group conversations with the children about reading.

The second world event, that of anti-racism protest following George Floyd's murder in the US by a White policeman, further influenced the research, particularly the analysis of my interactions with the children. Like thousands of others, I took part in protests and joined an anti-racism discussion group. I began reading material, largely written by Black, Indigenous and other People of Colour, that challenged my self-view as a White life-long anti-racist (e.g., Akala, 2019; Kimmerer, 2013; Menakem, 2021). Growing up, I was socialised with conversations at home about the injustice of racial inequality and its deep roots in capitalism. From my teenage years I protested against and challenged racism acted out by others and felt by others.

It was this belief that racism happens 'over there', in hatred, that has been most challenged since 2020. Eddo-Lodge (2017, p. 64–65) eloquently describes how racism is also enacted in "silently raised eyebrows (and) snap judgements made on perceptions of competencies." DiAngelo (2018) highlights the sense of superiority internalised by White people of which they are often unaware or can't admit to themselves. I was relieved to read this because I recognised the unwelcome racialised judgements that sometimes arise in my own mind. I found hope in her words because if White people can be conditioned into White superiority, then I could be unconditioned, even if as DiAngelo also suggests, this is always a work-in-progress. These insights sent me back to my field material to question how my Whiteness, my racialised assumptions and comfort-zones, showed up in my relationships with the children in the study and the stories I tell of these relationships; I elaborate on this in Chapter 4.

Stories

The children's stories, told either in their own words or narrated by me, are the beating heart of the book. They are the medium through which more abstract meditations on reading, reading groups, identity and power are formed and made more relatable. In this epistemological centring of story, I find myself in the good company of working-class feminist academics who demonstrate the affective and analytical power of elaborate participant narratives (e.g., Lareau, 2011; Luttrell, 2020; Reay, 2002, 2017). In a well-worn pamphlet, entitled *Stories and Meanings* (1985), Rosen talks of the enduring place of story in human experience, stories which crisscross geography, ethnicity, class, gender and generations. It is so universal that it must, he concludes, be wired into the core processes of what make us human. We select and interpret from a hotchpotch of events, people and objects, much as we do in telling the story of a research project (Lawler, 2014).

Ethnography allows stories to be told that have a different centre of gravity from the adult social scientist's concerns and assumptions. In the children's words and affective movements, they are the knowers of their positions, feelings and actions. They were also the known, to the extent that I was the listener, watcher and interpreter of their perspectives. I am motivated to tell these stories by the possibilities they hold of showing complexities of children's reading experience. In short, I hope the stories afford the children the complicated emotional and intellectual lives that are often hegemonically denied to those less economically or socially powerful in society (Steedman, 1987). Although all knowing is partial, contextual, interpretative and situated in relationships of power, I am motivated to give as faithful and plausible an account of the children's perspectives as I can.

Analysing and telling stories of children's reading was as much about feeling as about being methodical, though I was also methodical through thematic analysis of fieldnotes, conversation transcripts and reflexive journaling. In trusting to feeling I was encouraged by Reay (2017, p. 6) who describes her analysis as "an incomplete patchwork of narratives … that owes as much to intuition and feeling as it does to scholarly rigour." I began the interpretive process by composing narrative portraits of children in the 'bottom' reading group. The term *narrative portrait* was devised by Rodríguez-Dorans and Jacobs (2020) to describe a composition made from selecting and reordering fieldnotes, interviews and other documents to construct narratives that foreground and prioritise the stories people tell about themselves (2020). It can interrupt the privileging of researcher analysis and interpretation. The authors acknowledge, however, as I do, that the depriviging of the researcher is always partial. Narrative portraits, through selection and ordering, will still reflect the stance of the inquirer.

Composing the narrative portraits involved slow, iterative and close reading of fieldnotes, searching them for mention of particular children, and listening again to audio tapes and reading transcribed conversations. By beginning with the individual child, my appreciation of each participant grew, and I noticed their more subtle ways of being in the world that might have been overlooked. The portraits serve a triple purpose. Firstly, each one that appears in the book was chosen and developed to illustrate significant themes that I identified in the empirical material, in conversation with Bourdieu's conceptual tools, which are described in Chapter 2. Secondly, narrative portraiture provided the space for multisensory forms of communication to convey meanings rather than cutting off parts of speech from the context in which those words were spoken. And thirdly, the portraits make the individual children more present in the book. I hope this personalisation increases the emotional and intellectual connections between the book's subject and the reader. To develop this quality of presence, I also invited children to draw self-portraits, some of which appear in the book.

And so, narrative portraiture overlapped with, informed and was informed by a thematic analysis of the empirical material. I transcribed all the conversations with children myself, which allowed me to listen not just to the words but how the words were said, the tone, volume and prosody of the words. While transcribing, I noted children's feeling states mentioned in fieldnotes from the day of the conversation. As such, the transcription was a multimodal process as well as a reflexive one, as I thought through the ethical and sociopolitical implications and limitations of representing the children's words using standard and non-standard orthographies. Since the book is concerned with sociocultural influences on ability-grouped reading and in appreciating children's individuality, I chose to evoke the character of the speaker in ways that did not flatten their linguistic differences. In this there was no attempt at a full phonological transcription, which I believe would risk losing the meaning of the words in the unreadability of the text for most readers (Roberts, 1997). In addition, Jaffe (2000) makes the point that 'standard English' is an abstraction from how all people actually speak, even those who are more likely to be portrayed as 'standard' speakers, i.e., those who are more culturally dominant in society. The realisation that I more easily noticed local accents, the use of Scots and the grammar differences of children relatively new to English, sent me back to the audio recordings to listen more carefully to how the 'standard' speakers expressed themselves.

My inquiry and analysis was further guided by a newspaper interview with the poet Vanessa Kisuule (2020), which discouraged tendencies towards hearing constraint more loudly than children's agency and resistance. She was asked if she would write more about Black Lives Matter after her poem about the statue-toppling of slave trader, Edward Colston. Her response challenged how I engaged with race and class in the study, as a White, hybrid working/middle-class woman. She says,

> I think I am much better speaking to our joy, our mundaneness, all the things that people don't afford us. The establishment is obsessed with [black people's] trauma. Those are the stories they keep commissioning from us … They have fetishised our pain … Obviously we have to speak to our reality, to the struggle, but not for the titillation of white liberals.

In her caution about "white liberal" obsessions with others' trauma I can hear my starting point, my concern for the pain and constriction of those placed in the lowest group in a reading hierarchy. I hope it will be clear in the book that I have heeded this caution. I have attended closely and reflexively to children's words and silences, movement and stillness. Through this I have come to very different understandings of the relationships between reading and children's identities in the lowest positioned reading group. These reflexive shifts in understanding will be told through Chapters 3–7.

A Personal Reflection

Echoing Reay (2017, p. 2), in the spirit of honesty I want to make clear my, "passionate partiality", which has inspired, guided and misguided this ethnographic inquiry into children as readers. I wish for and work towards a socially just world in which all children of whatever race, faith, class, gender, dis/ability and sexuality, are free to fulfil their potential, educational and otherwise. The wish and work involve recognising and challenging educational orientations that curtail some groups' experience of learning. This book is part of that work; it has always had activist intent. One of my favourite novels is George Eliot's *Middlemarch* (2012). Every so often Eliot writes so directly it is as if she has just walked into my living room in her slippers. It is thrilling, intimate and disconcerting. At times, I write in this intimate voice that talks conversationally with you, my imagined reader. I do it partly because I want the research and stories it contains to affect you. Why would I not, when I am writing from a celebration of working-class children of all ethnicities, and from an anger and sadness that their potential can be constrained within neoliberal education systems that do not always teach in their interests (Finn, 1999; hooks, 1994; Patrick, 2013). When Reay (2017) talks about her passionate partiality, as I do here, I hear concern that the passion can lead to over-simplifications and I echo her intention to come closest to emotional truth, despite this passionate partiality.

The study evolved and changed in its doing. A process of reorientation and adaptation was prompted by external conditions, as described, but also by inner reflection. I have needed to examine my positionality, for example, in order to further understand my relationships in the field and what has influenced my interpretations. I will reflect in this section on how social class, in particular, has shaped me and shaped how I show up in the research. I think through how I might reflexively step aside (though this is almost like trying to out-jump one's shadow) to appreciate more clearly the workings of power that affect children's experience of reading in school.

I began my study with a hunch that viewing children's experience of reading groups through a sociological lens would help make sense of that experience for an academic and practitioner audience. What I did not anticipate was that issues of class and race would be the most emotionally and intellectually challenging aspects of the project for me, but this is how it proved to be. I began with a crusading spirit and believed I was, as a working-class woman, culturally aligned with working-class children in the 'bottom' reading group. The motivation for the study included the possibility it held of amplifying their voices, which, even in school, are less heard, in the interests of social justice and emancipation. But I found there are many ways of being working class and I had to contend with my unexamined assumptions that set me at odds with aspects of the children's lives, as I will discuss in Chapter 5.

I grew up in a White class-conscious working-class home, in which socialist politics was always in the air. When, aged 7, I sold my Curly Wurly chocolate bar for two pence profit, my mum angrily told me that this was "the unacceptable face of capitalism". At the time, this phrase was more commonly reserved for the worst excesses of capitalist exploitation (Gimson, 2016). Recalling Lawler (2014) who describes identity being made through story, the markers of my class were woven through events like that of the Curly Wurly. They were also made through stories told of my parents', grandparents' and ancestors' dignity and resistance to the economic constraints into which they were born and lived. I come from a long line of domestic servants and coal miners. My mum became a different kind of care worker (an auxiliary nurse) and building society cashier and my dad, a joiner and chargehand who worked for the council. I never met my maternal great-grandfather but know him from a photo shared of him and two pals in an open-topped motor car in the US, their fedoras tilted jauntily. He had caused trouble for the coal bosses, been banned from every pit in Lanarkshire and fled to America, before being thrown out of the US for being a communist.

Another story often told was of my mum and dad's intelligence, and the socioeconomic conditions that thwarted their chances of a university education. My mum had been the only girl in her primary school to pass the eleven-plus and go to the local grammar school. My nana spent a large chunk of the meagre compensation she had received on my grandfather's death in a pit accident to purchase my mum's grammar-school uniform. From the first day my mum felt like the proverbial fish out of water, separated from her friends and surrounded by middle-class girls whose home lives were so different from hers. On many occasions she had to skip school to do my nana's shift as a primary-school dinner lady because my nana's health never recovered from the shock of my grandfather's death. After the auspicious entry to grammar school, dressed in the uniform of educational privilege, my mum soon couldn't wait to leave. Education remained a vision for both my parents, however, and was emphasised as the exit route for me and my sister if we didn't want to "end up working in the factory" looming at the top of our road.

These stories helped form the identity I have brought to this study but so too did the dis-identifications (Islam, 2020; Skeggs, 1997) that set us apart from other families on the council estate where I grew up. While my dad resisted co-option as an intermediary between workers and management by refusing to wear a suit, my mum spoke of cultural difference from her neighbours. Bourdieu (1984) shows the oppositional character of social and cultural habits and choices, which seek distinction from other class groups as my mum did. Although Bourdieu focuses on distinction-making in the middle classes, Skeggs (1997) shows how working-class people, like my family, also seek distinction, though the pay-off is usually more limited. In her study of working-class women on care courses, Skeggs argues that the distinctions of "respectability" and "caring" were claimed by the women to distance themselves from stigmatised portrayals of working-class lives.

My mum felt she had inherited a snobbery from her mum, who despite abject economic hardship held herself above the community she had always been a part of. The snobbery was often gendered. If a woman left her washing on the drying green overnight, for example, this would be noted as the kind of slovenly behaviour that my mum and nana would never engage in. The source of their distinction was a novel and contradictory one. My nana was born with the word illegitimate on her birth certificate. And so, my mum believed her mother had been fathered by the 'gentleman' of the big house where her grandmother had worked as a domestic servant. It was this imagined act of, at the very least, sexual exploitation that accounted for our perceived middle-class brains and cultural ways, from my nana to my mum to my sister and me. We were middle class in disguise, or so the story goes.

Going to university in the 1980s and subsequent employment as a teacher, lecturer and literacy researcher has altered my class identity. It has taken me geographically, academically, occupationally, culturally and socially into more commonly identified middle-class territory. It continues to be an uneasy transition and I describe my adult self as a working/middle-class hybrid. The literacy habits of middle-class friends and colleagues who have children resonated with my love of reading. They also introduced me to an unfamiliar but appealing world of daily intergenerational reading, bedtime stories and bookshelves heaving with children's books. I imperceptibly shifted to a view that reading was the best vehicle in which to travel to emotionally and economically fulfilling futures, in a society that rewards fluency in print-based literacies. I have come to see the classed sub-plot to this view. If working-class families could only adopt the literacy practices I associated more with middle-class families, then working-class children would fare better educationally and beyond. Bourdieu and Passeron's (1990) notion of "the cultural arbitrary" proved significant in revealing my prejudice. It captures the idea that no cultural practice is inherently more valuable but that cultural practices of the powerful come to be legitimised as such.

I write about the classed stories that have helped shape me for the following reasons. Understanding social class as a lived experience, as I have done through my own experience, is central to investigating how ability-grouped reading does and does not reproduce educational inequalities. By reflecting on the idiosyncrasies of my own influences I point to the impossibilities of talking homogenously about class. There are indeed many ways of being working class, not least gendered and racialised ways of being working class. I have had to uncover prejudices and assumptions that unwillingly at times put me at odds with my participants and led me to misperceive deficits in children's home and literacy lives. It is this quirkiness of experience, while still producing recognisable patterns of culture and power, as well as emotionally acute experiences of class, that makes class so difficult but crucial to discuss throughout this book (McKenzie, 2015; Skeggs, 1997, 2004).

Reading Development, Literacy, Emotion and Identity

The theoretical understanding of reading development in the book draws on a complimentary mix of affective, psycholinguistic, sociocultural and multimodal perspectives on reading. I will outline them here to provide the background that informs the discussion of ability-grouped reading and the subsequent directions the fieldwork and analysis took.

The affective turn in literacy research (e.g., Anwaruddin, 2016; Leander & Bolt, 2013; Leander & Ehret, 2019) stresses that acts of reading, or talking about reading, are infused with shifting emotion. To understand children as readers, these affective/emotional dimensions of reading, played out in relationships, must be heard and understood. Also important when considering affect is the availability of reading material that might engage children and make them feel part of the reading world (Bishop, 1990; Cremin, 2019). It is much easier to concentrate on reading when the subject and format resonates with your interests. When literacy researchers pay attention to affect and emotion, different understandings about children's reading can emerge than might emerge from more decontextualised literacy studies.

Intersecting with affective aspects of reading are the sociocultural and sociopolitical dynamics and contexts of reading. Reading happens within relationships of power and control and is constantly in conversation with family, peers, cultures, knowledge and other texts (Govender, 2020; Bishop, 1990; Street, 2002, 2013). In reading texts, we are also reading the world. Within this sociocultural-political understanding, I assume a multimodal understanding of what reading is. Literacy is understood in the book to incorporate the myriad mediums and ways that meanings are made/conveyed in diverse fields and sociocultural groups, including the everyday practices involved in, for example, social media, music and art.

This widening of meaning from the narrower definitions of literacy as solely reading and writing print flows from the concept of *living literacies*, coined by Pahl and Rowsell (2020), which builds on the work of Heath (1983) and of New Literacy Studies (e.g., Street, 2013). Living literacies focus on how literacies are lived, through gesture, visuals, sound and words, and are concerned with affect and power. Meanings are conveyed through printed words but also through visual and auditory mediums and their interplay (Cope & Kalantzis, 2000; Kress, 2000; Pahl & Rowsell, 2020). When referring to the reading of printed words specifically, as I do at different points in the book, I will distinguish this by using the term print reading unless it is obvious from the context that print reading is signified. There is an important caveat to my use of the term print reading, however, which is that few instances of children reading are purely print based. Rather, it frequently involves a mediation between print and visuals, such as in picturebooks and comics.

Lastly, psycholinguistic views of reading are assumed in the book and these work with the affective, sociocultural and multimodal understandings of reading so far discussed.

Psycholinguists emphasise the active, problem-solving and meaning-making nature of reading (e.g., Goodman, 1967; Liu, 2022; Tennant et al., 2016). Four cueing systems interrelate when the reader makes sense of what they read. These are: graphophonic, attending to letter/sound relationships; syntactic, which is grammatical awareness of what would make sense; semantic, relating to meaning and context; and pragmatic, the purpose and function of the text. A fluent reader would use these four cues automatically, and each would refine the others. You might, for example misread blue as blub, but realise that this doesn't make semantic or syntactic sense in the sentence. Literacy scholars and practitioners have found that interlinked cueing works best to maintain sense of what is read when children can read at least 90% of the words in the text accurately (Bodmin & Franklin, 2014).

Reading pedagogy based on affective and psycholinguistic views of reading encourages children's active engagement with the text. They are coached in reading strategies, based on the four cueing systems above, to work out words and maintain sense of what they read (Hall, 2005). Coaching for reading strategies is common in guided reading and was practised in my project schools, as teachers prompt children on what to do if stuck on a word. Books are selected for and by children from levelled or banded book collections, which offer them a reading challenge of easy difficulty, i.e., of reading with between 90% and 95% word accuracy. It is on this basis that guided reading is organised into ability groups, so that children will read the level of text they can maintain sense of. There can be tension between this practice of banding books and the affective attraction of choosing books purely on interest. However, there can also be a negative effect on motivation if books are too difficult to make sense of when they are read independently. Conceptualisations of reading, as outlined in this section, are relevant to understanding what happens in ability-grouped reading as well as considering the pedagogical viability of mixed-attainment alternatives trialled in the study. Reading is never merely a set of cognitive skills but is indeed alive with affect.

Outline of the Book

This chapter has been an introduction to the study and to how I am situated in within it. In efforts at transparency and reflection, I have written of the personal, political and social conditions that have influenced my thinking before and during the research process. Although it is an introduction to the book, it has been written towards the end of a long journey through reading, fieldwork, analysis and self-scrutiny. As such, it has allowed me to reflect on my initial intentions, who and what I was directing my research to and against (Kramsch, 2010). It has also allowed me to hint at how my inquiry proceeded beyond my initial curiosity of children's experience of reading groups, without pre-empting the intricate work of findings and analysis that are the subject of Chapters 3–7. I have included conceptualisations of reading in the book, which I hope will help the reader orientate in the chapters that follow.

Chapter 2 explains how social class is conceptualised and put to work in the book, specifically in relation to the work of French sociologist, Pierre Bourdieu on habitus and capitals, including cultural capital. The historical development of guided reading from the 1990s is viewed in the context of literacy as cultural capital within the rise of neoliberalism and the knowledge economy. Specifically, research on ability-grouped reading, ability grouping in general, and the sociopolitical and emotional contexts of literacy in education and society are discussed. Through this discussion the scarcity of children's perspectives on ability-grouped reading becomes evident, and it is to this relative lack that the research questions in the study were directed.

Chapter 3 begins to acquaint the reader with some of the children who were in the 'bottom' reading group in the study. It does so by reflecting on how reading fits into the matrix of their rich lives. The decision to begin with the children's complex feelings for reading establishes a challenge to common deficit portrayals characterised by the referent 'bottom' to describe their position. Children are first portrayed as lovers of stories in the myriad mediums through which stories are told. How books, specifically, fit into their home lives is then told before describing the affective intensities observed when the children were required to read print for themselves in school.

Chapter 4 shifts focus to children's identities mediated by ability-grouped reading. Utilising and stretching Bourdieu's (1984) notion of distinction, I examine the positions children take up in relation to the different groups. Always I have the question in mind: who benefits from this organisation of reading that is hierarchically structured from the (allegedly) least to most fluent readers? The chapter explores how positions, sometimes gendered, are pushed back, accepted, accommodated and refused, in anger, resignation, optimism and neutrality.

Chapter 5 continues to keep power and privilege in the frame, by thinking through how social class, in particular, comes to matter in the workings of ability-grouped reading. Drawing on Bourdieu's (1990) notion of class habitus in relation to reading and other family pastimes, I argue that ability-grouped reading advantages those families that prioritise book reading in daily life. Going further, using Lareau's (2011) notion of concerted cultivation, I suggest parents can intentionally seek advantage for their child through this prioritisation by securing a place in the 'top' reading group. Once secured, there is considerable social status and educational benefit accrued from the position, which help reproduce classed advantage and disadvantage in distinct ways.

Chapter 6 diverges from the holistic analysis of ability-grouped reading to consider affective experience and social constructions of literacy for one particular subset of children in the 'bottom' reading group; that is, children experiencing profound difficulties in reading print. Through the close analysis of one child, Cash, and his engagement with print, theories of phonological processing difficulties are, in turn, accepted and troubled by issues of power, culture and affect. The impact of contexts like ability-grouped reading are questioned, while resisting the urge to reach for overly simplistic solutions to the challenges that reading difficulties can bring.

Chapter 7 tells individual and collective stories of disruption and challenge that can help change the hand dealt to working-class children of all ethnicities when they begin to read in school. The chapter explains practical alternatives to ability-grouped reading, in particular mixed-attainment reading, which holds egalitarian promise and is grounded in empirical evidence from the study. Reading hierarchies do not form or disappear, however, because of one pedagogical practice. They are complicated and influenced by societal complexities of power, ideology, identity and resources as well as by children's desire to distinguish themselves as readers. The chapter therefore contains a more fundamental challenge to print's dominance as a hallowed medium of communication. Practical pedagogies are introduced that may disrupt this dominance, creating more equitable conditions for all young readers to flourish.

Chapter 8, the final chapter, offers conclusions from the study's key findings as well as discussing the takeaways from the theoretical and epistemological perspectives that have informed the book. The chapter ends with a provocation: what might be the egalitarian potential of making disruption of hierarchies the guiding principle of literacy, in terms of policy, pedagogy and practice? The book may not have provided a final answer and instead gestures towards ongoing efforts needed by teachers, pupils, parents, academics and policymakers to always challenge assumptions on what constitutes reading practices and readers.

Notes

1 All names of children, schools, classes and reading groups are pseudonyms.
2 In the book I will place single scare quotes around words such as top, middle and bottom in relation to reading groups to trouble the hierarchical assumptions of their common usage. I use single inverted commas rather than double to distinguish scare quotes from quoted speech.

3 The Renfrewshire Literacy Approach, https://pureportal.strath.ac.uk/files-asset/72042928/Ellis_etal_2018_Report_on_the_renfrewshire_literarcy_approach_august_2015_july_2017.pdf
4 In 'reading' the children as White I acknowledge the possibility of misrecognition. *The Vanishing Half* by novelist Brit Bennett (2020) about two light skinned Black sisters, one who is read as White and the other Black, reminds me of the potential inaccuracy and racialised assumptions influencing my perceptions as well as being a reminder of the socially situated nature of 'race'. The capitalisation of 'Black' in the book reflects the widely used convention to signify a collective (though diverse) racial identity and history of people whose ancestors were born in Africa, and also its political use, beyond, African ancestry, to include other minoritised non-White populations to represent a shared experience of oppression in a White supremacist world. 'People of Colour' is also capitalised in the book, as well as associated phrases such as 'Children of Colour'. Although there are anti-racist arguments for and against the capitalisation of White for people of European origin with white skin, I have chosen to capitalise it in order to draw attention to the shared if not homogenous history of privilege experienced by White bodies and to the social construct of race that produces Whiteness. To capitalise Black and not White risks misrecognising Whiteness as neutral and 'normal' from which other racialised groups deviate (Appiah, 2020; Nguyên & Pendelton, 2020; Tharps, 2014). Ethnic groups will also be capitalised, e.g., South Asian and Indigenous.
5 The area falls in SIMD 1. The Scottish Index of Multiple Deprivation (SIMD) is a Scottish government tool for measuring relative levels of deprivation in different geographical areas (ranging from 1 as most deprived to 10, least) based on income, employment, education, health, access to services, crime and housing. https://www.gov.scot/collections/scottish-index-of-multiple-deprivation-2020/.
6 The fieldwork was planned for one year, May 2019 to May 2020. This timeframe was extended because of school closures in March 2020, in response to the COVID-19 pandemic. When schools closed, the research continued virtually through involvement in the children's online learning communities and conversations with the teachers. When schools reopened in August 2019 the mixed-attainment reading, which we had previously introduced in February, continued at St Jude's. I learned about its progress in monthly virtual meetings with the two teachers involved in the study. It was not until May 2021, when schools were again open to visitors, that I was able to return to St Jude's to complete the fieldwork in person. I did not return to Fairfield as changed circumstances meant mixed-attainment reading could not be introduced.
7 Initial research plans had included interviews with parents and teachers, as well as children, but this changed for three reasons. Firstly, and most importantly, the study draws epistemologically on feminist standpoint theory (e.g., Smith, 2002, Hill Collins, 1990, Hartsock, 1983). I qualify my use of standpoint theory to insist that there is no universal children's standpoint, and that children can be positioned very differently to each other. And still, novel insights emerge from the standpoint of children compared to top-down culturally dominant investigation. Secondly, there was a small number of teachers involved in the study ($N = 5$ teachers and 3 head teachers). For reasons of confidentiality their presence is largely absent from the book although we shared insights. All were keen to question the established practice of ability-grouped reading and to experiment with mixed-attainment reading and other pedagogies that might make literacy more egalitarian. Thirdly, pragmatic reasons based on time and volume of data additionally influenced the decision not to interview parents.

The initial research design had also included the use of standardised reading assessments to quantify and compare reading attainment in ability-group and mixed-attainment reading. However, a delay in sourcing reading tests for Fairfield, coupled with school closures (COVID-19), meant comparative assessments could not be undertaken. A consequence of the delay was that mixed-attainment reading was not introduced at Fairfield before schools closed since the intention was to do reading assessments before introducing mixed-attainment reading. Once schools reopened, changed circumstances at Fairfield meant mixed-attainment reading was not introduced, and the school did not continue in the study. Although initial reading assessments were done at St Jude's, a comparative second assessment was not undertaken because of the unexpected additional variable of school closures, which affected children's reading progress. Consequently reading assessment played no part in the analysis of the research data.

8 For ease of reading in subsequent chapters I sometimes omit the words *facilitated* and *audio-taped* but when children's words are quoted they have always come from these facilitated audio-taped contexts.

References

Akala. (2019). *Natives: Race and class in the Ruins of Empire*. Two Roads.
Anwaruddin, S. M. (2016). Why critical literacy should turn to 'the affective turn': Making a case for critical affective literacy. *Discourse: Studies in the Cultural Politics of Education*, 37(3), 381–396.
Appiah, K. A. (2020, June 29). The case for capitalizing the B in Black. *The Atlantic*. https://www.theatlantic.com/ideas/archive/2020/06/time-to-capitalize-blackand- white/613159/
Bennett, B. (2020).*The vanishing half*. Riverhead Books.
Bishop, R. S. (1990, March). Windows and mirrors: Children's books and parallel cultures. In M. Atwell & A. Klein (Eds.), *California State University reading conference: 14th Annual Conference Proceedings*. pp. 3–12. California State University.
Bodman, S., & Franklin, G. (2014). *Which book and why*. IOE Press.
Bourdieu, P. (1984). *Distinction: A social critique of the judgement of taste*. Routledge & Kegan Paul.
Bourdieu, P. (1990). *The logic of practice*. Stanford University Press.
Bourdieu, P., & Passeron, J. C. (1990). *Reproduction in education, society and culture*. SAGE.
Calderón López, M., & Thériault, V. (2017). Accessing a 'very very secret garden': Exploring the literacy practices of children and young people using participatory research methods. *Language and Literacy*, 19(4), 39–54.
Christensen, P. H. (2004). Children's participation in ethnographic research: Issues of power and representation. *Children & Society*, 18(2), 165–176.
Clay, M. M. (1993). *An observation survey of early literacy achievement*. Heinemann Educational Books.
Cope, B., & Kalantzis, M. (2000). *Multiliteracies: Literacy learning and the design of social futures*. Routledge.
Cremin, T. (2019). Reading communities: Why, what and how? *NATE Primary Matters Magazine, Summer*.
DiAngelo, R. (2018). *White fragility: Why it's so hard for White people to talk about racism*. Beacon Press.
Dunn, J. (2004). Naturalistic observations of children and their families. In S. Greene & D. Hogan (Eds.), *Researching children's experience* pp. 87-101. SAGE.

Eddo Lodge, R. (2017). *Why I'm no longer talking to White people about race*. Bloomsbury Publishing.

Eliot, G. (2012). *Middlemarch*. Penguin Classics.

Finn, P. J. (1999). *Literacy with an attitude: Educating working-class children in their own self-interest*. State University of New York Press.

Gimson, A. (2016). *The return of the unacceptable face of capitalism*. Conservative Home. https://conservativehome.com/2016/07/25/the-return-of-the-unacceptable-face-of-capitalism/

Goodman, K. (1967). Reading: A psycholinguistic guessing game. *Journal of the Reading Specialist*, 6(4), 126–135. 10.1080/19388076709556976

Govender, N. (2020). Literacy, language and power. *Stride, Global Citizenship Magazine for Schools*. http://www.stridemagazine.org.uk/features/item/467-literacy-language-and-power

Hall, K. (2005). *Listening to Stephen read: Multiple perspectives on literacy*. Open University Press.

Hartsock, N. C. M., (1983). The feminist Standpoint: Developing the ground for a specifically feminist historical materialism. In S. Harding & M. B. Hintikka (Eds.), *Discovering reality: Feminist perspectives on epistemology, metaphysics, methodology, and philosophy of science* (pp. 283–310). D. Reidel Publishing.

Heath, S. B. (1983). *Ways with words: Language, life and work in communities and classrooms*. Cambridge university Press.

Hill Collins, P. (1990). Black feminist thought in the matrix of domination. In P. H. Collins (Ed.), *Black Feminist thought: Knowledge, consciousness, and politics of empowerment* (pp. 221–238). Unwin Hyman.

hooks, b. (1994). *Teaching to transgress: Education as the practice of freedom*. Routledge.

Islam, A. (2020). *'Not just a housewife': Gender, class, and labour in the new economy of urban India* [Unpublished doctoral dissertation, University of Cambridge]. https://doi.org/10.17863/CAM.46576

Jaffe, A. (2000). Introduction: Non-standard orthography and non-standard speech. *Journal of Sociolinguistics*, 4(4), 497–513.

Kimmerer, R. (2013). *Braiding sweetgrass: Indigenous wisdom, scientific knowledge and the teachings of plants*. Milkweed Editions.

Kisuule, V. (2020, June 28). Poetic justice: Black lives and the power of poetry. *Guardian Newspaper*. https://www.theguardian.com/books/2020/jun/28/black-british-poets-black-lives-matter-linton-kwesi-johnson-grace-nichols-raymond-antrobus-kayo-chingonyi-malika-booker-vanessa-kisuule

Kramsch, C. (2010). Pierre Bourdieu: A biographical memoir. In J. Albright & A. Luke (Eds.), *Pierre Bourdieu and literacy education* (pp. 11–26). Routledge.

Kress, G. (2000). Multimodality: Challenges to Thinking about Language. In B. Cope & M. Kalantzis (Eds.), Multiliteracies: Literacy Learning and the Design of Social Futures (pp. 182-202). Routledge.

Lareau, A. (2011). *Unequal childhoods: Class, race, and family life*. University of California Press.

Lawler, S. (2014). *Identity: Sociological perspectives* (2nd ed.). Polity Press.

Leander, K., & Boldt, G. (2013). Rereading "A pedagogy of multiliteracies": Bodies, texts, and emergence. *Journal of Literacy Research*, 45(1), 22–46. https://doi.org/10.1177/1086296x12468587

Leander, K. M., & Ehret, C. (2019). *Affect in literacy learning and teaching: Pedagogies, politics and coming to know*. Routledge.

Liu, X. (2022). Making the invisible visible: Young Chinese heritage language learners' reading process through retrospective miscue analysis. *Journal of Early Childhood Literacy*, 0(0). https://doi.org/10.1177/14687984211067633

Luttrell, W. (2020). *Children framing childhoods: Working-class kids' visions of care*. Polity Press.
Mantell, H. (2020). *The mirror & the light*. Harper Collins.
McKenzie, L. (2015). *Getting by: Estates, class and culture in Austerity Britain*. Policy Press.
Menakem, R. (2021). *My grandmother's hands: Racialized trauma and the pathway to mending our hearts and bodies*. Penguin UK.
Nguyễn, A. T., & Pendelton, M. (2020, March 23). *Capitalize "Black" and "White"*. Center for the Study of Social Policy. https://cssp.org/2020/03/recognizing-race-in-language-why-we-capitalize-black-and-white/
Pahl, K., & Rowsell, J. (2020). *Living literacies: Literacy for social change*. MIT press.
Patrick, F. (2013). Neoliberalism, the knowledge economy, and the learner: Challenging the inevitability of the commodified self as an outcome of education. *International Scholarly Research Notices*. https://doi.org/10.1155/2013/108705
Reay, D. (2002). Shaun's story: Troubling discourses of white working-class masculinities. *Gender and Education, 14*(3), 221–234.
Reay, D. (2017). *Miseducation: Inequality, education and the working classes*. Policy Press.
Roberts, C. (1997). Transcribing talk: Issues of representation. *TESOL Quarterly, 31*(1), 167–172.
Rodríguez-Dorans, E., & Jacobs, P. (2020). Making narrative portraits: A methodological approach to analysing qualitative data. *International Journal of Social Research Methodology, 23*(6), 611–623. https://doi.org/10.1080/13645579.2020.1719609
Rosen, H. (1985). *Stories and Meanings*. National Association for the Teaching of English.
Savage, M. (2015). *Social class in the 21st century*. Pelican Books.
Skeggs, B. (1997). *Formations of class & gender: Becoming respectable*. SAGE.
Skeggs, B. (2004). *Class, self, culture*. Routledge.
Smith, D. E. (2002). Institutional ethnography. In T. May (Ed.), *Qualitative research in action*. SAGE.
Steedman, C. (1987). *Landscape for a good woman: A Story of two lives*. Rutgers University Press.
Street, B. V. (2002). *Literacy and development: Ethnographic perspectives*. Routledge.
Street, B. V. (2013). *Social literacies: Critical approaches to literacy in development, ethnography and education*. Taylor and Francis. https://doi.org/10.4324/9781315844282
Tennent, W., Reedy, D., Hobsbaum, A., & Gamble, N. (2016). *Guiding readers-layers of meaning: A handbook for teaching reading comprehension to 7–11 year olds*. UCL IoE Press.
Tharps, L. L. (2014, July 28). *I refuse to remain in the lower case*. My American Melting Pot. https://myamericanmeltingpot.com/2014/06/02/i-refuse-to-remain-in-the-lower-case/

Children's Literature References

Blyton, E. (1943). *The magic faraway tree*. Newnes.
Riddell, C. (2010). *Ottoline and the yellow cat*. Macmillan Children's Books.

2
SOCIOPOLITICAL AND EMOTIONAL LANDSCAPES OF ABILITY-GROUPED READING

Introduction

How social class, and its intersections with gender and race, come to matter in ability-grouped reading is a key preoccupation of the book. It is a preoccupation that finds echo in wider critiques of social reproduction in education in Britain and beyond (e.g., Bourdieu & Passeron, 1979,1990; Gillborn et al., 2021; Taylor, 2012). As there are different sociological understandings of class and of its influence in education this chapter explains how social class is conceptualised and used in the book. In *Social Class in Educational Research,* I introduce conceptualisations of social class, intersecting with race and gender, that have provided theoretical ground for the study, guided fieldwork and informed interpretations of children's reading in ability groups. The greatest influence on my understanding of class is the writing of French sociologist Pierre Bourdieu (e.g., 1984, 1986; Bourdieu & Passeron, 1979, 1990) and feminist sociologists who have engaged critically with his work (e.g., Lareau, 2011; Reay, 2004, 2017; Skeggs, 1997a, 2020). I introduce his conceptual tools and explain how I use these when exploring children's words, feelings and actions. Given a central concern of the study was how social inequalities intersect with ability-grouped reading, it was necessary to locate the children in terms of class. This was a messy, partial but carefully considered process, which drew on Bourdieusian principles from Savage's (2015), Great British Class Survey. The complexity of this process is elaborated on in the next section, *Capital Assets, Social Class and Children in the Study.*

In *Guided Reading and Literacy Capital,* the political landscape and trends in literacy scholarship are explained within which ability-grouped reading developed from the 1990s. Little critical research has been published on the subject since that time, despite the prevalence of the practice, and I position myself in conversation with such absences and possibilities. The chapter then examines the larger research output on ability grouping in general, in *Ability Grouping Across Age Phases and Subjects* (e.g., Bradbury and Roberts-Holmes, 2017; Gillborn et al., 2021; Francis & Tereshchenko, 2020). I use the term ability grouping to refer to three distinct forms of pupil organisation: streaming, setting, and within-class attainment grouping. Streaming refers to placing secondary-school pupils in the same hierarchical group for all subjects. Setting, found in both primary and secondary schools, places pupils in separate classes for different subjects based on their 'ability'. Within-class ability grouping, which is more common in primary settings, organises children by the so-called ability within the same classrooms for all or specific subjects. Much of the literature on ability grouping concerns secondary school pupils and is not focused on literacy education. However, issues of social inequity, and the affective and situational affordances and constraints revealed by this research have guided my inquiry into the impact of grouping young readers hierarchically.

The chapter then shifts, in *Affective Movements in Reading Lives*, to foreground affect in literacy and learning (e.g., Duckworth, 2013; Leander & Ehret, 2019; Williams, 2017). Connections are made between emotion and social positioning, such as in reading and writing groups, which may influence reader identities and life trajectories. The chapter concludes by returning to the gaps in knowledge around ability-grouped reading and presents the guiding research questions for the study that emerged from this gap.

Social Class and Educational Research

Understandings of social class have had many iterations in the last 50 years (Savage, 2016, 2015; Tyler, 2020). Its sociological relevance has been questioned and conceptualisations contested (e.g., Giddens, 1991a & 1991b). It is necessary, therefore, to tease out how class will be put to work in understanding the experience and effects of ability-grouped reading. There are two very different strands in how class has been historically understood (Skeggs, 2020). One strand stratifies people according to their position in society and the other conceptualises class within capitalist relationships of domination and exploitation. The first strand, that of classification, is based mainly on employment and economics (e.g., Goldthorpe, 1992). This form of classification, according to Skeggs, is largely undertaken by those in power for purposes of control. There are many issues with this form of class conceptualisation. Not least of these issues is that women's class position and that of immigrants have rarely been so easy to map onto employment as that of predominantly White men (Skeggs, 1997a; Tyler, 2013). However,

I agree with Savage (2016) that such socioeconomic classification can still be utilised for emancipatory purposes. Classification could, for example, be used to draw statistical attention to unequal distributions of socioeconomic groups within a stratified education system. In a limited way, I draw on such class conceptualisations to question whether children from different socioeconomic backgrounds are more likely to occupy one reading group or another. Nevertheless, class conceptualisations based on stratification alone are not enough to understand how inequalities are felt or reproduced in education.

The second strand, which is also employed in the book, is that of conceptualising class within relationships of power; it focuses on how class shapes our lives and possibilities. It is an important *and* difficult concept to work with (McKenzie, 2015; Skeggs, 1997a, 2004). Since the 1970s, rich economies, like the UK, have been characterised by deindustrialisation and the rise of neoliberalism. The neo-liberal project reframes life chances as less to do with birth and more to do with making the 'right' lifestyle choices. An intentional consequence of these politico-economic shifts is that class identity becomes less relatable for many (Tyler, 2013). Yet, at the same time classed advantages and slights continue to be felt deeply in people's lives (Savage, 2015).

A consequence of this fragmentation and disidentification with class is that classed analysis cannot begin from the assumption that class is a subjective individual or group identity (Skeggs, 2020). In my study the children rarely alluded directly to themselves in class terms even if it was signalled in many of their peer relationships. When considering how educational practices like ability-grouped reading may or may not challenge or sustain intergenerational privilege it is fruitful to ask not what class *is* but what class *does* (Taylor, 2009). Bourdieu's work is transformative here, as is that of feminist theorists who have used and stretched his work (e.g., Lareau, 2011; Reay, 1995b, 2004, 2017; Taylor, 2007).

Bourdieu (1984) compares classes to forests or clouds, discernible but with no hard demarcation lines. This analogy is particularly apt when traditional boundaries between working and middle classes are fuzzier than ever (Savage, 2015). But, while acknowledging this nebulous middle, and the messiness of objective and subjective identifications of class, I think there is efficacy still in using the terms *working class* and *middle class* as Skeggs (2020) and Reay (2017) do, not to pin children into categories that don't quite fit, but to keep attention on inequality and how privilege is reproduced. In some instances, I describe children as being in the hazy middle between working class and lower middle class.

The conceptual tools Bourdieu developed, and which I use, to probe inequality offer models of class based on how class matters, is lived and felt. His enduring concern was to expose the injustices and delusions of a so-called meritocratic capitalist society. This concern makes his work valuable when interrogating educational practice (Costa & Murphy, 2015). Central to his proposition are the concepts of *habitus, capitals* (in the economic, cultural and social sphere), *legitimation* and *symbolic violence*. Bourdieu uses *habitus* to represent how the social is embodied in the self (Lawler, 2014). The concept allows subjective activity to be investigated within "structuring structures" (Bourdieu, 1979, p. 72) and structures to be interrogated within small interactions (Reay, 1995b). Bourdieu (1984) defines habitus as dispositions inculcated from birth. These dispositions influence ways of being in the world, as a "feel for the game", expressed in "a durable way of standing, speaking, walking, and thereby of feeling and thinking" (Bourdieu, 1990, p. 70); it also includes ways of reading and of writing. Habitus is never only an individual embodiment – it holds the collective histories of the family into which one is born. Those histories are classed as well as gendered and always inflected by the different material effects of the social construction of race (Skeggs, 2004; Rollock, 2014; Singh, 2022).

While the concept of class habitus recognises agency and the multiplicity of individual practices, it also points to classed patterns of lifestyle. These patterns are born of the "necessities and facilities characteristic of that class of (relatively) homogeneous conditions of existence" (Bourdieu, 1984, p. 95). Habitus is not fixed; it is responsive to the social conditions it encounters in different fields of action. Early socialisation can however sediment and have a powerful influence in (childhood and) adult encounters (Lawler, 1999).

Although he insists that habitus is generative (rather than determining) of life trajectories within social constraints, social constraint can weigh heavily in Bourdieu's work. Yet, as he stresses, his weighting of agency and structural constraint must be read in the historical context of its production (Bourdieu & Passeron, 1990). Bourdieu was writing in the era of neoliberal declarations of meritocracy and the end of class. His writing reveals why the social conditions into which we are born still have a profound generative effect on our life trajectories. Nevertheless, there is an element of rebalancing required to appreciate empirically and theoretically how social agents resist, adapt and accommodate the social conditions of their existence. I agree with McNay (2004) that Bourdieu does not linger enough on "intention" and reflexivity as central aspects of human agency. I think he also misses the originality that can arise within working-class "virtue(s) of necessity" (Bourdieu, 1984). Preferences for replica paintings and such like, recorded in *Distinction,* can obscure the kind of ingenuity and humour that is conveyed in, for example, McKenzie's (in Savage, 2015) interviews with working-class people for the Great British Class Survey.

The social relations and space that children are born into provides access to different amounts of capital assets, which have different capacities for capital accumulation. *Economic capital* refers to monetary assets including inherited wealth and income. As Marx (1992 [1867]; 2004 [1867]) shows so clearly, the more money you have the easier it is to accumulate more. Bourdieu (1984) extends this theory of accumulation beyond the economic into cultural and symbolic spheres, and I use this to examine children's experience of reading.

Cultural capital has three aspects. It is embodied within habitus, as described above, as ways of talking, moving, thinking and feeling. It is objectified in cultural goods such as furniture, art and books. And it exists in institutional states as, primarily, educational qualifications. *Social capital* refers to one's network of social relations through which one can accrue economic and symbolic value. Although all children are born into a network of social relations, the advantage that can be gained from these social networks is unequal. The more valued the cultural and social capital one has, the easier it is to accrue more advantage. *Symbolic capital* is a term Bourdieu uses in different ways but most commonly to describe any of the other capitals when they are recognised and legitimised in a particular field. It is also important to recognise that the ability to accrue advantage from one's capitals is unevenly raced, as Rollock et al. (2016) show in their study of Black Caribbean middle-class parents in a UK education system that centres Whiteness.

The concept of *legitimation*, and its relation to *field* (Bourdieu, 1984), is key to understanding how such cultural and social resources are unequally converted into symbolic power and advantage. Fields, such as education, are structured social spheres in which cultural practices and knowledge are legitimised and delegitimised through struggle (Costa & Murphy, 2015). This notion of cultural legitimation and delegitimation has proved critical both to questioning my own positionality but also to making sense of children's experience of reading in the study. Class operates relationally within particular fields often through the valorisation of cultural dispositions, artefacts and knowledge of the more powerful in society (Bourdieu, 1984; Tyler, 2020). Rollock (2014) has extended Bourdieu's work to show that this process of valorisation is raced as well as classed. Through legitimation of, for example, certain genres of reading, privilege is maintained and extended. Conversely, the cultural practices and competences associated with those who are marginalised are frequently delegitimised and stigmatised (Tyler, 2013, 2020). Bourdieu and Passeron call this cultural stigmatisation, *symbolic violence* (1990), which is the imposition of tastes and values of dominant groups as if they are innately superior. As Skeggs makes clear, "the inability to trade one's cultural capital because it has only limited value or is not recognised in the places where value can be accrued is a substantial disadvantage to and a sign of being born working-class" (1997b, p. 129).

Capital Assets, Social Class and Children in the Study

The children's limited identification with class raised similar methodological issues to those encountered by Skeggs (1997a) in her groundbreaking study of women on care courses. She locates the women as working class using various 'objective' markers of class, such as parental employment and housing. This location allowed her discussion of women's disidentification with the class to which they are ascribed. I too use 'objective' markers of class as I will further explain but, like Skeggs, my aim is not to categorise but to help explore what class does in children's reading lives, including whether allocation to prestigious reading groups reflects class backgrounds. It has been an emotionally difficult and messy process as classed differences in culture and disposition, including accent and embodiment, are not framed as a benign 'difference' – the working classes, however heterogeneous, are pathologised (Lawler, 1999; Tyler, 2020). I am aware of this and afraid that in talking of class habits and culture, it may re-pathologise working-class children. But to understand how class matters in reading hierarchies it is necessary to talk about class in cultural as well as economic terms.

Information was gathered from the children talking about their lives, and from head teachers and teachers. My subjective identification of children's class position is adapted from Savage's (2015) Bourdieusian interpretation of groupings based on economic, social and cultural capital. Savage measures economic capital in terms of household income, savings and house value. Since I did not have access to this financial information, I drew partly on children's eligibility for support through the Pupil Equity Fund.[1] The local authority also provided data on families' economic circumstances based on eligibility to school clothing grants and free school meals.[2] Some parental occupations, mentioned by children and teachers, also suggested levels of economic capital, and some fell into traditional categories of working-class and middle-class occupations. These included low-paid work as refuse workers, cleaners, carers and delivery drivers and middle-class identified jobs such as lawyers, doctors, journalists and television producers.[3] Other jobs fell into more ambiguous class territory between working and lower middle class such as nurses and administrative office-based work.

Savage measured social capital by the social status of respondents' connections. I knew little of the families' social connections but identified some of the out-of-school social connections between children, such as the sharing of books during lockdown. To identify cultural capital, Savage considered the composition of interests declared by respondents, categorised as "highbrow" and "low-brow" cultural pursuits, and by their level of educational qualifications. In terms of cultural pursuits, I included the centring and decentring of book-based literacies along with the space taken up by other pastimes such as spending time with extended family and playing outside independently (both borrowed from Lareau, 2011). Some children spoke about their parents' education, often when parents had degrees or higher qualifications. I assumed, with great potential for inaccuracy, that if children did not talk about their parents' education it may be because higher education had not featured significantly in their lives. These assumptions were combined with information on parents' work since some jobs required a higher qualification while others did not.

Accent and the use of Scots[4] also influenced the assumptions I made about children's class position although these assumptions could be inaccurate when considered with other aspects of children's capitals. I assumed one boy to be working class by his accent before learning that his father's job was often located in the hazy middle between working and middle class, and that the boy owned a horse, a pet I associate more with the middle classes. Locating class through accent is also troubled when children speak English as an additional language. Their accent could be inflected by accent in their first language, with which I was unfamiliar, and they were also perhaps more influenced in the first two years by the accent of those they spent most time with at school. I learned this in London, as an EAL teacher,[5] when children who had recently arrived from Chile, spoke their first words in English with a Scottish accent like mine.

Notwithstanding the inconsistencies of perceiving class through accent, if children spoke with an accent and dialect that rooted them in their locality, and which sometimes I found difficult to understand, this informed an assumption they were working class, but only in combination with other capitals. If their accent was a closer match to standard written forms this would contribute to locating them as middle class. In one conversation, for example, a boy talked about a book, "The Stink Afore Rismas".[6] When I didn't understand, another boy interjected with "The Stink Before Christmas", his speech closer to 'standard' English. Through this exchange, though not alone, I assumed the first boy to be working class and the second, middle class. The confidence displayed by the second boy, assuming I would understand when *he* articulated the words, I also perceived as an embodied middle-class disposition in Bourdieusian terms. All of the above highlights the difficult, subjective and partial nature of classed categorisation I employed in the study but my attempts have been rigorous and deliberate.

Guided Reading and Literacy Capital

In the last quarter of the twentieth century, as industrialisation in the world's richest countries ceased to guarantee economic wealth, 'knowledge' came to the fore as valuable global capital (Olssen & Peters, 2005). The emergence of this *knowledge economy* repositioned education as a key driver of wealth production. Consequently, the 1980s and 1990s witnessed large-scale revision of education policy by many governments in the Global North and South (Patrick, 2013; Peters, 2001; Peters & Humes, 2003). Underpinning these revisions were the neoliberal paradigms of enterprise, marketisation, globalisation, competition and personal responsibility (Brancaleone & O'Brien, 2011; Olssen & Peters, 2005). These changes had profound impact on the way children's learning was organised. Following an era of comprehensive mixed-attainment teaching in England in the 1960s and 1970s, for example, ability grouping re-emerged as a practice deemed more likely to meet growing government demands for pupil progress, mediated by high-stakes testing (Bradbury & Roberts-Holmes, 2017).

The rise of the knowledge economy has prompted state intervention in *literacy* education in particular. Since, as Brandt (2005) argues, text becomes the main product in knowledge-intensive industries, companies' reputation and profits come to rely on the literacy skills of knowledge workers. Moral panics around falling literacy standards are nothing new, as Williams (2007) illustrates through a history of such literacy panics. But with the knowledge economy, crises in literacy standards become linked to the economic health of the nation. In Scotland, for example, 'poor literacy outcomes' and their potential to exclude future adults from knowledge-based employment has been a recurring theme from the last days of the Scottish Office to more recent Scottish Government National Improvement Frameworks (NIFs)[7] (Scottish Office, 1999; Scottish Government, 2015).[8]

In the drive to improve literacy outcomes in England, the New Labour government introduced the National Literacy Strategy (NLS) (DfEE, 1998), which stipulated content and how literacy should be taught in primary schools. Literacy teaching was to be organised around *The Literacy Hour*, a key component of which was *guided reading*. Guided reading is organised by the so-called ability as children are grouped together to read and discuss a book matched to their level of print fluency. It is interesting to observe that those promoting ability grouping, as the NLS does, often do so using similar language to those who oppose it, that of challenging social inequality. In its 1998 foreword, New Labour's David Blunkett presented the NLS as a means by which social disadvantage could be ameliorated by helping all children achieve good standards of literacy. Subsequent governments have continued to fuse ability grouping to 'high standards' in discourses around poverty and children's educational attainment (Francis et al., 2017b). However, numerous studies over many years have found that allocation to ability groups is vulnerable to classed, raced and gendered biases that work against equality (e.g., Cassen & Kingdon, 2007; Joseph- Salisbury, 2020; Siraj-Blatchford & Troyna, 1993).

Although the National Literacy Strategy has been superseded by subsequent government interventions, specifically the teaching of synthetic phonics[9] (Rose, 2006; DfE, 2022), guided reading remains a common practice in English schools. Unlike the NLS, Scotland's Curriculum for Excellence (CfE) (Education Scotland, 2023) does not specify *how* reading instruction should be organised,[10] and so has never prescribed that reading be taught in ability groups. Local authorities in Scotland also retain more autonomy in pedagogical matters than they do in England, meaning there is less government-directed practice. Nevertheless, influential guidance produced by some Scottish local authorities[11] promotes guided reading and this guidance has helped make ability-grouped reading a common practice in Scottish primary schools. Hamilton and O'Hara (2011) in their survey of Scottish teachers found that ability grouping children for literacy was a common and favoured practice for children as young as 5 years old.

Guided reading does aim to do valuable pedagogical work, such as collaborative development of children's response and comprehension of children's literature. As such, it received a positive reception from influential literacy scholars in the countries in which it was first introduced, namely the UK and US[12] (Fountas & Pinnell, 1998; Hobsbaum et al., 2006; Tennent et al., 2016). These authors each produced award-winning handbooks to support guided reading. However, the emotional and motivational effect of organising reading hierarchically by reading fluency is not questioned in the handbooks. Nor is it interrogated in many of the studies that have explored different pedagogical aspects of guided reading (e.g., Fisher, 2008; Skidmore, 2003; Young, 2019). This theoretical and practical uptake of guided reading, I believe, helped relegate critical research into ability-grouped and alternative mixed-attainment reading to the educational hinterland.

Indeed, I found only three studies that have looked specifically at the *ability-grouped aspect* of group reading and each was done prior to the promotion of the particular form of group reading that is known as guided reading (Cunningham et al., 1991, 1998; Cunningham, 2006;[13] Grant and Rothenberg, 1986; Haller and Davis, 1980). All three studies were US based, as follows. In 1980 Haller and Davis challenged a commonly voiced proposition, and one I make in this chapter, that ability grouping helps reproduce parents' social status in their children. Yet, Haller and Davis grapple with, and actively reproduce, contradictory ideas in this analysis of ability-grouped reading. Firstly, they found that allocation to the highest and lowest reading groups *did* follow socioeconomic patterns. Economically poor children were statistically more likely to be in the lowest reading group. This confirms part of that common assumption their study aimed to refute. Secondly, they describe how the children's placements were justified by their "reading ability". This statement highlights the authors' lack of engagement with how differentiated educational outcomes can be the product of an education system that reflects and rewards middle-class norms (Bourdieu, 1986). Instead, Haller and Davis appear to assume a view of intelligence as hereditary and innate, which results in more middle-class children in higher reading groups.

How hierarchical reading groups might indeed contribute to classed outcomes in reading attainment is illustrated by Grant and Rothenberg's (1986) study. With reading groups reflecting class divisions, the authors noted behaviours and their frequency that galvanised a sense of belonging and pedagogical advantage in the top groups, as summarised in Table 2.1.

For all these reasons, the authors argue, social inequality is reproduced intergenerationally within ability-grouped reading. These conditions could help explain why some children do better in terms of reading fluency than others, and challenges Haller and Davis's (1980) lack of criticality around the notion of "reading ability".

Grant and Rosenberg's (1986) study helped direct my gaze in the field towards the hospitable and inhospitable nature of school-based reading for different children. They describe discrimination that may be felt keenly as personal experience but sit within structures that reproduce inequality. Think here, for example, of the "good" Pixies you met in Chapter 1 and the fact that no children from the 'bottom' reading group ever became a Pixie. Five years after Grant and Rosenberg's article appeared, Cunningham et al. (1991) reported on a mixed-attainment alternative to ability-grouped

TABLE 2.1 Educational advantage in ability-grouped reading

Classroom practices	*Highest reading group*	*Lowest reading group*
Pupil/teacher communication.	Warmer, conversational, more equal.	Children rebuked for more informal chat with teacher.
Cultivation of personal, and reading, characteristics.	Initiative and independence encouraged in making sense of text.	Instructed to complete reading in unison and "not race ahead".
Life trajectories associated with the above characteristics.	Initiative and independence are important in educational success and valued in adult leadership roles.	Quality of compliance valued in non-professional workers.
Teacher's use of praise.	Unqualified.	Qualified.
Criticism by teacher.	Often softened, e.g., noting a mistake as out of character.	Direct, unsoftened.
Reading resources.	Reading books and word boxes demarcated for their sole use.	Children reprimanded for touching reading material demarcated for higher group.
Reading sessions.	Infrequently interrupted.	Frequently interrupted.

(Grant & Rothenberg, 1986)

reading which they had devised, entitled the Four Block Framework. The framework attends to the social, emotional and pedagogical needs of all children, including the least fluent readers. The four blocks are: modelling reading through shared big books, self-selected reading individually and socially, making words and writing. The studies reported encouraging results in hundreds of schools that adopted the Four Block Framework across US states (Cunningham et al., 1998; Cunningham, 2006). Schools using the method appeared to be bucking the trend of literacy attainment in high-poverty contexts. Children, including less fluent readers, were reading on average six months ahead of those in ability groups. The authors attribute these results in part to a maintenance of enthusiasm and self-belief in children with less print experience on school entry who would previously have been placed in the 'bottom' reading group.

Again, this series of studies offered guiding direction to my own research. It prompted exploration into fluidity and fix between reading groups particularly for less print-experienced readers on starting school. It also encouraged equal attention to the social, affective and pedagogical dimensions of reading, as well as experimentation with mixed-attainment alternatives to ability-grouped reading. However, the studies (Cunningham et al., 1991, 1998; Cunningham, 2006), like that of Grant and Rothenberg (1986), did not include the perspectives of children and this absence left me curious about the lived experience of children within mixed-attainment and ability-grouped reading.

Ability Grouping across Age Phases and Subjects

Research on ability-grouped reading may have been sparse since the introduction of guided reading but the subject of social equity and ability grouping *in general* continues to attract significant research interest. An England-based study by Francis and Tereshchenko (2020) involving 126 secondary schools, for example, found a large minority of students were placed in maths and English sets that did not fit their Key Stage 2 SATS results but instead reflected classed, raced and gendered stereotypes.[14] The authors found, for example, gender stereotypes reproduced in the greater prevalence of boys in the lowest set for English (60% compared to 40% for girls) and highest sets for mathematics (56% compared to 44% for girls). White pupils also dominated top groups for English, at 81%, and for mathematics at 77%. Black and mixed heritage pupils were over-represented in lower groups for both subjects, and Asian[15] pupils for English. The Centre for Research in Race and Education (Gillborn et al., 2021) draws on numerous qualitative studies to report similarly raced patterns of allocation. The greater proportion of Black pupils in lower sets, compared to White pupils of the same social class and gender, can be influenced by teachers' persistently low expectations of Black pupils (Gillborn & Youdell, 2000; Gillborn et al., 2021). For example, Joseph-Salisbury's (2020) interviews with teachers on race and racism in schools revealed an awareness of negative stereotyping of Black pupils among the staff.

In addition, pupils from economically poor families, of all ethnicities, are significantly over- represented in middle and low academic sets, according to multiple studies across curriculum subjects and ages (e.g., Dunne et al., 2007; Francis et al., 2017b; Kutnick et al., 2005; Ireson et al., 2002). Bradbury and Roberts-Holmes (2017) found children as young as four years old being allocated to ability groups based on teachers' classed assumptions about home literacy practices. One teacher in their study remarked on this by saying, "I think we end up with middle-class and *not-middle-class* groups" (p. 40, emphasis added). According to the UK's Social Mobility Commission (Shaw et al., 2016), if economically poor children are placed in lower ability groups at a young age, they make less educational progress than they do in mixed-attainment settings.

A rationale for ability grouping is that it is responsive to children's learning, with children moving between groups depending on their progress. However, once in a lower set (often at a very early age) pupils' educational trajectories are curtailed in ways that mean they are more likely to remain there (Dunne et al., 2011; Gillborn et al., 2021; Hallam & Ireson, 2006, 2007). In a review of research on teachers' and pupils' experience of setting in England and Wales, Wilkinson and Penney (2014) explain this lack of mobility. Firstly, systems can be inadequate to help teachers re-assess children's groupings based on their achievement. Schools can also overestimate movement between groups, unaware of its static nature. In addition, pupils in lower groups are usually taught a simplified or alternative curriculum, at a slower rate, often by less qualified adults, which includes disbarment from working for higher qualifications in secondary school. Slavin (1990) also found teachers were often reluctant to teach lower sets and had poor expectations of outcome. This combination of factors works against the possibility of 'catching up' and shifting groups (Gillborn & Youdell, 2000).

Parents can also exert influence both on their child's group position and on the perpetuation of ability grouping itself. According to Lareau's (2011) study of education, class and race in the US, and Taylor's (2009) study of lesbian and gay parenting in the UK, middle-class parents are significantly more proactive and effective in favourably influencing school practice for their children compared to working-class parents, including in the area of ability grouping. Working-class parents may feel less at home in dealing with school and more likely to defer to the perceived expertise of teachers (Lareau, 2011; Taylor, 2009; see also Francis et al., 2017b). For middle-class parents, fear of losing social and economic advantage can be deeply rooted in their psyche, suggests Reay (2017), and ever more so as economic and professional possibilities for their children are squeezed. In one study of White middle-class choices of urban secondary schools, being in the top set was regarded as insulation from the "undesirable Others" (Reay et al., 2011). The success of such middle-class capital to influence school practice is also racialised. Rollock et al. (2016) have shown that despite having similar capitals and educational strategies as White middle-class parents, the payoff for Black middle-class parents can be unequal as they challenge racism in their child's educational experience.

Despite reservations about ability grouping so far presented in the chapter it is still important to consider if ability grouping has a positive effect on academic attainment, and if so, whose academic attainment. In a survey of Scottish teachers, a majority of the respondents believed ability grouping made their teaching more effective *and* raised attainment for all pupils (Hamilton & O'Hara, 2011). By narrowing the 'ability' range they had to teach, ability grouping was perceived to encourage targeted support, increase interaction between children and teachers and, consequently, improve motivation and self-esteem among pupils.

This positive view of ability grouping appears to be supported by the English charity, Education Endowment Foundation (EEF).[16] Although they report that within-class ability grouping does have a positive impact on educational achievement, improving outcomes by two months, they acknowledge the weakness of the data supporting this claim (EEF, 2016, 2018). On close reading of the studies upon which their claim is made, for example, it becomes clear that the two-month increase in attainment is limited to mathematics and is based on studies that are more than 50 years old. Slavin, for example, concluded, in 1987, that there was insufficient evidence from research studies to evaluate the impact on attainment of ability-grouped reading. Evidence is also limited in what Lou et al. (1996) term their meta-analysis of studies on reading attainment. Although the studies they analysed showed a small overall improvement on attainment for ability-grouped reading, pupils in the lowest group fared less well in ability groups than in mixed-attainment settings. In 2010, Puzio and Colby conducted another meta-analysis, which included only studies conducted in the previous 30 years. Although they found that ability grouping for reading appeared to increase reading proficiency by six months, no indication was given of the effect size for different ability groups. It cannot, therefore, be ascertained from their analysis how the least fluent readers fair in ability-based reading groups. A further caution on the evidence upon which the EEF's report is based: it is unclear from the studies when ability-grouped reading was being compared to whole-class reading and when it was compared to mixed-attainment group reading.[17]

It is interesting to note too that at least two of the literature reviews drawn on by the EEF, that of Kulik and Kulik (1992) and Lou et al. (1996), appeared after an influential and damning critique of ability grouping in the US by Oakes (1985). Oakes criticises the practice for the barriers it creates for minoritised ethnic groups and those from low socioeconomic communities. The timing of these reviews could be interpreted as an effort to reassert ability grouping, which had been significantly challenged by Oakes's work. Indeed, James Kulik was part of The National Centre for the Gifted and Talented and who criticised Oakes's work for its threat to "their brightest learners ... if they were required to move at a common pace" (Kulik, 1992, p. 73).

And so, ability grouping can be understood as an educational system that, in the words of Kulik, allow the "brightest learners" to advance. This advancement is secured at the expense of pupils who are assigned to lower sets in the group hierarchy. There is scant evidence that ability grouping for reading or other subjects improves attainment (EEF, 2016, 2018). In fact, conditions within ability grouping serve to constrain educational trajectories of pupils in lower groups (Dunne et al., 2011; Hallam & Ireson, 2006, 2007). Allocation to such groups can happen as young as 4 years old (Bradbury & Roberts-Holmes, 2017) and, once there, children are more likely to remain there than shift groups (as the rationale for ability grouping might suggest). These group placements are susceptible to classed, raced and gendered stereotyping and sometimes to parental pressure, which results in disproportionate numbers of working-class children of all ethnicities being assigned to the lower positioned group (Frances & Tereshchenko, 2020; Gillborn et al., 2021).

Emotion, Affect and Ability Grouping

The chapter turns now to consider how pupils in lower groups feel about their position, and how they are positioned by others. Although the EEF (2016, 2018) summaries focus on attainment, worries about pupil morale come up so frequently in the studies they consulted that they stress the need to monitor impact on confidence and engagement of pupils in lower groups. The EEF also makes the point, as this chapter does, that "disadvantaged pupils" are more susceptible to low teacher expectations leading to over allocation to lower groups. In this regard alone, in-class ability grouping appears unlikely to close the poverty-related attainment gap. However, from personal experience as a teacher and researcher, I know that not all teachers hold such low expectations. Early in the study I was struck by how passionately a teacher spoke of the progress children were making in the lowest reading group, and how this was reflected in their changing self-view as readers.

A recurring theme in Reay's account of her 25 years of researching with children and young people is that ability grouping creates "fragile, unconfident learner identities" (2017, p. 16). She has found it common for pupils in the bottom sets to see themselves as hopeless, placed in groups marked by educational failure where they feel written off. Similar feelings are expressed by students in Boaler's (2005, 2015) studies of maths groups. The students attribute their despondency, and lack of achievement and motivation, to membership of a lower set. Middle-class parental pressure to move their children from low-positioned groups also highlights the perceived stigma of occupying lower groups (Davies et al., 2003; Lareau, 2011).

If this stigmatisation happens in literacy teaching it could be doubly injurious, given the role reading and writing play in affecting identities, educational progress and life trajectories (Duckworth, 2013; Duckworth & Cochrane, 2012; Tett, 2016). In Moss's (2000, 2007, 2021) work on gender and reading, she found that when boys are spatially marked as struggling readers, in ability groups for example, they develop avoidant reading behaviours that hamper their progress. In Chapter 4, I bring Moss's work on gender and reading into conversation with my study's findings.

Feelings of despondency and poor learner identities correspond with psychological research showing how profoundly people are affected when they believe others expect them to fail (Reay, 2017). This in turn reduces their capacity for success. But as well as hearing feelings of failure from those in the lower group, Reay also hears outrage that they are unfairly allocated less resources and teacher expertise. In primary schools, group naming can attempt to conceal the hierarchy embedded in the groups, which is still recognised by children as a hierarchy. This is clear from numerous children's comments in Marks' (2013, p. 5) study of primary mathematics, with one child explaining, "The Blue Table means you don't have a clue." Within this hierarchical relationship, children who themselves are subject to such slights can seek to distinguish themselves from those they regard as further down the hierarchy (Reay, 2017).

When we ask such questions about how children feel in different pedagogical contexts and how those feelings affect their sense of identity, positioning and learning, we begin to engage with a turn to affect in literacy scholarship. This affective turn invites the educator and the researcher to notice the embodied intensities, faint, muffled and strong, that are evoked in doing literacy (Anwaruddin, 2016; Leander & Ehret, 2019; see also Zembylas, 2021, for the related affective turn in educational theory). The term *affect* is used in the book to represent the sometimes elusive energetic intensities within and across beings. The term includes emotions but also more attitudinal reactions like enthusiasm and disengagement. Perhaps inevitably, there will be a shifting slippery coupling and uncoupling of the terms *affect*, *emotion* and *agency* in the book as there is in the literature. This follows Ahmed (2010, p. 231) who suggests that although affective reactions can be discerned separately from emotion, this is not how they are experienced in practice. "In fact," she argues, "they are contiguous; they slide into each other; they stick and cohere, even when they are separated."

There are also scholars, whose work is less closely associated with the 'affective turn', but who offer valuable insight into affect, emotion and agency in doing literacy (e.g., Duckworth, 2013; Reay, 2017). Williams (2017, p. 19), for example, who explores emotion and agency in students' writing development, helpfully defines emotion as "embodied-meaning making *and* performance" (original emphasis and hyphen). He stresses this coupling because emotions are felt and played out in the social transactions in which they arise. I also use the concepts of affect and emotion as Dutro (2019) does, with power and structure in sight, recognising that they both constrain and yield to affect.

Speaking, reading and writing are expressions of our deepest humanity (Leander and Ehret, 2019). Through them we connect to others and narrate ourselves, our histories and memories. Literacy also mediates many social, economic and cultural relationships. Whether we can read and write proficiently in a range of contexts can have significant and potentially life-defining consequences (Williams, 2017). As such, reading and writing are potent aspects of cultural capital (Bourdieu, 1986; Bourdieu, 1984). They are capitals because they confer "strength, power, and consequently profit on their holder" (Skeggs, 1997a, p. 6). They are not evenly distributed in a classed, raced and gendered society.

Through solitary and shared reading experiences, we can make sense of our lives, and increase empathy and understanding of others, according to Kidd & Castaño (2013). 'Empathy' is understood in the book as a reaction more akin to the traditional meaning of sympathy, in which one gains a sympathetic understanding of and general identification with others as fellow humans and other sentient beings (Boler, 1999). Yet, coupling reading novels with empathy, as Kidd and Castaño do, can ignore classed differences in how empathy is generated. There are continuous reminders of working-class 'habits' not orientated towards books, but this should not equate to a lack of working-class empathy or imagination. I came to understand this vital distinction through the words of author Douglas Stuart[18] in a radio interview in 2021: "I don't think not having books made us any less creative or compassionate or curious. We were all those things as kids. It's just we didn't feel invited into the world of literature." A focus of this book is the inner affective experience of learners navigating through literacy landscapes with smaller pots of legitimated cultural capital than others, who may not "feel invited into the world of literature".

The role of emotions in affecting and being affected by literacy experiences is well illustrated in *Literacy Practices and Perceptions of Agency* (Williams, 2017), which recounts 30 years of literacy participatory research in the US, Britain and Kazakhstan. Williams explains how early emotional reactions in literacy events create dispositions, which in turn affect self-view, performance and outcomes in reading and writing. I use the term *literacy event,* as Pahl and Rowsell (2020) do, by bringing affective movements into Heath's (1983) concept of any event that is, in some way, mediated by reading or writing (Heath, 1983; Pahl & Rowsell, 2020). How children and adults are viewed and positioned by others as readers and writers can profoundly influence their disposition or self-view. As Reay (2017, p. 77) has found "when we expect to be viewed as inferior our abilities seem to be diminished, and this sense of inferiority is particularly strong in the bottom sets." Aligning with feminist theorists (e.g., Duckworth, 2013; Reay, 2004, 2017), Williams argues that when affect and emotion are unconsidered, opportunities are missed to address structural barriers and to fight for more equitable literacy practices.

How children see themselves as readers may impact more on their identity than other curriculum subjects do because of the common association of reading with notions of intelligence. The linguistic and psychological coupling of reading difficulties with stupidity can be heard in the words of many of Duckworth's (2013) adult basic-skills participants. The word "thick" is peppered through the participants' discourse on finding reading difficult. Some participants described themselves as childlike because of their unconfident relationship with reading and writing. Arriving at college brought up the same fears of being judged and dismissed that many had experienced in school. And yet, the participants also describe affective acts of resistance, taking themselves out of hostile environments and "wagging school".

Refusal to accept the roles assigned by society takes many forms, in childhood and adulthood. It can be heard in Taylor's (2007) working class lesbian participants "who are necessarily, unavoidably, painfully and pleasurably, living out the intersections of class and sexuality." It can be discerned in the envy and longing of Steedman's (1987) mother as she refused to embody the role assigned to poor working-class women like herself. And it can be witnessed in the child who struggles with reading in Scherer's (2016) research. The child grabs an animal puppet and 'bites' the researcher while emitting a battle-like roar when asked why some children are better at reading than others. Although experiences can sediment and form dispositions, these dispositions, our habitus, are malleable. They are responsive to the field and to the rules of the field that are encountered. If educational contexts are changed to become more equitable and sensitive to affect, dispositions can also change, even if as Bourdieu (1990, p. 54) makes clear "the dispositions of the habitus … give disproportionate weight to early experiences." If we believe that dispositions are fixed there would be little reason to struggle for fairer, more equitable and kinder educational practices, as my research does. With regard to the common practice of placing children in 'bottom' reading groups, we might reflect on its emotional residue, both positive and negative. We can further speculate on how reading practices that foster collaboration and social integration may impact on children's sense of agency and self-view as readers.

Conclusion

With this book, I reclaim and reopen a debate about the emotional/affective and socioeconomic dimensions of guided (ability-grouped) reading. Bourdieu's theories of habitus, capitals, legitimacy and symbolic violence have been explained and are put to work in the following chapters to explore how children welcome, resist, accommodate and reject the positions entangled within ability-grouped and mixed-attainment reading. I use these tools as they have been laid out in this chapter, with a reorientation towards complexities, instabilities, resistance and ingenuity in children's experience. It is important to be clear, however, that I see this reorientation as a shift in gaze and emphasis rather than suggesting it is absent from Bourdieu's work: it is not (e.g., Bourdieu, 1999). And as Reay (1995b) says, there is something about the indeterminacy and messiness of habitus that makes it an apt tool when examining the complicated messiness of real life. I will show how different class habitus, including literacy practices, meet the reading practices valorised in school and show up in ability-grouped reading. Ability grouping, argues Reay (2017, p. 25), is one of the key mechanisms by which some children thrive at the expense of others resulting "in a very overt form of class labelling".

The chapter also presented research and scholarly literature on ability grouping that gives background to, and has guided, my ethnographic study of children's experience of ability-grouped reading and mixed-attainment reading. No source thus far has demonstrated positive social, emotional or egalitarian outcomes for ability grouping. The evidence on attainment is also unconvincing; the impact on reading attainment in particular is unproven. Conversely, the attainment outcomes for US studies of mixed-attainment reading (Cunningham, 2006; Cunningham et al., 1991, 1998) suggest something potentially life-affirming and barrier-breaking about mixed-attainment reading instruction. This promise warranted the further interrogation in the UK context that my study has provided. Little was known about children's emotional and social experience of ability-grouped reading from their perspective, a gap I felt compelled to probe. I welcome the affective turn in literacy scholarship as described by Leander and Ehret (2019), which engages with ambiguity, complexity, contradictions and the messy middle of things. I hope I have researched in ways that are attentive to affective surges and small emotional movements within and among children as they engage and disengage as readers. The reality of reading groups is more complex than I imagined when I envisioned the study. It is timely to reopen a

40 Identity, social class and learning

debate around emotional and motivational effects of ability-grouped reading that has been quiet through the years of neoliberal education policy and the promotion of guided reading by literacy scholars. The questions that guided my study are as follows:

- Does ability-grouped reading affect children's identity and feelings for reading and, if so, in what ways?
- How do social inequalities around class, race and gender intersect with the practice of ability grouping for reading development?
- What effect does mixed-attainment reading have on children's identity and attitudes to reading?

Notes

1 The Pupil Equity Fund is allocated by Scottish Government to schools, via local authorities, based on the number of families whose lives are impacted by poverty. Its intended purpose is to help close the poverty-related attainment gap. This phrase, 'the poverty-related attainment gap', has been used frequently by the Scottish Government, including in their National Improvement Frameworks since 2016. See, e.g., https://www.gov.scot/publications/closing-poverty-related-attainment-gap-report-progress-2016-2021/.
2 A school clothing grant, which is available to parents on low incomes, provides help to buy school clothes. I have used this as an indicator of economic circumstances more frequently than eligibility for free school meals because of the universal availability in Scottish schools of free school meals for children up to, and including, P3 at the time of the study.
3 I identify 'low paid' as receiving close to the minimum hourly wage in Scotland, which in 2022 was £9.50 for workers over the age of 23. According to the recruitment agency, *indeed*, the average hourly rate of a care assistant was £10.81, a cleaner, £9.91, a delivery driver, £10.53 and a refuse collector, £10.48.
4 Although the Scots language has varied status in class terms, it is often ridiculed in popular media as 'bad English' and as a working-class language or dialect (Lowing, 2017).
5 An EAL teacher was a teacher whose priority was to support the learning of children who were at various stages of learning English as an additional language.
6 'Afore' in 'The Stink Afore Rismas' is an example of Scots. He refers to the book, The Stink Before Christmas by Nixon & Rhodes (2017).
7 The Scottish Office was a department of the UK Government with a wide range of governing functions pertaining to Scotland until the Scottish Government was established in 1999 following devolution.
8 Although there have been no direct connections made between literacy and the knowledge worker in more recent NIFs, the linking of literacy with social inclusion remains a prominent aspect of the NIF.
9 Synthetic phonics is a way of teaching reading and writing in which words are broken down into, or built up from, the smallest units of sound, i.e., phonemes.
10 The CfE covers experiences and outcomes for children rather than prescribing how these experiences are to be taught or organised.
11 Most notably, Highland Literacy: Literacy for Practitioners, https://highlandliteracy.com/reading-2/guided-reading-2/ , accessed June 2024.

12 In terms of 'influence' it is worth noting that the US dominates the global education market. In 2021, the US share of global revenue from the education technology market was 35% (Grand View Research, 2022). Heinemann, based in the US, is one of the world's largest educational publishers. *Guided Reading*, written by Fountas and Pinnell in 1998, was still Heinemann's best-selling title in 2021, more than 20 years after publication (Peak, 2022). The adoption of guided reading in South Africa, for example, cites Fountas and Pinnell as the key influence (Kruizinga & Nathanson, 2010).
13 The papers by Cunningham et al. (1991, 1998) and Cunningham (2006) refer to the same study at different times.
14 SATs tests, which stand for Standard Assessment Tests, are national tests in English, mathematics and arithmetic at the end of Key Stage 1 (Year 2) and Key Stage 2 (Year 6) in England. The results of the Key Stage 2 SATs are believed to inform secondary school placement of pupils in ability streams and sets.
15 Francis and Tereshchenko do not specify whether this group is South, East or Southeast Asian or a combination but based on individual testaments in the book, 'Asian' is most likely to refer to South Asian heritage.
16 The EEF aims to give accessible research summaries on the impact of various educational initiatives. Their stated aim is to help "break the link between family income and educational achievement." https://educationendowmentfoundation.org.uk.
17 Whole class reading takes different forms but could include the practice of children taking turns to read a shared text aloud to the class. Issues around such practice include the pressure it puts on pupils to perform, the public nature of making errors, and the lack of text suitability for children at different stages of print fluency. This whole-class practice contrasts with the mixed-attainment reading explored in this book, in which texts are matched to children's reading fluency, reading is practised without public exposure, there is more concentrated interaction between the teacher and the small group of pupils, and more opportunities for collaboration between the pupils.
18 Douglas Stuart is the Scottish author of the Booker prize-winning novel, Shuggy Bain. The book echoes his own working-class upbringing as a White queer boy navigating poverty, homophobia and his mother's alcoholism in a community affected by deindustrialisation in the 1980s. Reading had not been a common pastime growing up.

References

Ahmed, S. (2010). *The promise of happiness*. Duke University Press.
Anwaruddin, S. M. (2016). Why critical literacy should turn to 'the affective turn': Making a case for critical affective literacy. *Discourse: Studies in the Cultural Politics of Education*, 37(3), 381–396.
Boaler, J. (2005). The 'psychological prisons' from which they never escaped: The role of ability grouping in reproducing social class inequalities. *Forum*, 47(2), 125–134. Symposium Journals.
Boaler, J. (2015). *Mathematical mindsets: Unleashing students' potential through creative math, inspiring messages and innovative teaching*. John Wiley & Sons.
Boler, M. (1999). *Feeling power: Emotions and education*. Routledge.
Bourdieu, P. (1984). *Distinction: A social critique of the judgement of taste*. Routledge & Kegan Paul.
Bourdieu, P. (1986). The forms of capital. In J. Richardson (Ed.), *Handbook for theory and research for the sociology of education*. Greenwood Press.
Bourdieu, P. (1990). *The logic of practice*. Stanford University Press.

Bourdieu, P., & Accardo, A. (1999). *The weight of the world: Social suffering in contemporary society*. Stanford University Press.
Bourdieu, P., & Passeron, J.-C. (1979). *The inheritors: French students and their relation to culture*. University of Chicago Press.
Bourdieu, P., & Passeron, J. C. (1990). *Reproduction in education, society and culture*. SAGE.
Bradbury, A., & Roberts-Holmes, G. (2017). *Grouping in early years and key stage 1– "A Necessary Evil"?* National Education Union, London. https://discovery.ucl.ac.uk/id/eprint/10039076
Brancaleone, D., & O'Brien, S. (2011). Educational commodification and the (economic) sign value of learning outcomes. *British Journal of Sociology of Education*, 32(4), 501–519. https://doi.org/10.1080/01425692.2011.578435
Brandt, D. (2005). Writing for a living: Literacy and the knowledge economy. *Written Communication*, 22(2), 166–197. https://doi.org/10.1177/0741088305275218
Cassen, R., & Kingdon, G. (2007). *Tackling low educational achievement*. Joseph Rowntree Foundation.
Costa, C., & Murphy, M. (2015). *Bourdieu, Habitus and Social Research: The Art of Application*. Palgrave Macmillan.
Cunningham, P. M. (2006). High-poverty schools that beat the odds. *The Reading Teacher*, 60(4), 382–385. https://doi.org/10.1598/RT.60.4.9
Cunningham, P. M., Hall, D. P., & Defee, M. (1991). Non-ability grouped, multilevel instruction: A year in a first-grade classroom. *Reading Teacher*, 44(8), 566–571
Cunningham, P. M., Hall, D. P., & Defee, M. (1998). Nonability-grouped, multilevel instruction: Eight years later. *Reading Teacher*, 51(8), 652–664.
Davies, J., Hallam, S., & Ireson, J. (2003). Ability groupings in the primary school: Issues arising from practice. *Research papers in Education*, 18(1), 45–60.
Department for Education. (2022). *The Reading Framework: Teaching the Foundations of Literacy*. https://assets.publishing.service.gov.uk/government/uploads/system/uploads/attachment_data/file/1050849/Reading_framework_Teaching_the_foundations_of_literacy_-_July_2021_Jan_22_update.pdf
Department for Education and Employment. (1998). *The National Literacy Strategy: Framework for teaching*. DfEE.
Duckworth, V. (2013). *Learning trajectories, violence and empowerment amongst adult basic skills learners*. Routledge.
Duckworth, V., & Cochrane, M. (2012). Spoilt for choice, spoilt by choice: Long-term consequences of limitations imposed by social background. *Education+ Training*, 54(7), 579-591.
Dunne, M., Humphreys, S., Dyson, A., Sebba, J., Gallannaugh, F., & Muijs, D. (2011). The teaching and learning of pupils in low-attainment sets. *Curriculum Journal*, 22(4), 485–513.
Dunne, M., Humphreys, S., Sebba, J., Dyson, A., Gallannaugh, F., & Muijs, D. (2007). *Effective teaching and learning for pupils in low attaining groups*. University of Sussex. https://dera.ioe.ac.uk/6622/
Dutro, E. (2019). How affect theory can support justice in our literacy classrooms: Attuning to the visceral. *Language Arts*, 96(6), 384–389.
Education Endowment Foundation. (2016). *Teaching and learning toolkit, setting and streaming*. https://educationendowmentfoundation.org.uk/resources/teaching-learning-toolkit
Education Endowment Foundation. (2018). *Teaching and learning toolkit, within-class attainment grouping*. https://educationendowmentfoundation.org.uk/resources/teaching-learng-toolkit
Education Scotland. (2023). *Curriculum for excellence*. https://education.gov.scot/documents/All-experiencesoutcomes18.pdf

Fisher, A. (2008). Teaching comprehension and critical literacy: Investigating guided reading in three primary classrooms. *Literacy*, 42(1), 19–28. https://doi.org/10.1111/j.1467-9345.2008.00477.x

Fountas, I. C., & Pinnell, G. S. (1998). *Guided reading: Good first teaching for all children*. Heinemann.

Francis, B., Connolly, P., Archer, L., Hodgen, J., Mazenod, A., Pepper, D., Sloan, S., Taylor, B., Tereshchenko, A. & Travers, M. (2017b). Attainment grouping as self-fulfilling prophesy? A mixed methods exploration of self-confidence and set level among year 7 students. *International Journal of Educational Research*, 86, 96–108.

Francis, B., & Tereshchenko, A. (2020). *Reassessing ability grouping: Improving practice for equity and attainment*. Routledge.

Giddens, A. (1991a). *Modernity and self-identity: Self and society in the late modern age*. Polity Press in association with Basil Blackwell.

Giddens, A. (1991b). *The consequences of modernity*. Polity Press.

Gillborn, D., Bhopal, K., Crawford, C., Demack, S., Gholami, R., Kitching, K., Kiwan, D., & Warmington, P. (2021). *Evidence for the commission on race and ethnic disparities*. University of Birmingham CRRE. https://doi.org/10.25500/epapers.bham.00003389

Gillborn, D., & Youdell, D. (2000). *Rationing education: Policy, practice, reform, and equity*. McGraw-Hill Education (UK).

Goldthorpe, J. H., & Marshall, G. (1992). The promising future of class analysis: A response to recent critiques. *Sociology*, 26(3), 381–400. https://doi.org/10.1177/0038038592026003002

Grand View Research. (2022). *Education technology market size, share & trends analysis report by sector (preschool, K-12, higher education), by end-user (business, consumer), by type, by deployment, by region, and segment forecasts, 2023–2030*. https://www.grandviewresearch.com/industry-analysis/education-technology-market

Grant, L., & Rothenberg, J. (1986). The social enhancement of ability differences: Teacher-student interactions in first-and second-grade reading groups. *The Elementary School Journal*, 87(1), 29–49.

Hallam, S., & Ireson, J. (2006). Secondary school pupils' preferences for different types of structured grouping practices. *British Educational Research Journal*, 32(4), 583–599.

Hallam, S., & Ireson, J. (2007). Secondary school pupils' satisfaction with their ability grouping placements. *British Educational Research Journal*, 33(1), 27–45.

Haller, E. J., & Davis, S. A. (1980). Does socioeconomic status bias the assignment of elementary school students to reading groups? *American Educational Research Journal*, 17(4), 409–418.

Hamilton, L., & O'Hara, P. (2011). The tyranny of setting (ability grouping): Challenges to inclusion in Scottish primary schools. *Teaching and Teacher Education*, 27(4), 712–721.

Heath, S. B. (1983). *Ways with words: Language, life and work in communities and classrooms*. Cambridge University Press.

Hobsbaum, A., Gamble, N., & Reedy, D. (2006). *Guiding reading: A handbook for teaching guided reading at key stage 2*. Institute of Education, University of London.

Ireson, J., Hallam, S., Hack, S., Clark, H., & Plewis, I. (2002). Ability grouping in English secondary schools: Effects on attainment in English, Mathematics and Science. *Educational Research and Evaluation*, 8(3), 299–318. https://doi.org/10.1076/edre.8.3.299.3854

Joseph-Salisbury, R. (2020). *Race and racism in English secondary schools*. Runnymede Trust. https://assets-global.website- files.com/61488f992b58e687f1108c7c/61bcc0cc2a023368396c03d4_Runnymede%20Secondary%20Schools%20report%20FINAL.pdf

Kidd, D. C., & Castano, E. (2013). Reading literary fiction improves theory of mind. *Science, 342*(6156), 377–380.

Kruizinga, A., & Nathanson, R. (2010). An evaluation of guided reading in three primary schools in the Western Cape. *Per Linguam, 26*(2), 67–76.

Kulik, J. A. (1992). *An analysis of the research on ability grouping: Historical and contemporary perspectives*. University of Connecticut, The National Research Center on the Gifted and Talented.

Kulik, J. A., & Kulik, C.-L. C. (1992). Meta-analytic findings on grouping programs. *Gifted Child Quarterly, 36*(2), 73–77.

Kutnick, P., Sebba, J., Blatchford, P., Galton, M., Thorp, J., MacIntyre, H., & Berdondini, L. (2005). *The effects of Ppupil grouping: Literature review* (Vol. 688). Department for education and skills, Research Report RR688. https://dera.ioe.ac.uk/18143/1/RR688.pdf

Lareau, A. (2011). *Unequal childhoods: Class, race, and family life*. University of California Press.

Lawler, S. (1999). 'Getting Out and Getting Away': Women's narratives of class mobility. *Feminist Review, 63*, 3–24.

Lawler, S. (2014). *Identity: Sociological perspectives* (2nd ed.). Polity Press.

Leander, K. M., & Ehret, C. (2019). *Affect in literacy learning and teaching: Pedagogies, politics and coming to know*. Routledge.

Lou, Y., Abrami, P. C., Spence, J. C., Poulsen, C., Chambers, B., & d'Apollonia, S. (1996). Within-class grouping: A meta-analysis. *Review of Educational Research, 66*(4), 423–458. https://doi.org/10.3102/00346543066004423

Lowing, K. (2017). The Scots language and its cultural and social capital in Scottish schools: A case study of Scots in Scottish secondary classrooms. *Scottish Language, 36*, 1–21.

Marks, R. (2013). "The blue table means you don't have a clue": The persistence of fixed-ability thinking and practices in primary mathematics in English schools. *Forum: For Promoting 3–19 Comprehensive Education, 55*(1), 31–44.

Marx, K. (1992 [1867]). *Capital: Volume III*. Penguin UK.

Marx, K. (2004 [1867]). *Capital: Volume I*. Penguin UK.

McKenzie, L. (2015). *Getting by: Estates, class and culture in Austerity Britain*. Policy Press.

McNay, L. (2004). Agency and experience: Gender as a lived relation. In L. Adkins & B. Skeggs (Eds.), *Feminism after Bourdieu* (pp. 175 –190). Blackwell Publishing.

Moss, G. (2000). Raising boys' attainment in reading: Some principles for intervention. *Reading, 34*(3), 101–106.

Moss, G. (2007). *Literacy and gender: Researching texts, contexts and readers*. Routledge.

Moss, G. (2021). Literacies and social practice: Sociological perspectives on reading research. *Education 3–13, 49*(1), 41–51. https://doi.org/10.1080/03004279.2020.1824701

Oakes, J. (1985). *Keeping track: How schools structure inequality*. Yale University Press.

Olssen, M., & Peters, M. A. (2005). Neoliberalism, higher education and the knowledge economy: From the free market to knowledge capitalism. *Journal of Education Policy, 20*(3), 313–345. https://doi.org/10.1080/02680930500108718

Pahl, K., & Rowsell, J. (2020). *Living literacies: Literacy for social change*. MIT Press.

Patrick, F. (2013). Neoliberalism, the knowledge economy, and the learner: Challenging the inevitability of the commodified self as an outcome of education. *International Scholarly Research Notices*, 2013(4), 1–8. https://doi.org/10.1155/2013/108705

Peak, C. (2022, November 10). *Heinemann's billion-dollar sales have nationwide reach*. APM Reports. https://www.apmreports.org/story/2022/11/10/heinemann-sales-by-school-district

Peters, M. (2001). National education policy constructions of the 'knowledge economy': Towards a critique. *Journal of Educational Enquiry*, 2(1), 1–22.

Peters, M. A., & Humes, W. (Eds.). (2003). Education in the knowledge economy. *Policy Futures in Education*, 1(1), 1–19.

Puzio, K., & Colby, G.T. (2010). The Effects of within Class Grouping on Reading Achievement: A Meta-Analytic Synthesis. *Society for Research on Educational Effectiveness*.

Reay, D. (1995b). 'They employ cleaners to do that': habitus in the primary classroom. *British Journal of Sociology of Education*, 16(3), 353–371. https://doi.org/10.1080/0142569950160305

Reay, D. (2004). Gendering Bourdieu's concept of capitals?: Emotional capital, women and social class. In L. Adkins & B. Skeggs (Eds.), *Feminism after Bourdieu* (pp. 57–74). Blackwell Publishing.

Reay, D. (2017). *Miseducation: Inequality, education and the working classes*. Policy Press.

Reay, D., Crozier, G., & James, D. (2011). *White middle-class identities and urban schooling*. Palgrave Macmillan.

Rollock, N. (2014). Race, class and 'the harmony of dispositions'. *Sociology*, 48(3), 445–451.

Rollock, N., Gillborn, D., Warmington, P., & Demack, S. (2016). *Race, racism and education: Inequality, resilience and reform in policy*. University of Birmingham.

Rose, J. (2006). *Independent review of the teaching of early reading: Final report*. https://dera.ioe.ac.uk/5551/2/report.pdf

Savage, M. (2015). *Social class in the 21st century*. Pelican Books.

Savage, M. (2016). The fall and rise of class analysis in British sociology, 1950–2016. *Tempo Social*, 28, 57–72.

Scherer, L. (2016). 'I am not clever, they are cleverer than us': Children reading in the primary school. *British Journal of Sociology of Education*, 37(3), 389–407. https://doi.org/10.1080/01425692.2014.948989

Scottish Government. (2015). *National Improvement Framework and Improvement Plan (NIF)*. https://education.gov.scot/parentzone/learning-in-scotland/national-improvement-framework/

Scottish Office. (1999). *Targeting excellence—modernising Scotland's schools*. The Stationery Office Edinburgh.

Shaw, B., Menzies, L., Bernardes, E., Baars, S., Nye, P., & Allen, R. (2016). *Ethnicity, gender and social mobility*. Social Mobility Commission. https://assets.publishing.service.gov.uk/government/uploads/system/uploads/attachment_data/file/579988/Ethnicity_gender_and_social_mobility.pdf

Singh, A. (2022). Exploring the racial habitus through John's story: On race, class and adaptation. *The Sociological Review*, 70(1), 140–158. https://doi.org/10.1177/03611981211051519

Siraj-Blatchford, I., & Troyna, B. (1993). Equal opportunities, research and educational reform: Some introductory notes. *British Educational Research Journal*, 19(3), 223–226.

Skeggs, B. (1997a). *Formations of class & gender: Becoming respectable*. SAGE.

Skeggs, B. (1997b). Classifying practices: Representations, capitals and recognitions. In P. Mahony & C. Zmroczek (Eds.), *Class matters: 'Working-class' women's perspectives on social class* (pp. 123–139). Taylor & Francis.

Skeggs, B. (2004). *Class, self, culture*. Routledge.

Skeggs, B. (2020, July 28). Does class still matter? Webinar with Beverley Skeggs and Andrew Sayer. *Lancaster Sociology Webinar*. https://www.youtube.com/watch?v=mE-GCiVgqyc

Skidmore, D., Perez-Parent, M., & Arnfield, S. (2003). Teacher-pupil dialogue in the guided reading session. *Reading, 37*(2), 47–53.

Slavin, R. E. (1990). Achievement effects of ability grouping in secondary schools: A best-evidence synthesis. *Review of Educational Research, 60*(3), 471–499.

Steedman, C. (1987). *Landscape for a good woman: A story of two lives*. Rutgers University Press.

Taylor, Y. (2007). *Working-class lesbian life: Classed outsiders*. Palgrave Macmillan.

Taylor, Y. (2009). *Lesbian and gay parenting: Securing social and educational capital*. Palgrave Macmillan.

Taylor, Y. (2012). *Educational diversity: The subject of difference and different subjects*. Springer.

Tennent, W., Reedy, D., Hobsbaum, A., & Gamble, N. (2016). *Guiding readers-layers of meaning: A handbook for teaching reading comprehension to 7–11 year olds*. UCL IoE Press.

Tett, L. (2016). Learning, literacy and identity: 'I don't think I'm a failure any more'. *Journal of Sociology of Education, 37*(3), 427–444. https://doi.org/10.1080/01425692.2014.939265

Tyler, I. (2013). *Revolting subjects: Social abjection and resistance in neoliberal Britain*. Zed Books.

Tyler, I. (2020). *Stigma: The machinery of inequality*. Zed Books.

Wilkinson, S. D., & Penney, D. (2014). The effects of setting on classroom teaching and student learning in mainstream mathematics, English and science lessons: A critical review of the literature in England. *Educational Review, 66*(4), 411–427. https://doi.org/10.1080/00131911.2013.787971

Williams, B. T. (2007). Why Johnny can never, ever read: The perpetual literacy crisis and student identity. *Journal of Adolescent & Adult Literacy, 51*(2), 178–182.

Williams, B. T. (2017). *Literacy practices and perceptions of agency: Composing identities*. Routledge.

Young, C. (2019). Increased frequency and planning: A more effective approach to guided reading in Grade 2. *The Journal of Educational Research, 112*(1), 121–130. https://doi.org/10.1080/00220671.2018.1451814

Zembylas, M. (2021). The affective turn in educational theory. In *Oxford research encyclopedia of education*. https://doi.org/10.1093/acrefore/9780190264093.013.1272

Children's Literature Reference

Nixon, S., & Rhodes, M. (2017). *The stink before christmas*. Scholastic.

3
A FEELING FOR READING

Introduction

This ethnography was guided by a central concern, that of ability-grouped reading and its effects on children's identity and feelings for reading, and how social inequalities around class, race and gender intersect in this reading practice. Yet, as mentioned in Chapter 1, these concerns still risk missing aspects of children's reading that may be obscured by the adult social scientist's preoccupations and assumptions about ability grouping. And so, I begin, with this chapter, to portray more generally how reading mattered and did not matter to the children in the 'bottom' reading group. I show how reading identities and reading events were felt in the body, expressed with words and in the emotional tone of those words. The chapter is primarily about children in the 'bottom' reading group, and where children from other reading groups are introduced, this will be made clear.

Three themes are presented to illustrate the children's affective relationship with reading, assuming a multimodal understanding of what reading can involve (Jewitt 2008; Kress, 2000; Pahl & Rowsell, 2020). The first of these themes, *Enthusiastic Lovers of Stories*, introduces the children as inquisitive appreciators of stories, stories that come in many forms including visual, oral and print. When books are referred to, it is in the specific context of stories being read to them in school. The second theme, *Books in the Matrix of Children's Lives*, shifts location, to how books, specifically, fitted into children's home and social lives. In the final section, *Reading Can Also Be a Wee Bit Nerve-Wracking*, I illustrate how children felt and acted when they read print for themselves in school, as opposed to when others read to them. The three themes are developed through narrative portraits

(Rodríguez-Dorans & Jacobs, 2020) that exemplify rather than fragment their voices, offering a more holistic view of complex personhoods (Wilson & Milne, 2016). I attend as closely to the children's joy and agency as to their anxieties and constrictions. Towards the end of the chapter, I specifically explore the act of deciphering and making sense of printed words, and for clarity I distinguish this as print reading. The reading of words still involves an interplay with the reading of visuals, such as in picturebooks and comics. However, deciphering the written code is such a key focus for children's reading development that it can be saturated with particular emotions and meaning.

Enthusiastic Lovers of Stories

One of the first things that struck me in the study was what enthusiastic lovers of stories the children were. This love of story is itself a less told story in much of the research literature. By beginning here, I contrast my findings with work that more often foregrounds disaffection, concealment and emotional stress around reading for children in, for example, the lowest positioned reading group (e.g., Hempel-Jorgensen et al., 2018; Moss, 2007; Scherer, 2016). Children's appreciation of stories can be missed when attention is drawn to problems around reading as it is taught and organised in school.

Almost all the children in the 'bottom' reading group ($N = 10$ of 14) expressed delight in stories. This was observed in words, through bodies bent towards books and comics, through light in their eyes and requests for more stories. Their delight in book-based stories was particularly clear when the stories were read *to* them, by me, their teachers or friends; that is, when the children did not have to grapple with deciphering print for themselves. In these contexts, they were not disengaged from books at all, fictional or factual. This observation chimes with one influential study on The Power of Reading Project run by the Centre for Literacy in Primary Education in London (O'Sullivan and McGonigle, 2010). The authors reported the positive impact on children who were positioned as struggling readers when books were read aloud by the teacher. From my own study, the following narrative portrait of Jamie, a White working-class boy of Scottish heritage, is illustrative of the agency and engagement in story expressed by most children in the lowest positioned group. The narrative portrait was composed from fieldnotes and audio-taped conversation.

A Feeling for Reading   49

FIGURE 3.1   Self-portrait by Jamie.

Jamie: A Narrative Portrait

Jamie is in the lowest positioned reading group, and he loves a good story. He flags his interest in stories the very first time I read with him, in the following way. Laying out a selection of picture books, I say, "Shall we have a little read? I can tell you a bit about them if you w--" Jamie cuts me off mid-flow, with a smile dancing through his words. "There's one book I'm staring at right now," he says. He is ahead of me, already picking out what he would like to read. This turns out to be Hermelin by Mini Grey, a story of lost objects found by a small detective mouse. The following sequence captures an affective engagement with the story, expressed through unwavering attention, smiles and talk-back that was characteristic of us reading a book together. The text from the book is written here in italics, to distinguish it from our chat.

Jess:	*Lady Chumley-Plumley was talking on the phone but also dangling her arm out of the window.*
Jamie:	So, I'm guessing that's her!
Jess:	I think that's a pretty good guess. I would guess that.
Jamie:	Wait! Does it say 'mumbling'?
Jess:	It says *Lady Chumley was talking on the phone.*
Jamie:	Awww.
Jess:	But '*blah blah blah*' is like talking, isn't it? It's like pretend talking.

Jamie: It's like pretend but it's also like mumbling!
[The reading continues with Jamie commenting on each new event]
Jamie: That's going to fall out the windae [window]! It's even sitting on the windae ledge!
Jess: (laughs) Precarious! *Captain Potts was trying to feed Parsley, his cat.*
Jamie: He's ee'in' [eating] the fish!
Jess: He's ee'in' the fish. I bet that's Parsley. *Emily at Number 33, was pouring herself a serving of Crunchy Flakes.*
Jamie: It even says '*Crunchy Flakes*'!
Jess: Oh so it does. *Baby McMumbo had just thrown his toast into the flower bed.*
Jamie: Aye, see wance [once]…that's just like ma big brother. 'Cause see wance, he had like a wee pen and he dropped it on the road. And he dropped it on the road because he's clumsy… I'm no clumsy and I'm seven!

Jamie, Fairfield, Kelvin

I laughed along with Jamie as he recounted his brother's clumsiness. It was such a pleasure to read with him; his enthusiasm for stories was infectious. He seemed completely absorbed in the characters and events as they unfolded, connecting different parts of the story, thinking ahead, asserting opinions and relating the story to his own life. His intimate dialogue with the story revealed the very opposite of a disengaged reader. He was doing what engaged readers generally do according to Chambers (2011) in his important work, *Tell Me: Children, Reading and Talk*. If you listen in to people's book talk, Chambers suggests, it will meander along the three intersecting paths in Jamie's book chat: sharing enthusiasms, sharing puzzles or confusions and making connections within the text and with things previously read, seen or experienced. In addition, reading *Hermelin* with Jamie had the conditions that Cremin (2019, p. 6, 8) argues are crucial for children's development as agentic readers: it was "reader-led, reader-owned … social, affective and relational". If there is value in cultivating this love of reading, and I believe there is, then adults and peers may have a vital role to play through engaging authentically with children in these intimate informal "book blethers" as fellow readers (Cremin, 2019, p. 7).

But there are many ways to enjoy a good story. While Jamie's enthusiastic engagement in sharing a book in school was not uncommon among those in the lowest positioned group, some enjoyed their stories in other ways. Puzzle,[1] for example, created her own stories through recalling and reworking stories told to her by her mum. She also incorporated elements from her computer games and her collection of small plastic characters she called The Grocery Gang. In one audio-taped conversation she told me stories for

FIGURE 3.2   Self-portrait by Puzzle.

30 minutes, without pausing for breath it seemed, and spent less than three minutes answering questions I asked about reading books. Her response to my question of what she thought about reading was, "it's kinda boring". In the following narrative portrait, composed only from her words, she weaves together aspects of her life into characterful oral stories.

Puzzle: A Narrative Portrait

>Sometimes I play with ma toys called Grocery Gang. I can show you them. They're like cool little guys. Try not to lose them. I think this guy has poop on his head. I just call him Poop-Duck. This guy, I haven't got this guy's name yet.

>Mmmm, maybe Alex might do. Alex left the school by the way. This guy's called Crazy because he is *crazy*. This is a Rare. I've a secret Rare in ma house. He's so tiny. I could lose him really easily. Mustardy, Watermelon Sugar, Frankenstein, Blue Ketchup, that's all ma guys. Ma mum has like a secret bit where she'll like open her bed and there's like thousands of books. They're like ideas for her so she likes telling me them, so then I can fall asleep quicker. Reindeer at the Window, that's the best. Ma mum made it up basically when I was like four years old, sometimes in Polish

and sometimes in English. There was like a reindeer out the window. I was playing the Xbox and (ma brother) wouldn't let me play the computer, then we were in a little fight and then the reindeer at the window said em, "If you fight one more time, I'll take all the stuff away and you won't get it ever again." Then there's Reindeer out the House instead of Reindeer out the Window. Part three is Reindeer on the Roof. Part four is Reindeer on the Toilet. That's quite funny.

Puzzle, St Jude's, Avon

Re-reading my reflective journal about this conversation I was surprised to read that the focus of my attention was on the believability of her words, not because I thought children less believable but for the many social reasons people are selective in what they share (Plummer, 1995). Was she recounting her mum's stories, I wondered, or had Puzzle adapted these into cautionary tales? It seems now that this misses the most interesting thing about them. The importance of her words surely lies in her as a creator of stories, in which events and ideas from many areas of her life flow together to create unique humorous tales. Puzzle's stories also point to impermanency of experience since when I returned to school a year later, Puzzle had forgotten all about the Grocery Gang. She was now an avid reader of cartoon books, specifically the *Dog Man* series by Dav Pilkey.

Cash, a White working-class boy of Scottish heritage, also told stories when we chatted and read together, about the adventures of his new pet tortoise, Micky, named after Michelangelo from *Ninja Turtles*; of flying dinosaurs called pterodactyls that he discovered through watching programmes on Netflix; and the narrative games he and his friends played in the playground, like *Zombie Apocalypse*. The words seemed to tumble out of him as he told me about these things. He also enjoyed listening to stories in books. When I asked what his favourite thing was to do in school, he told me it was reading café. In the reading café children got to choose reading material and read socially together. He said,

I love it, and you get like a little biscuit or a drink or something too. And you can talk to like your people next to you about your book and all that. 'cept sometimes see … the teacher actually reads to us sometimes in our reading café. Like if people (have) like trouble with their reading, like you can go down to the teacher and like read a book and all that.

Cash, St Jude's, Clyde

While transcribing this part of our conversation, I paused on the topic of the reading café and wondered whether Cash was telling me what he might think a book-obsessed adult like myself may want to hear. But I also hear that, just like Puzzle, there are many narrative pathways in his imagination. Some of these were nourished by a similar sociability around reading that was heard in Jamie's story.

Each of these examples illustrate the rich, multidimensional and contextualised nature of children's reading that was grounded in their lives. These accounts challenge deficit portrayals of working-class language and life that blame the poverty-related literacy attainment gap on "poor" early language in "lower social classes" (Siraj et al., 2021; see also Fernald & Weislender, 2015). Children's love of stories also complicates a dualistic portrayal of readers as either engaged or disengaged. How these children show up as readers depends on the context. This point is made by Learned's (2016) in her study of adolescents positioned as struggling readers in the US. The school allocated pupils to "engaged" and "unengaged" reading classes. When allocated to "unengaged" reading classes, pupils reported feelings of demoralisation, injustice and doubt about their intelligence. Yet, when the same pupils were in cross-curricular contexts, where co-construction was embedded in the pedagogy, they enacted very different reader identities. Only in this context would they persevere to develop reading-related skills. Likewise, the intention of this chapter is to eschew any homogenising of children's experience as readers or feelings about reading. The importance of context has been emphasised in their enactment of reader identities and affective responses to reading.

While this section has explored the role stories play generally in their lives, the next section focuses specifically on the place and weight that books occupied in their home and social lives.

Books in the Matrix of Children's Lives

For the majority of children in the 'bottom' reading group ($N = 13$ of 14) books seemed to occupy a relatively unimportant place in their home and social lives. Other things, such as time spent with siblings and cousins, playing outside with friends, pets, computer games and toys took up more affective space when they talked of their lives. The following narrative portrait of Millie, a White working-class girl of Scottish heritage, is illustrative of the relationship with books that many of the children in the 'bottom' reading group described having at home. The narrative portrait is composed from fieldnotes and audio-taped conversations with Millie.

54 Identity, social class and learning

FIGURE 3.3 Self-portrait by Millie.

Millie: A Narrative Portrait

Millie is seven years old. She has lots of friends, all girls. She likes to dance and is an enthusiastic member of the Lunchtime Zumba Club in school. Reading books is part, but not the be-all and end-all, of her rich life. In my conversation with her and her friend Ellie, I can hear how reading fits into her life as a daughter, a sister, a reader and a future adult self. Reading is neither stressful, absent or singularly defining in the way she talks about her life. She has a few books at home, some got from trips to *McDonalds*, the fast-food restaurant, and she reads them, she tells me, mainly by herself. If she is not reading it is because there are other things that she wants to do, things she sees others in her family do.

She loves her stepsisters and as she talks of them her voice becomes stronger and more effervescent, her body more animated. When they come to her house at the weekend, she would rather play with them than read a book, she says. I ask whether she thinks she will read a lot when she is an adult, and her response again illustrates the comfortable non-dominant place that reading occupies in her life. She says, "Em, maybe not because when you're older … you would have something else that you really like. And like you might want to go out and all that, and you like to go places … When you're older you can, you'll have a car… I don't think

I want to drive when... I'm really bigger so I want to when I'm a teenager because my sister did."

Millie, St Jude's, Avon

Millie talks of a life full of people, activities and things she values and enjoys. Reading fits in to her life; it is just doesn't take centre-stage. Many, though not all, children in the lowest positioned reading group enacted reader identities similar to Millie's, that asserted their affective disinterest in reading books at home and in their free time. The pastime of reading books was often found in the margins of their lives, off-centred by their enthusiasm for computer games, toys, playing, dancing, pets and family life. It was easy for a literacy researcher like me, who brought a strong belief in the emotionally, intellectually and economically transformative power of reading books, to perceive a deficit in these stories that is not there.

Something that underpins deficit views of working-class lives is a binary that presents books as either absent or ever-present in children's daily lives (Anderson et al., 2003). Although this will be returned to more extensively in Chapter 5, the next short section begins to complicate this binary by illustrating the flexible affective relationship that children in the lowest positioned group had with books. In turn, this flexible relationship further challenges categorisations of readers as either engaged or disengaged. I do this by sharing stories of Jeffy, a White working-class boy of Scottish heritage. Like Millie, Jeffy told me in passing one day that he would much rather play with his toys than read a book. Yet the following narrative portrait composed from field notes shows that books do feature in the abundant things that capture Jeffy's interest. Extracts from the book we were reading are written in italics to help you, the reader, navigate through the cacophony. What is revealed is that books can matter differently in different moments and contexts.

Jeffy: A Narrative Portrait

I invite Jeffy to come and read and chat today. As we enter (the nurture room) he spots two large boxes on the floor, brimming full of toys. A bright red plastic hyper-muscled man catches his eye. He really wants to buy him, he says. We move to the couch, and I ask if he would like me to read to him from the selection of books I have spread out on the floor. He chooses *Pugs of the Frozen North*, by Philip Reeve and Sarah McIntyre, which his teacher has been reading to the class. Already, writing these field notes a couple of hours afterwards I can't quite remember what order the following conversation came in. It all happened in a jumpy-about way, but it went something like this.

56 Identity, social class and learning

FIGURE 3.4 Self-portrait by Jeffy.

Very quickly, Jeffy says, "Oh is that a puppet over there?" He goes to investigate, sees a duck puppet, and Ducky comes with him to hear the story. Jeffy tells me that he usually comes to school in his dad's van. His dad works in a garage fixing cars. He's good at fixing cars, he says. I ask if his mum works, and he says she works in a big shop. She's a seller. *Meanwhile Professor Shackleton Jones has arrived to begin the race. The professor, hearing of the coming of winter that signals the beginning of the race, had gone straight to the airport.* "Maybe it was Glasgow airport," says Jeffy. He likes Glasgow airport. Next year, he and his family, mum, dad, grandparents and sister are going to PortAventura. They are flying Jet2. He likes colourful planes like Jet2 and Easy Jet, not plain white ones. *Now Sir Basil Sprout-Dumpling arrives.* "He's a meany," says Jeffy and Ducky's face makes a perplexed expression. "Look Jess," he says, pointing to Ducky's quirking mouth. At some point the Black and Decker workbench calls his attention. He used to have one like this, he says. His favourite things are cars. He has an ambulance station at home with two ambulances in it. He also loves egg sandwiches. He had an egg roll with coleslaw yesterday for his lunch. I ask him a few times if he would like me to read a little more and each time he says yes. I read about a paragraph at a time, before we meander off on another interesting tangent.

Jeffy, St Jude's, Clyde

Far from an impoverished inner wasteland devoid of the richness of books, this extract shows Jeffy's inner life bursting with colour, ideas and fascinations. The book did catch his attention among the many other things that capture his attention. And at times the book prompted connections with those many other things, like airports, colourful planes and holidays. The extract also reveals a relationship with books that complicates the binary of engaged and disengaged readers in much of the discourse about boys' underachievement in reading (e.g., Frater, 1997; Hoff Sommers, 2015; Whitmire, 2010). In Moss's (2000, 2007) work on children's literacy and gender, for example, she identifies three categories of readers: *can and do* readers (those who can read and chose to read), *can and don't* readers (those who can read but don't chose to read) and *can't yet/don't* readers (those who cannot yet read print independently). Although these categories illuminate useful patterns when exploring influences on children as readers, they may also conceal the slipperiness of interest and attention. This fluidity means that, in any moment, the so-called disengaged readers can be engaged in books and vice versa. This observation is important because it challenges debates around boys and reading which, as Scholes et al. (2021, p. 2) point out, "often homogenise young males as reluctant, disengaged and, at times, adversarial readers", particularly working-class boys. It is a deficit view which may conceal sparks of engagement, which if fanned, could ignite in more sustained concentration and enjoyment of books and other printed material.

Indeed, when I returned to St Jude's a year on from the pre-pandemic fieldwork both Millie and Jeffy expressed different feelings about books. When I visited Jeffy's class, he put his hand up and told me he was reading David Walliams' *Billionaire Boy* in bed at night. In Avon class I frequently observed Millie reading side by side with her friend Ellie, both absorbed in their own copies of *Dork Diaries* by Rachel Renée Russell. Feelings shift both within reading events and with changing times and influences. One influence on the children's shift in reader identity, among many others, could be their involvement in this study, which was all about reading. Their desire to tell me, the researcher, about their engagement with reading could reveal influence of the researcher on the researched (Oswald et al., 2014).

Encountering Bourdieu's notion of what he terms, "the cultural arbitrary" (Bourdieu & Passeron, 1990, p. 8) proved a turning point in how I heard children's stories of home and inner lives that did not necessarily pivot around the reading of books. Bourdieu uses the term *cultural arbitrary* to argue that what gains cultural legitimacy has *no innate superiority* but masquerades as such when asserted by the more economically and culturally powerful in a society. As a White, university-educated woman, I fit the demographic of those most likely to read books and to proclaim their value (Griswold et al., 2005). Through misrecognition, the reading habits of this group to which I belong are elevated above other pastimes and come to signal being better, cleverer and more 'refined' (Atkinson, 2016). It is this notion of cultural arbitrariness that underpins Bourdieu's concept of symbolic violence. Through assuming the superiority of certain reading habits, for example, the cultural lives of those with less economic and cultural power are delegitimised and portrayed as unworthy and trashy (Skeggs, 2013; Jones, 2011; Tyler, 2020). This delegitimising portrayal is symbolic violence. To appreciate the worth in children's stories of their lives I had to recognise and challenge the partiality of my own elevation of reading. In addition, I began to recognise that categorising children as either caring little about reading, as Millie's narrative portrait might convey, or being hooked by reading as she later appeared to be, obfuscates subtle and not so subtle affective shifts around reading, which risks fixing children in place.

Reading Can Also Be a Wee Bit Nerve-Wracking

I now move on to look specifically at the children's emotional relationship with reading when they were asked, or required, to read print (and illustrations) for themselves. This might involve reading aloud in a group or in one-to-one sessions with the teacher or other adult as part of a learning-to-read programme. When the children were required to read, their affective responses were vivid and varied but infused with more anxiety and uncertainty than when engaging with stories in other ways. As with all patterns, there were exceptions, such as Angel, a member of the 'bottom' reading group in Clyde, St Jude's, who conveyed her confidence as a reader by declaring to her class that she used not to be able to read but could now. But Angel's confidence *was* an exception. A more common emotional response for those in the 'bottom' group involved elements of anxiety.

The following narrative portrait of Lucia Jasmine, a White working-class girl of Scottish heritage, offers a feel for how reading aloud was experienced moment by moment by most of the 'bottom' reading group, in shifting sensations of anxiety, relief, hesitancy and joy. The portrait is constructed from classroom observations, incidental chats and three longer audio-recorded sessions in which Lucia Jasmine read and chatted to me outside the classroom. Again, words from books are written in italics. As the portrait reveals, these reading sessions were, in the words of Leander and Boldt (2013, p. 32), "sites where affect, imagination, passion and energy (were) constantly being produced". Anxiety is present, but within a constantly changing flow of emotion, connections and shifting attention.

Lucia Jasmine: A Narrative Portrait

> From my time in Kelvin class, I recall Lucia Jasmine's regular refrain, "Can I tell you something Jess?" as I pass by or sit near her. "Guess if I have a brother or not." I guess that she has, and I am right. He is 11 and in

A Feeling for Reading **59**

FIGURE 3.5 Self-portrait by Lucia Jasmine.

high school. When she tells me she is going to stay with her aunty because it is her birthday soon, she smiles with her whole face. Lucia Jasmine often asks if she can read with me and we have read together numerous times over the year. On one occasion, as we walk along the corridor on the way to the library, Lucia Jasmine skips and gives a high five to two girls passing by.

In the library she opens the book she has chosen to read, *Little Mouse's Big Book of Fears*. She talks of her fears: big giant daddy long legs and big mummy long legs. On the opening page there is small relatively dense print containing a message from the author, Emily Gravett. Lucia Jasmine's body goes still, and her eyes settle on the small dense words. "This is too small," she says, "let's not read this one." Do I witness another of her fears in this moment, that of reading small dense print? She picks another, *Ten Things I Can Do to Help My World*, by Melanie Walsh. Her mum works in a florist, she tells me, and she chose the book because of the flowers inside. As she reads, she tells me stories about her mum's best friend at the florist who isn't really a best friend. "She's actually a bit bossy," she says. She reads tentatively, each word voiced with the intonation of a question. She encounters the word 'may' a few times and, with shoulders and voice dropping, she says, "I keep forgetting that."

On another occasion, she is reading *Nobody Got Wet*, from the reading scheme, Oxford Reading Tree. The book is from a higher level than the level she is currently on. "This level's a bit hard," she says but she leans over the book and applies herself to the task with a steely upbeat energy. "Oh, I haven't met this family before," she says, as she bends in and looks closely at them. Back on the print she says, "I know that word, I know that word, I know that word," jumping out of her chair, "that was in my *Jumble Sale* book!" At another point she says, "Oh I keep forgetting *down*." The image that often plays in my mind as she reads is that of a plucky girl with high hopes as she sets off to do a long jump, only to feel deflation if the jump falls short, if a familiar word cannot be recalled, or if the flow of text breaks down.

Mice reappear when she is reading *Green Eggs and Ham*, by Dr Seuss. "*Do- you- like- green- eggs- and- ham?*" she reads, pausing between each word. When she gets to the phrases '*Would you like them in a house? Would you like them with a mouse?*' she reverts to sounding out each letter of 'mouse' and comes up with "m-o-u-s-e, monster". To help, I point to the visual similarity between 'mouse' and 'house', and when I say the sound 'ouse', her affective reaction is vibrant. She shouts out, "Mouse!" She calls it out with gusto, repeats it for good measure, and then starts to clap her hands. I hear achievement in her voice and in her hands clapping.

Lucia Jasmine, Fairfield, Kelvin

The narrative portrait charts the many small elations, deflations and connections Lucia Jasmine made as she applied herself to the business of reading print. And it did feel like 'business', that reading print aloud was a task she braced herself for, and frequently stumbled in. There were vibrant moments of revelation when a word rose from the page and popped into her mind, and she knew she had it. However, anxiety was never far away, particularly when she couldn't recall a word that she knew she had read before. I heard anxiety too in the way each word she read was phrased as a question, as if she did not feel confident enough in her knowledge to commit herself.

In the following exchange, Tom and Alf articulated similarly anxious feelings about reading. Tom is a working-class boy, a Child of Colour, with Pakistani heritage[2] and Alf is a White working-class boy of Scottish heritage. The conversation happened while I chatted and painted with them in Fairfield.

Jess: Can I ask you a question while you are painting? [There is a chorus of 'yehs' that sound upbeat.]
Jess: Can you tell me what you feel about reading?
Tom: Eh, I feel a bit, ah, I feel a bit, a wee bit nervous.

Jess: Can you tell me a little bit more about that? What makes you feel nervous?

Tom: Oh because I don't really like to read the books. Sometimes like I get mixed up with the words.

Alf: Sometimes I get mixed up because there's tons uh [of] words in ma book ... I choosed a level book but see when I looked in it ... tons uh words.[3]

Conversation with Tom, Alf and Jamie, Fairfield, Kelvin

This feeling of anxiety when presented with 'tons of words' reminds me of the halt in Lucia Jasmine's body when she opened *Little Mouse's Big Book of Fears*, saw dense text, and opted for another book with bigger font and less words per page. In these examples, the children were talking about reading aloud to an adult or peers in order to practise reading. To understand what may be happening in these reading encounters it is important to keep in mind the intertwining of social and personal elements of emotion (Williams, 2017). In the context of reading to an adult, there is a relationship of power. The children are obliged to read, even though they may also want to learn to read print. It is also a context in which children may feel embarrassed in front of their peers if they make mistakes.

The children in the lowest positioned reading group were not alone, however, in finding this stressful. Performative reading anxiety was also expressed by children in the 'top' group, including Will, in a conversation with him and two friends, Bingo and Kevin.[4]

Will: Yes, I'm not a good reader.

Jess: You don't think you're a good reader?

Will: nnn [his voice is quieter now and less projected than it has been throughout the chat]

Bingo: But you're really clever!

Jess: So ... what makes you say you don't think you're a good reader?

Will: I'm not confident at reading in front of the class ... I just think I'm a bad reader.

Jess: ... How do you feel about reading when you're just reading on your own?

Will: I feel fine ....

Jess: Is that ... maybe more to do with being a bit shy in front of the group rather than you not being a good reader?

Will: Well, I think I'm ok at reading. It's just I'm a bit, I get a bit shy.

Conversation with Will, Bingo and Kevin, St Jude's, Clyde

In this extract Will talked of feeling shy when reading aloud, while Tom, earlier, talked of feeling a wee bit nervous about reading. Although they appear in similar emotion terrain, there are wider discourses and positions operating that create different "conditions of possibilities" (Renold & Mellor, 2013) for Will, a White middle-class boy in the highest group and Tom, a working-class Boy of Colour in the lowest group. Firstly, Bingo questioned that Will could be a poor reader since he was clever. This allowed Will to occupy a position of cleverness while saying he didn't feel confident reading print. As the next chapter will argue, this position is much less tenable for those in the lowest positioned reading group because of associations made by peers between intelligence and reading in the different groups. Secondly, when I interrogate my role in both exchanges, I find that I offered Will a way of explaining how he feels that maintained his position of 'good reader' and I did not do this with Tom or Alf. I did not question it when they spoke of feeling anxious about reading perhaps because I had assumed that, being in the 'bottom' reading group, they would feel anxious.

Sometimes when the children told me that they were not good at reading this was conveyed in the body as much as in words, as illustrated by in the following example.

> Jeffy and I had gone to the nurture room[5] in the school to chat and browse some books I had brought along. I say to Jeffy, "Maybe you could read to me?" He stops still and turns to me. "I'm not really good at reading," he says quietly. This stillness is in contrast to his almost constant body and eye movement since entering the nurture room.
>
> *Fieldnotes, St Jude's, Clyde*

Puffy, a White working-class boy of Scottish heritage, made a similar assertion, both embodied and verbal, in the following exchange, which took place during a book browsing session. He had selected *Little Mouse's Big Book of Fears* for us to read together. The *Kipper* books he mentions in the following extract are from the early levels of Oxford Reading Tree.

Jess: So do you want to have a little read at this one?
Puffy: (quietly) Yeh.
Jess: Or you can choose any of these books and I can either read to you or --
   [Puffy's next words cut in when I say 'or']
Puffy: (very quietly) I can't read.
Jess: What's that?
Puffy: (a little louder) I can't read.
Jess: You can't read, can't you?
Puffy: I only can read the Kipper ones...they're like the easy ones.
   Conversation and book browse with Puffy, Fairfield, Kelvin

A Feeling for Reading **63**

FIGURE 3.6 Self-portrait by Puffy.

In both cases, the boys expressed the belief that they *can't* read print, rather than they are *learning* to read, as I suggest they are doing. Confirming Moss's work, the pattern of revelations around 'can't read' was gendered, expressed by boys in the lowest positioned group rather than girls (Moss, 2000, 2007, 2021), a pattern that will be explored more in the next chapter. It seems so early in the reading lives of Puffy and Jeffy, two and three years respectively, to identify as someone who can't read. In the quietness of these utterances, I hear a confession rather than an assertion, a confession that must be whispered. We need to look to the relationships and structural conditions that contribute to the dynamic, sometimes anxious, emotional dance that children in the 'bottom' reading group engage in when reading print. Dispositions towards reading such as these do not emerge from isolated individualised emotional reactions but are forged in a web of relationships and dominant cultural symbols (Bourdieu, 1984; Pahl & Rowsell, 2020). As Wetherell (2012, p. 87) suggests, "The affective pattern is ... distributed across the relational field and each partner's part becomes meaningful only in relation to the whole affective dance." In the next chapter I will look more deeply into this dance, of how children position themselves and are positioned by others within and across hierarchical reading groups.

Conclusion

This chapter has introduced children in the lowest positioned reading group by exploring themes that foreground their feelings as readers, their moment-by-moment embodied experiences with reading, and with books. By "coming alive to affect" (Leander & Ehret, 2019, p. 9) the children's relationship with reading can be known differently than it can by attending to words alone. Affective movements can be perceived in the tone, volume and prosody of voice, in silence, in body movements and stillness, facial expression and audible inhales and exhales of breath. By drawing on definitions of reading that encompass multiple sources, including television, playground games, comics and books, the children's relationship with stories comes alive. They are engaged and knowledgeable about stories they tell or are told to them through varied media. This interest in story challenges common portrayals of less confident print readers, particularly working-class boys, as disengaged in reading. These portrayals, as Asplund and Prieto (2018) point out, are often based on a narrow view of what counts as reading and on large scale test data that fails to capture nuanced understandings of young readers (e.g., McGrane et al., 2017; OECD, 2015). This chapter does a vital job in troubling these damaging myths around reading that, as Asplund and Prieto again point out, can compound the cultural and social marginalisation of predominantly working-class boys.

The second theme developed in the chapter focused on the emotional space that books took up in the children's lives, something that will be returned to in Chapter 5. Books often occupied a relatively minor place in the rich lives of children in the lowest positioned group. This was evident in Puzzle's description of reading as "kinda' boring" while telling the most fantastic stories. It was also evident in Jeffy's preference for toys over books and in Millie's dreams of going out as a teenager rather than staying in and reading. Book reading is often legitimated as superior to other cultural pastimes, a consequence perhaps of it being a pastime favoured by dominant groups, particularly White middle-class women (Atkinson, 2016; Griswold, 2005). In asserting their preferences for toys, games and playing with their siblings I imagine the children pushing back against this arbitrary cultural dominance of reading. And at the same time, it is crucial to appreciate the fluid nature of the children's relationship with books. Towards the end of the study some who had been disinterested in books were enacting very different reader identities, including that of avid readers.

Lastly, I shifted attention to the feelings around reading when children in the lowest positioned group were engaged in reading to adults and peers in school. Anxiety was heightened in this context, compared to the other circumstances explored in the chapter. Although children in other groups expressed similar anxiety around reading in front of others, it was a stronger and more persistent presence in the words and actions of children in the lowest positioned group. It was in this context that they said, in hushed tones, "I can't read". However, even in this context there was also enthusiastic interaction with the book as they read, and there were moments of revelation and joy when a word was remembered or worked out. Always there are multifarious factors that influence identity construction (Lawler, 2014) but hierarchical reading groups may contribute to identities such as Puffy's 'can't read' and it is to these questions of positionality that the next chapter turns.

Notes

1 Puzzle was a White girl of Polish heritage who had moved to Scotland with her family about two years before. Although I identified her as working class, largely on the basis of her dad's manual work (her mum didn't do paid work), class identifications are made more complex and ambiguous when families migrate; that is, they could have occupied a different class position in Poland.
2 Although I apply the same caveat to identifying Tom as working class as I did with Puzzle, given the possibility they led middle-class lives in the country they had recently left, I situate Tom as working class partly by the decentring of print-based literacies (in Urdu and English) in his accounts of family life.
3 When Alf talks about a "level book" he refers to a book from the reading scheme, in which the books are levelled to match a child's reading fluency. By mentioning this I think Alf is saying he chose a book he should have been able to read but was instead presented with more words than he was comfortable with.
4 Although I identified Kevin, Will and Bingo as White middle-class boys of Scottish heritage my knowledge of their family background and pastimes was sketchy. Accent played a part in identifying them as middle class, as did some of their parent's jobs. Bingo's mum was a doctor, for example. Other jobs were harder to place, however, like working with machinery and for the council. I knew little of the place reading occupied at home.
5 The nurture room was a room in the school, furnished with comfortable couches and kitchen facilities, that was used for a variety of purposes including support for children who were feeling upset.

References

Anderson, J., Anderson, A., Lynch, J., & Shapiro, J. (2003). Storybook reading in a multicultural society: Critical perspectives. In A. v. Kleeck, S. A. Stahl, & U. B. Bauer (Eds.), *On reading books to children*. Routledge.

Asplund, S.-B., & Pérez Prieto, H. (2018). Young working-class men do not read: Or do they? Challenging the dominant discourse of reading. *Gender and Education*, *30*(8), 1048–1064. https://doi.org/10.1080/09540253.2017.1303825

Atkinson, W. (2016). The structure of literary taste: Class, gender and reading in the UK. *Cultural Sociology*, *10*(2), 247–266. https://doi.org/10.1177/1749975516639083

Bourdieu, P. (1984). *Distinction: A social critique of the judgement of taste*. Routledge & Kegan Paul.

Bourdieu, P., & Passeron, J. C. (1990). *Reproduction in education, society and culture*. SAGE.

Chambers, A. (2011). *Tell me: Children reading and talk*. Thimble Press.
Cremin, T. (2019). Reading communities: Why, what and how? *NATE Primary Matters Magazine, Summer*.
Fernald, A., & Weisleder, A. (2015). Twenty years after "Meaningful Differences," it's time to reframe the "Deficit" debate about the importance of children's early language experience. *Human Development, 58*, 1–4. https://doi.org/10.1159/000375515
Frater, G. (1997). *Improving boys' literacy: A survey of effective practice in secondary schools*. The Basic Skills Agency.
Griswold, W., McDonnell, T., & Wright, N. (2005). Reading and the reading class in the twenty-first century. *Annual Review of Sociology, 31*(1), 127–141.
Hempel-Jorgensen, A., Cremin, T., Harris, D., & Chamberlain, L. (2018). Pedagogy for reading for pleasure in low socio-economic primary schools: Beyond 'pedagogy of poverty'? *Literacy, 52*(2), 86–94. https://doi.org/10.1111/lit.12157
Hoff Sommers, C. (2015). *The war against boys: How misguided policies are harming our young men*. Simon & Schuster.
Jewitt, C. (2008). Multimodality and literacy in school classrooms. *Review of Research in Education, 32*(1), 241–267. https://doi.org/10.3102/0091732x07310586
Jones, O. (2011). *Chavs: The demonization of the working class*. Verso.
Kress, G. (2000). Multimodality: Challenges to Thinking about Language. In B. Cope & M. Kalantzis (Eds.), Multiliteracies: Literacy Learning and the Design of Social Futures (pp. 182-202). Routledge.
Lawler, S. (2014). *Identity: Sociological perspectives* (2nd ed.). Polity Press.
Leander, K., & Boldt, G. (2013). Rereading "A pedagogy of multiliteracies": Bodies, texts, and emergence. *Journal of Literacy Research, 45*(1), 22–46. https://doi.org/10.1177/1086296x12468587
Leander, K. M., & Ehret, C. (2019). *Affect in literacy learning and teaching: Pedagogies, politics and coming to know*. Routledge.
Learned, J. E. (2016). "Feeling like I'm slow because I'm in this class": Secondary school contexts and the identification and construction of struggling readers. *Reading Research Quarterly, 51*(4), 367–371. https://doi.org/10.1002/rrq.157
McGrane, J., Stiff, J., Baird, J.-A., Lenkeit, J., & Hopfenbeck, T. (2017). *Progress in International Reading Literacy Study (PIRLS): National report for England*. Department for Education. https://assets.publishing.service.gov.uk/government/uploads/system/uploads/attachment_data/file/664562/PIRLS_2016_National_Report_for_England-_BRANDED.pdf
Moss, G. (2000). Raising boys' attainment in reading: Some principles for intervention. *Reading, 34*(3), 101–106.
Moss, G. (2007). *Literacy and gender: Researching texts, contexts and readers*. Routledge.
Moss, G. (2021). Literacies and social practice: Sociological perspectives on reading research. *Education 3–13, 49*(1), 41–51. https://doi.org/10.1080/03004279.2020.1824701
OECD. (2015). *The ABC of Gender Equality in Education: Aptitude, Behaviour, Confidence*. PISA, OECD Publishing. http://dx.doi.org/10.1787/9789264229945-en
O'Sullivan, O., & McGonigle, S. (2010). Transforming readers: Teachers and children in the Centre for Literacy in Primary Education Power of Reading project. *Literacy, 44*(2), 51–59.
Oswald, D., Sherratt, F., & Smith, S. (2014). Handling the Hawthorne effect: The challenges surrounding a participant observer. *Review of Social Studies, 1*(1), 53–73.

Pahl, K., & Rowsell, J. (2020). *Living literacies: Literacy for social change*. MIT Press.
Plummer, K. (1995). *Telling sexual stories: Power, change and social worlds*. Routledge. https://doi.org/10.4324/9780203425268
Renold, E., & Mellor, D. (2013). Deleuze and Guattari in the nursery: Towards an ethnographic, multi-sensory mapping of gendered bodies and becomings. In R. Coleman & J. Ringrose (Eds.), *Deleuze and research methodologies*. Edinburgh University Press.
Rodríguez-Dorans, E., & Jacobs, P. (2020). 'Making narrative portraits: A methodological approach to analysing qualitative data'. *International Journal of Social Research Methodology*, 23(6), 611–623. https://doi.org/10.1080/13645579.2020.1719609
Scherer, L. (2016). 'I am not clever, they are cleverer than us': Children reading in the primary school. *British Journal of Sociology of Education*, 37(3), 389–407. https://doi.org/10.1080/01425692.2014.948989
Scholes, L., Spina, N., & Comber, B. (2021). Disrupting the 'boys don't read' discourse: Primary school boys who love reading fiction. *British Educational Research Journal*, 47(1), 163–180. https://doi.org/10.1002/berj.3785
Siraj, I., Mathers, S., Gross, J., & Buchanan, C. (2021). *The role of early language development and social mobility*. BERA Presidential Roundtable Seminar Series.
Skeggs, B. (2013). *Interview with Professor Beverley Skeggs* [Interview]. YouTube. https://www.youtube.com/watch?v=8xqR1Y307dc
Tyler, I. (2020). *Stigma: The machinery of inequality*. Zed Books.
Wetherell, M. (2012). *Affect and emotion. A new social science understanding*. Sage.
Whitmire, R. (2010). *Why boys fail: Saving our sons from an education system that's leaving them behind*. American Management Association.
Williams, B. T. (2017). *Literacy practices and perceptions of agency: Composing identities*. Routledge.
Wilson, S., & Milne, E. (2016). Visual activism and social justice: Using visual methods to make young people's complex lives visible across 'public' and 'private' spaces. *Current Sociology*, 64(1), 140–156. https://doi.org/10.1177/0011392115592685

Children's Literature References

Gravett, E. (2008). *Little mouse's big book of fears*. Two Hoots.
Grey, M. (2015). *Hermelin: The detective mouse*. Red Fox.
Hunt, R., & Brychta, A. (2011a). *Nobody got wet*. OUP Oxford.
Hunt, R., & Brychta, A. (2011b). *The jumble sale*. OUP Oxford.
Hunt, R., Page, T., & Brychta, A. (2011). *Kipper's laces*. OUP Oxford.
Pilkey, D. (2016). *Dog man*. Scholastic Corporation.
Reeve, P., & McIntyre, S. (2015). *Pugs of the frozen North*. OUP Oxford.
Russell, R. R. (2009-present). *Dork diaries* series. Aladdin Paperbacks.
Seuss, D. (1960). *Green eggs and ham*. Random House.
Walliams, D. (2010). *Billionaire boy*. Harper Collins.
Walsh, M. (2009). *Ten things I can do to help my world*. Walker.

4
SOCIAL POSITIONING IN HIERARCHICAL READING GROUPS

Introduction

In the previous chapter, I deliberately extended my initial frames of reference to introduce the children in terms of their feelings for reading, rather than by my specific interest in the effects of ability grouping. In this next chapter I inquire into those specific concerns, that is, how ability-grouped reading affects children's identities, agency and emotions. I utilise and extend Bourdieu's (1984) concept of *distinction* to theorise how children relate within and across hierarchical reading groups. While Bourdieu is concerned primarily with children as inheritors of parental capital, I extend this to foreground children's agency in accumulating social and cultural advantage as actors in their own social worlds.

The first section of the chapter, *Appreciation for Ability-Grouped Reading*, considers the neutral or positive reasons some children expressed for being satisfied with their place in the lowest positioned reading group. This satisfaction is then complicated by attending, beyond words, to the prosody of those words and how words are held in the movement and expression of the body. The second section, *"It's like Football Top 5": Elite Positioning in the 'Top' Reading Group*, explores how children in the highest positioned reading group distinguished themselves as socially and intellectually superior to those in the lowest positioned group. In the third and final section, *Resistance, Accommodation and Compliance: Responses to Positioning as a Struggling Reader*, I suggest that most children in the lower group *were* aware of how they were positioned by others in the reading hierarchy. The section examines agentic patterns of accommodation, resistance, anger and refusal of this positioning and argues that reactions were, to an extent, gendered.

Appreciation for Ability-Grouped Reading

When children from the 'bottom' group were asked about reading groups, not all alluded to the hierarchical organisation of groups around print fluency. Some gave practical reasons for the organisation of groups while others gave reasons why their group suited them best. These children's words expressed mildly positive or neutral feelings about their reading group. When I asked Tom, Alf and Jamie about their group, for example, their responses focused on practical issues rather than positioning, as illustrated in the following conversation.

Tom: We got a reading book called *A Bad Dog* …
Alf: Yeh. Cause the dog, Floppy, she's Floppy, she ate the washing, she's breaking everything. …
Jess: Can you tell me about The Triangles?
Tom: Triangles? … I don't know about them.
Jess: How do you think they might feel about reading? Can you imagine?
Tom: I think they em (inaudible word) a wee bit good. …
Jess: So why are you in these different groups?
Alf: Then, if we're not in groups, see then you have to go a giant group and go around.
Tom: And (inaudible) we don't have the same reading books.
Jess: So why do you have different reading books?
Tom: Reading books? Because em can't have the same because sometimes we have to have different books because,
Jamie: Because sometimes you can listen and then you just see what they've said.
Tom: … what they're reading about.
　　　　Conversation with Tom, Alf and Jamie, Fairfield, Kelvin

How Alf, Tom and Jamie describe their reading groups suggests some unawareness or lack of concern that reading groups were organised hierarchically around print fluency.

Firstly, the boys identified groups by book name and there was no mention that these books were from different levels of the reading scheme. Rather, they were given different books so everyone could listen to different stories. Alf also gave an organisational explanation for the existence of reading groups. It wouldn't make sense to read in one huge group because it would take too long to hear everyone read. There is one small sign that Tom might be aware the groups were organised by print fluency when he said that

70 Identity, social class and learning

Triangles, the highest positioned group, probably felt "a wee bit good" about reading when he'd talked earlier about feeling a "wee bit nervous". If Alf, Tom and Jamie were largely unaware of the hierarchy, the system may not be negatively affecting their self-view as readers at all.

The smallness and familiarity of the 'bottom' reading group may also have felt welcome to Tom, who had joined the school just over a year before, when his family had come to Scotland from Pakistan. His first language was Urdu and he had been learning English for about a year when the study began. In the following narrative portrait, composed only of Tom's words, a sense is conveyed of what the group might mean to him. The portrait opens with his comments about a book on penguins we had read together.

Tom: A Narrative Portrait

> Do penguins run? Maybe they don't run but they do skate on the ice. I think the baby one's Peppy. And I want to tell you, see when last time when we was painting with you well there's a boy called Alf, and Jamie and me as well. And see the boy who called Alf, he has two sisters and one sister she called Poppy. So Poppy and Peppy. We're in Stars. I don't know about the Triangles or Circles [other reading groups] because I

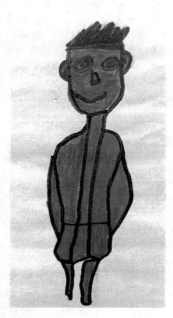

FIGURE 4.1   Self-portrait by Tom.

don't know what their book's called. I don't like books really. Sometimes like I get mixed up with the words when I get a new book, a wee bit tricky.

See the games the (other children in the class) talk about, I don't know the games. I don't understand them about the games stuff. I don't play those games because I don't know what game they are, and I don't know how to play them. I know about Minecraft but not like other games. And what do you call that thing again? Audio (recorder)? I would like one of them. But I don't think ma dad, don't know what o, o, recorder. Can you just write it so then I can tell ma dad about it? Just write it here I'll just put that in ma pocket. I speak two language. I speak one English and one Urdu. My whole family speak Urdu as well. Outside I don't because they don't speak that language. My dad told me (to speak English). Yeh, I still need to practice 'cause I don't know much English.

Tom, Fairfield, Kelvin

My overwhelming impression from this narrative portrait, composed from his words, was that, for Tom, his small reading group was a place of belonging and safety, where he knew the names of his classmates' siblings. At other times he told me about their pets and their habits. The classroom may not always have felt such an easy place of belonging. I observed instances of casual othering, when race and religion intersected to position Tom and the two other children of Pakistani heritage and of Muslim faith as outsiders in the taken-for-granted White and secular norms of the classroom. One such episode concerned a whole class writing exercise about children's favourite Haribo sweet. Tom had never heard of Haribos, he said, and sat quietly back in his chair as others huddled together, talked and wrote about their favourites. Haribos contain pork gelatine, which may explain why he was unfamiliar with them; eating them would be incompatible with halal practices.

Racialised othering can also be experienced in gesture and gaze, as attention slides over one child and lands on another (Rankine, 2020). In Rankine's example, she refers to the way White teachers, on hearing trouble, can scan the room, slide over White children and land on a child who is Black. I thought on Rankine's observation of racialised gaze in my own relationship with Tom, where conversely my attention could slide over Tom, and other Children of Colour, to land on a White child who was calling out to me. I was aware he seemed reserved with me, that when I caught his eye, he looked away, perhaps not expecting me to engage with him. But I had not recognised *my* awkwardness and othering, which was there as a White woman, in a largely White classroom, talking with a Boy of Colour with a different cultural heritage and first language to me. When transcribing our first conversation I could hear myself clumsily concerned with 'getting it right' when asking him, for example, of the different language scripts his family read at home. My self-concern got in the way of empathising with him at first when he talked about finding reading difficult – while transcribing conversations my responses seemed more clipped than when White children spoke of similar difficulties. This early awkwardness did fall away, and our relationship grew in affection when I became more interested in him than in *me* not appearing racist. But recognising and calling out this othering matters, given the authority and space that adult white skin assumes in the largely White space that Tom was navigating.

Tom collected words, like the *audio recorder* in the portrait above, to help him navigate these unfamiliar, and at times othering, linguistic and cultural waters in which many of his White peers swam easily. The comments he made about unknown computer games suggest he felt left out of this peer culture that he would like to be a part of. There were other aspects of classroom culture, like reading, that he may have been less inclined to join, when it felt hard and not particularly interesting. He gave little indication of how reading groups were organised or his positioning in it. Perhaps for him, in this moment, the comradery and belonging he found in his reading group mattered more to him than its position in a hierarchy of readers. There are, however, alternative ways of offering the kind of familiarity that Tom seemed to welcome without placing children in hierarchical groups. In the study, all children in their first two years of learning English as an additional language were in the 'bottom' reading group and not all welcomed their position there, as I will discuss later in the chapter.

As well as the comfort of familiarity, other reasons were expressed for why the 'bottom' group suited them best. These reasons sometimes centred on the reading group being perceived as a helpful place of learning. Millie, for example, conveyed satisfaction with her reading group in a conversation with her and her friend Ellie, who was in the highest positioned group. In the conversation, Millie expressed a quiet confidence as a reader. She remembers the first word she learnt to read and when she learnt it. The word was *the*, and she learnt it between the ages of 4 and 5 (in Primary 1):

> When I was in P1 that was ma first word because I was really close to finishing it. And then I was a wee bit older in P1, and then I was, em, I tried *the* again and I *got it*!
>
> *Millie, St Jude's, Avon class*

When I asked her how she felt about her group she whispered "good". If she had a choice of groups, she would choose it and gave the following reasons why the group helped her learn. It was the smallest group and she liked this. It also gives her practice with easier books and through this she would read harder books next year.

Social positioning in Hierarchical reading groups **73**

Millie's response of "good" when asked about her place in the 'bottom' reading group was echoed by others whose responses were either neutral or weakly positive. George,[1] for example, in Avon class at St Jude's, when asked which group he would choose said, "Eh none, any. 'cause I'm fine with any of them". Jamie, in Kelvin class at Fairfield, said he felt "fine" and thought he would always be in this group. Yet I also noted that these reasons were expressed with a stillness of body and a quietness of voice, often whispered, that could still suggest ambiguity about their position. George's words, for example, were positive but his body was completely still, his gaze fixed straight ahead, his speech clipped and quiet when he talked about reading. Millie too was still in body and her words whispered but when she, like George, talked of other things, like family, her voice projected, she elaborated, and her body was animated.

Yet the stillness and quietness in their utterances must be held in tension with agentic bursts of self-confidence around reading, and writing. Puffy, for example, had quietly told me he couldn't read but he also employed his wicked sense of humour to push the boundaries of what was permissible to read and write in school, as the following example illustrates:

> I invited Puffy to make some words using magnetic letters. I laid out some letters that I know can make short words. I said, "Could you make a word like ..." but before I could say which ones, he launched into the task with

FIGURE 4.2   Words made by Puffy with magnetic letters. Photograph by author.

gusto, searching for letters in the *unsorted* pile next to my curated set. He first found a 'p' then added 'oo' to it, smiling up at me and giggling. I giggled back. Next came '2jeT' which he called Jet2. This is the airline that's going to take the family on their next holiday abroad, he said.

Fieldnote, Fairfield, Kelvin

Puffy agentically created words that he wanted to create but that also challenged constraints in this educational space. I hear agency and self-belief too in Millie's responses when I asked her and her friend Ellie how others might see them as readers. In the following extract, Ellie goes first:

Ellie: I don't *know* because I'm not in other people's minds but ... it's just big long words, they just get me sometimes ... if they wanted me to read like *The Paper Dolls* or rhymes and all that, I would be quite good at that. They would be like *wow*. They would be impressed. Like, if I was reading, like, a big chapter book like Emma's got, a *big* chapter book, then they'd be like 'you're good at reading it's just, eh, some words' ... Yeah. that's what I think.
Millie: That's like the same to me. I'm not good at some words but I'm good at a lot of other words.
Jess: So there's some words?
Millie: Em, are tricking me, and chapters. It's a wee bit hard for me as well.

Conversation with Millie and Ellie, St Jude's, Avon

In this exchange, Millie asserted her own successful trajectory in learning to read print. She didn't signal awareness that others might claim a superiority over her or her reading group. In class I observed Millie choosing chapter books to read, which she said in the above extract were a wee bit hard for her. That said, the chapter books she chose had lots of pictures.

Through this choice she could enact a reader identity that placed her with the majority of the class who read chapter books, while still choosing books she could decipher because of the pictures they contained.

So far, I have presented children's affective relationship with reading in the lowest positioned reading group as complex, illustrating the push and pull between educational practices and children's agency within them (Reay, 2002, 2006, 2017; Reay & Wiliam, 1999). The children either did not mention the hierarchical organisation of reading groups or spoke convincingly of how their group suited them. I imagine they would not know there are non-hierarchical ways of creating the conditions they appreciated about their group. As a teacher I had not known of mixed-attainment alternatives to ability-grouped reading, for example, as I described in Chapter 1. But there is also something important in Jamie's belief, that he would always be in the same group, which suggests one's position can appear as the natural order

Social positioning in Hierarchical reading groups **75**

of things. In making this observation I draw on Bourdieu's (1977, 1984) concept of "doxa"; that is, when one's place in the social hierarchy, and the discriminatory conditions concealed within it, appear natural rather than fashioned by power inequalities. Jamie actually had a level of fluency matching that of children in the 'middle' and even 'top' group[2] yet he believed the 'bottom' reading group was where he belonged, something I will return to in Chapter 5. If hierarchical reading groups appear natural, it could limit what children in the lowest positioned group may envision for their reading life. The language used by children in the 'top' reading group is in stark contrast to that used by the children so far discussed, and it is to the 'top' reading group the chapter now turns.

"It's like Football Top 5": Elite Positioning in the 'Top' Reading Group

All children in the highest positioned reading group expressed awareness of the hierarchical organisation of reading groups and of their elevated position within that hierarchy. Words conveying superiority frequently cropped up when asked about their group: words like "top", "highest", "best" and words describing ascendancy like "going up". Kevin, in conversation with Bingo and Will, described their elite position with the following football analogy:

FIGURE 4.3 Self-portrait by Bingo.

Jess: You're all in the Red group?
Will: That's the top group.
Bingo: It's the best group.
Kevin: It's like Football Top 5.
Will: What? No! That's in football!
Kevin: No, like see the top five footballers like, they're like a top five group and that's the Red group, so like they're like the smartest ...
Bingo: They're the best readers, kinda ... And they've got the biggest book.
Kevin: I moved up!
Bingo: We've got huge chapters in the *Matilda* book.
Will: We've got 213 pages.
Bingo: And the Green Group, is like the lowest group down, which is basically like they have really small books.

Conversation and book browse with Kevin, Bingo and Will, St Jude's, Clyde

As well as using an elite analogy to describe their position, that of the world's best (male) footballers, the extract also includes a qualification, here represented by Bingo's "kinda". I grew accustomed to hearing such qualifications when children conveyed their elevated position to me, which I interpreted as an attempt not to appear boastful while still claiming this elevated position. The extract also highlights the way hierarchy was expressed through reading material. In my conversations with the top group there was frequent mention of the size of reading books, of who was reading chapter books, how thick those chapter books were and who were reading picturebooks.

Claiming distinction is always relational, only working in opposition to another social group, as Bourdieu (1984) makes clear. The social advantage of being in the top group was emphasised in the borders between groups. This emphasis was revealed when Bingo, Will and Kevin recalled Kevin moving to the 'top' group. The boys remembered this being announced during a parents' evening although their teacher did not recall it being so publicly announced. In the following reflection I consider the possible effects of what the boys remember as a public 'promotion'.

There is a certain 'coronation' feeling when this was recalled. Each of the boys remembered it happening. Everyone cheered when he was 'promoted'. But of course, this begs the question: how do the children feel in the group he is being 'promoted' from?

Reflexive notes while transcribing conversation with Kevin, Bingo and Will, St Jude's, Clyde

The memories of cheers when a child is elevated to the 'top' reading group suggest that top-group position was something children staked a claim in. It is a form of distinction that requires two conditions for those claims to be capitalised upon. Firstly, to gain legitimacy, those making the claim need to be in possession of sufficient authority in that field (Bourdieu, 1984, 1990). I suggest from the examples shared that children in the 'top' group had this authority. It was generated by their own volition, although often built on cultural capital inherited from their parents, as Chapter 5 will confirm. The second condition required for claims of distinction to stick is the presence of others who are not in possession of the valuable commodity, in this case that of 'top reader'. Without the lowest positioned group as a "foil" (Bourdieu, 1984, p. 171), reading in the 'top' group would lack the exclusiveness that allowed them to claim it as a form of distinction. As the following paragraphs will illustrate, the children in the 'top' group were active in patronising and portraying those in the lowest positioned group as not as good as them. Through their words it becomes evident why it was so compelling to stake a claim in this group.

Kevin pointed to one of the reasons why membership of the 'top' group was so valuable when he said that Red group was made up of "the smartest" children in the class. In fact, in the same conversation with Bingo and Will above, he attributed his smartness in *mathematics* directly to his promotion to the 'top' *reading* group.

> I wasn't really confident about like moving up 'cause I wasn't that smart at that time. I really knowed, like (with an audible inhale of breath) two times four and stuff like that. ... And now like since I've moved up to the Red group I've like, know like three times six ... I'm very good at maths.
> *Conversation and book browse with Kevin, Bingo and Will, St Jude's, Clyde*

This association between intelligence and membership of the 'top' reading group was commonly expressed by those in the highest positioned group. Emotional dispositions were also attached to different reading groups, as highlighted in the following conversation:

Kayla: The Red group is the people who are like ... more like confident and like mature [sound of a smile in her words, as the other two quietly giggle] ... So, like *our* group is like the more confident people. We feel like, sometimes feel like the children in Green are like, aww, sometimes they look a bit sad and we feel a bit bad for that.
Jess: Why do you think they feel sad?
Kayla: 'cause like we are in the other group, and I think they really want to get to our level.

78 Identity, social class and learning

FIGURE 4.4   Self-portrait by Kayla.

Claudia: They just, any time they do read they like, they don't show their confidence. It's like they're shy.
   Conversation with Kayla, Alexa and Claudia, St Jude's, Clyde[33]

These excerpts illustrate how children in the higher reading group patronised and looked down on children in the lower groups. It also shows how characteristics that have nothing to do with reading, such as intelligence, maturity and even happiness become disproportionately attached to children based on their reading group. In addition, a belief was expressed on more than one occasion, and exemplified in Amay's[4] words below, that those in the 'bottom' group would grow up to be unconfident adult readers:

Jess: Do you think everyone in the class are going to be as good readers as each other (when they are older)?
Amay: Probably but they will need help at some points if they've got really really tricky books like Flying Fergus and stuff, like Harry Potter books.
   Conversation with Jake, Ryan, Lewis and Amay, Fairfield, Kelvin

This projection that those in the 'bottom' reading group would struggle as adult readers suggests that the stigmatisation of ability-grouped reading could have a long tail. The coupling of these characteristics with low-status readers is echoed in Duckworth's (2013) study of Adult Basic Skills learners who had struggled with dominant literacies. Her participants recalled, with emotional intensity, being labelled by teachers and peers as "thick", "stupid" and "no-hopers". Experiencing such negative labelling by those with legitimised authority in the field of education can have an enduring impact on a person's reading identity (Williams, 2017). In the course of my research, I have heard people with a wealth of social, economic and cultural capital, including award-winning authors and university professors, recount vivid, disquieting memories of being placed in the 'bottom' reading group in school. In the case of Duckworth's study, participants described how positionings crystallised in low self-esteem, shame and feeling less adult than those who appeared as insiders in the world of dominant literacies.

When Kevin described his group as Football Top 5, he also revealed the social and emotional capital that can be accrued through membership of the 'top' reading group. Such advantages of status and belonging were also expressed in the linking of friendship with reading by those in the higher groups. For example, reading is portrayed as the connective tissue in the friendship of Kayla, Claudia and Alexa:

Kayla: We're like the girls in the class who like funny things.
Claudia: This is us, like all day [making gestures that signify joke-telling and hilarity].
Kayla: Like, *all* day ... sometimes we like really crazy funny books.
Alexa: And sometimes happy books.
Kayla: Yeh but we like all the nice smooth books because it reminds us of how long we've been together. And like our friendship is like so close; that's what books make us think of ... our friendship becomes bigger and bigger by books.
Conversation with Kayla, Claudia and Alexa, St Jude's, Clyde

My fieldnotes recorded the girls' intimacy; as they spoke, their bodies turned towards each other, they touch each other on the arm, and gently stroked each other's hair. They defined their friendship through books. A similarly gendered story of bonding through reading was told by Lilly and Jennifer, two White girls of Scottish heritage from the 'middle' reading group in Clyde, at St Jude's.[5] Lilly had been in the highest positioned group but, finding the books difficult to read, she was moved "down", as she described it, into the middle reading group where her friend Jennifer was. Jennifer recalls reassuring her by saying: "You don't need to be scared Lilly because ... you know that your bestie will help you." Talking it through with Jennifer had made Lilly feel happy, she said, and she now thinks she is good at reading.

Boys did not talk explicitly about friendship and reading as emotionally supportive and bonding, as the girls did. That said, the boys in the highest positioned reading group still appeared to generate social and emotional capital from the connections they made with others in the top group. This is evident in Bingo's response when I asked why he had selected *Captain Underpants* to read:

> I kinda' like *Captain Underpants*, cause the first time I watched the movie I found it really funny and 'cause like we, us three, always have to, like a laugh.
> [There are sounds of agreement and mild laughs from Will and Kevin]
> *Conversation and book browse session with Kevin, Bingo and Will, St Jude's, Clyde*

Bingo's response echoes the bonding role of humour in books that Kayla, Claudia and Alexa spoke of. Books also circulated among children in the highest positioned reading group in ways that reinforced connections between reading and friendship. At Fairfield, Cain told me one day that Kirkby[6] had passed on a book to him because they were friends. Jack, a White middle-class boy of Scottish heritage, also at Fairfield, told me he had sent a copy of his favourite *Ottoline* book to his friend Bella May, also White, Scottish and middle class, during the pandemic. In return she sent him a copy of her favourite book. When Jack mentioned this, I noted that despite also being good friends with Car, a White working-class boy of Scottish and English heritage in the lowest positioned reading group, Jack had not chosen to send the book to *him*. I had learned of Car and Jack's friendship through the teacher, and it was evident in their close camaraderie when they sat together in class.

In fact, there were no examples of children in the lowest positioned reading group talking of reading as something that cemented their friendships. For some in the lowest positioned group, reading print appeared a source of stress and something that had to be concealed, which is discussed later in the chapter. In these circumstances it may be emotionally risky to forge friendships orientated around reading. Perhaps, as was the case with Car, who was a fan of *Mr Men*, a series often associated with younger children,[7] he was not perceived as a significant fellow reading friend even when he was a friend.

Before beginning the research, I had questioned whether children who were visibly located at the bottom of a reading hierarchy might be socially ostracised by their peers, but I found this not to be the case. The children in the lowest positioned reading group often appeared popular members of the class. The following fieldnote captures the warmth of welcome when Gary,[8] a member of the 'bottom' reading group with high footballing credentials, arrived one morning.

> Gary arrives late and is met with cheers. I can't remember the actual words, but they were positive, along the lines of 'Yeah, Gary's here!' echoing round the class.
>
> *St Jude's, Clyde*

Cash, a White working-class boy of Scottish heritage, also in Clyde, had friendships like Gary's, that cut across the reading groups. This was evident in the friends he played with at school and on his Nintendo Switch video game console. When speaking about his friends, he led the conversation and spoke in a bouncy animated prosody. Yet, although children in the lowest positioned reading group had friends and popularity, they did not appear to have the prestige as readers within this hierarchical reading group structure to forge reading friendships. There was a coupling of friendship with reader identities, and an associated sense of belonging in the world of print, that appeared available only to those located towards the top of the reading group hierarchy, and this accrued valuable social capital.

Social capital, in Bourdieusian terms, refers to the network of social connections one has that can be capitalised upon. These social connections can elicit economic gains, such as advantageous employment. They can also elevate status in powerful fields and cultivate a sense of belonging to an exclusive club. One such exclusive club appears to be the 'top' reading group and children were active in fostering this social capital. With social capital comes *emotional capital* that develops from feeling connected and at home in this exclusive club. Emotional capital is not a term used by Bourdieu but has been applied to his concept of capitals (Nowotny, 1981, cited in Reay, 2004; Reay, 2004). I use the term in a slightly different way to that used by Reay. Reay focuses on emotional capital generated in the family realm through the emotional resources passed on mainly by mothers to children. I use it here to signify valuable feelings of emotional security that can come from feeling like an insider in the field of literacy education. In saying this I immediately qualify it with recollections of competition within the 'top' group itself, over for example who reads 'proper' chapter books. In a disagreement between Lewis and Jake (Fairfield, Kelvin),[9] the spectre of competition within, and potential displacement from, the highest reading group is evident. For example, Lewis commented, "Not really that many people in the Triangles *actually* have chapter books. I think it's only three people in the class have chapter books." Lewis was one of those three who read 'proper' chapter books. He is making a distinction here between those who had moved on to non-scheme chapter books and those in the 'top' group who still read chapter books from the reading scheme. In the rapid fire that seemed to propel Jake's response that he "did read chapter books" (albeit reading scheme ones) I read the threat Lewis's words held for Jake's identity as one of the top readers in the class. But despite these inner group tensions, I still suggest there were real emotional benefits gained from the insider status of the 'top' group.

Accommodation and Resistance to Positioning as a Struggling Reader

Most, although not all, children in the 'bottom' reading group showed an awareness of their stigmatised positioning by those in higher groups. How they reacted to the positioning was often influenced by their gendered identities, and this will now be teased out. By gendered identities I refer to children's affective dispositions, relationships and interests that align most commonly with those associated with the feminine or masculine, those most commonly associated with "doing boy" or "doing girl" (Renold, 2004).

Moss (2000, 2007), in her ethnographic studies of gender and reading in primary school, makes a key claim that I find helpful in examining gendered reactions to being visibly positioned by reading groups. Writing in a historical context of concern about boys' reading, she argues that when judgements on reading are made highly visible, girls and boys react differently, in ways that affect their progress. Girls who were positioned as struggling readers often complied with teachers' instruction, including acceptance of book recommendations that held little prestige among their peers. Boys, she found, were more resistant to stigmatised positioning and consequently spent more time avoiding reading.

Moss's proposition resonates strongly with my own findings when her categories are reframed as gendered rather than belonging to boys and girls per se. This chapter opened with accounts of children, mostly girls, who approached their group as a place that helped them learn (as Moss suggests) and, in the case of Tom, as a source of companionship. These qualities, of learning and companionship, seemed more important to them than the status or lack of it that attached to their reading group. However, and here I diverge from Moss, despite their agentic compliance there was still a push back from the stigmatisation of ability grouping for those enacting feminine qualities. I use the following narrative portrait of Angel, a White working-class girl of Scottish heritage, to exemplify the considerable emotional work that could be incurred to maintain a positive reader identity in the lowest positioned group.

The narrative portrait is composed from fieldnotes and audio-taped conversation extracts.

Angel: A Narrative Portrait

Angel, the only girl in the lowest positioned reading group in Clyde, seemed to love reading. One day, when Jim asked her what the biggest lie was she had ever told, Angel didn't respond. She appeared totally absorbed in a graphic novel called Far Out Fairy Tales by Louise Simonson. When I went over to her, she didn't stop reading or acknowledge my presence. I listened as her read the text aloud to herself in what sounded like an American TV accent. This is one of many similar accounts dotted throughout my fieldnotes of Angel being absorbed in books amidst the hustle and bustle of classroom life.

A few months into the field work, I had a conversation with her, Jeffy and Gary,[10] all members of the 'bottom' reading group. When I asked them what they thought of their group, Angel expressed satisfaction, which was met with derision from Jeffy and Gary. The conversation extract that follows is alive with affective significance.

Angel: So, the Green Group is the best group ever because it's only a six.
Jeffy: [with a surprised tone] What? How is it the best group ever?
Gary: No, the Red Group is the best.
Jeffy: 'cause they've got thousands of people. Lionel-CR7 is the fastest.[11]
Jess: But you Angel think Green Group is the best?
Angel: Yeh because Green Group always works with Miss B (the boys burst into giggles) or Miss or Miss (the boys continue giggling) … That's why the Green group is the best group … But I think the Red Group (mimes 'thumbs down').
  …
Jeffy: That's not nice.
Gary: I'm telling Lionel-CR7 that. …
Jess: So what do you think of the Green Group (Gary)?
Gary: Eh, it's good.
Jeffy: I like Red group better.
Gary: It's, I like the Red group better as well.
Jess: Why do you like the Red group better?
Gary: 'cause they get tricky words …
Jeffy: Because it's the best group and it's got thousands of people. I wish I joined.
Jess: So, if you could be in any reading group, which reading group would you be in?
Jeffy: [sings it out] Red.
Gary: [at the same time] Red.
Jeffy: I bet Angel would stay in the Green Group [both boys laugh]. Would you?

Angel: I would be in the [she pauses, as the boys giggle].
Gary: In the Green!
Angel: No, not *that* group. I'll choose one of the other two groups. I'd choose Blue.
Jess: Why would you choose Blue?
Angel: Because blue is my second favourite colour. Red is my last.

Angel, Clyde, St Jude's.

This narrative portrait reveals the emotional work that can be involved in trying to maintain a positive reading identity in the face of stigmatised positioning. Angel, usually so verbally surefooted, stumbled in the face of the giggling boys when she tried to defend her group, and ultimately distanced herself from it in the comment, "not *that* group". Jeffy, in particular, seemed to accurately read how his group was perceived negatively by others. He consequently wanted out of this group, with Gary following suit, and into the group perceived as the best of all. The odds, however, of joining that more prestigious group are stacked against them, as I will argue in Chapter 5 because ability-grouped reading is more likely to hold them in place. It is interesting here that Lionel-CR7 is held up as the one who is transgressed by Angel's irreverence towards Red group. Lionel-CR7 held a position of power in the class, considered by the children to be the best reader because he reads fast. I wanted to cheer when Angel, despite ultimately distancing herself from their stigmatised reading group, refused to accept Red group's superiority. She most likely lacked the social capital, however, to dent Red group's elevated position by her dismissal of them.

The ambivalent compliance portrayed in Angel's narrative is contrasted in the following section with resistance to stigmatised positioning in two children, Puzzle and George, who I suggest were more invested in masculinised enactments, particularly that of appearing knowledgeable (Renold, 2004). Yet, while setting this up as a gendered distinction I also want to blur it. Firstly, some of the boys (Tom, for example) in the lowest position group did not convey resistance to being positioned in the 'bottom' reading group. Secondly, Puzzle is a girl who identifies as a girl but whose interests, friendships, and dispositions frequently aligned her with common perceptions of "doing boy" (Renold, 2004).

I came to notice this alignment through sharing a narrative portrait of Puzzle at conferences. Despite me introducing her as 'she', the narrative portrait did not indicate her gender since it is composed solely of her words. I only realised this when the participants, losing sight of my gendered introductory reference to Puzzle, invariably assumed that Puzzle was a boy. On reflection, I wondered if this assumption was prompted by her use of gendered language, like "guys", her passion for computer games that her brothers also played, her battles with those brothers, her humour about stories that involve toilets, and her disinterest in reading, which is often regarded as a feminised activity (McGeown et al., 2012; Millard, 1997). I also perceived a competitiveness and fury in Puzzle that echoed George's reaction at being seen as a struggling reader.

Although it is important not to make too much of two children's experience, their reactions reflect Moss's (2000) larger findings on gender, reading and social positioning in schools. What follows is an exploration of the emotional work and strategies employed by Puzzle and George in resisting the stigmatised positioning that went with their reading group and the consequent effect on their progress as readers. I believe too that Puzzle had an additional cause for fury. All children in their first two years of learning English as an additional language were placed in the 'bottom' reading group where, because of how that group was perceived, they were stigmatised, as the chapter has shown. Because of her group position, Puzzle, whose home language was Polish and was in this early stage of learning English, would be regarded as unintelligent. This is despite successfully navigating the triple challenge of learning to read print, in a language she was learning to speak, and with books containing many unfamiliar cultural references (Gregory, 2008).

Although a couple of children in the lowest positioned reading group expressed disinterest in reading, children still wanted to be *seen* as someone who could and did read print. This echoes findings in the Hempel-Jorgensen et al. study (2018) of struggling readers in low socioeconomic 'reading for pleasure' schools as well as in Moss's (2000, 2007) work. The desire to stake a claim as a reader is unsurprising given the social and educational status afforded to reading print in education (Bourdieu, 1977). When this desire meets negative positioning by others it can engender anger, resistance and attempts to conceal lower levels of print fluency particularly for children identified with 'doing boy'. For Puzzle and George, their identity as readers became particularly precarious in performative reading events, as the following paragraphs will show. I use 'performative' as Goffman (1990) does to indicate the actions of a person during an activity which is done in the presence of observers and with awareness of the possible effect of the performance on those observers.

At various times both George and Puzzle seemed angry when I witnessed their struggles to decipher words when reading with the teacher. This raises questions about whether I should have observed them when I sensed their discomfort. Although I closed my notebook and moved away, I did continue to observe these reading events from a distance. I write about it because the events highlight how reading instruction often fails to minimise public exposure of ordinary struggles. Yet, by writing about it I am re-exposing it. For this reason, it is ethically conflicting. I perceived their anger in a freeze of their posture except for darting, piercing and unsmiling glances at me and my notebook. On occasions when I sat behind Puzzle her head jerked round and her eyes glared at me when she was unsure of a word in her book. This affective response was very different to the ease and joy Puzzle expressed when she *chose* to read me a section of her new favourite book, *Dog Man* by Dav Pilkey:

> Oh, this is the best page ever. Wait till I find it. [She sings the text in an American TV accent]: '*We fight for our freedom and that's our duty so everybody* [smile bursting through her words] *shake your booty, ohhhh baby baby baby baby baby shake your big big booty*' (laughing). Hilarious.
> Puzzle, St Jude's, Avon

These contrasting reading events reveal that it mattered to Puzzle how she was seen as a reader. When she was the knowledgeable one, sharing her choice of book that she knew she could read fluently, I perceived joy and authority. When she was positioned as a learner to the teacher's instruction, struggling over a word, witnessed by me, the researcher, she appeared tense and angry at being seen to struggle. This difference recalls again the students in Learned's (2016) study who enacted very different reader identities in the segregated "unengaged reader classes" to those enacted in collaborative problem-solving contexts. Being in the 'bottom' reading group was just one of the subordinated positions that Puzzle occupied in the classroom. Even without ability grouping she could not wholly step out of the power inequalities between learner, teacher and researcher. She could also not step out of the relationships of power that are mediated by the status of English over other languages spoken. However, being visibly marked in hierarchical reading groups as less fluent, less intelligent and less happy incurs avoidable injury and emotional work in resisting this positioning. And Puzzle did resist this positioning. One day, during a book browsing session, I heard her mutter, "I'm not stupid, I'm really not."

George, similarly, refused the role others assigned to him as a member of the 'bottom' reading group and he did this in argumentative affective surges. During group reading, for example, he argued with the teacher that "if there is a silent 'e' at the end of 'have' it should tell you it is silent." I *silently* cheered this fighting spirit, while simultaneously noting that his resistance was often constructed in opposition to the women and girls in the class. As a feminist, in the words of Reay (2002, p. 222), I perceived in his actions "the uncomfortable image of the familiar oppressor". This oppression is illustrated in the following incident.

> The teacher invites me [Jess] to read with Twinkle. As I go over to sit with her, George says loudly, "It's because Twinkle can't read." "Yes I can,"

says Twinkle in a tone that suggests hurt. Later, I am told by the teacher that in fact Twinkle reads more fluently than George.

Fieldnote, St Jude's, Avon

George's put-downs of girls as poor readers and his orthographic arguments with the teacher, who was a woman, could be understood as enacting hegemonic masculinity as explained by Renold (2004, p. 66) in her study of young sexualities. It refers to:

> ... a contested elusive idea that generally fails to empower the specific individual but nevertheless operates to produce 'culturally exalted' forms of (heterosexual) masculinity via domination of other men and subordination of women, femininity and other (non-hetero) sexualities.

Likewise, George's elusive claims to superiority in reading at the expense of girls continually threatened to be undone by his place in the 'bottom' reading group and required patterns of concealment to maintain his standing as a reader. This precarious course is illustrated by an encounter with one of the Pixies, who were introduced in Chapter 1.

> While at the table, George tells me that he is up to Chapter 3 in his book ... He tells me nothing else about the book. When asked what the title is he is unsure. The book is often closed on his desk. In an activity, facilitated by a Pixie, in which each child has to tell the others what their book is about, George strongly asserts that he is not going to do this. When one of the Pixies summarises his own book, in which animals fly to the moon, George ridicules these events by saying, "That's not possible because there's no air in space so they couldn't breathe."

Fieldnote, St Jude's, Avon

Pixies are afforded a prestigious 'teacher' role that requires others to act as their pupils and, in this extract, George refuses to comply with the subordinated role he is assigned. Instead, he asserts himself as more knowledgeable than the Pixie through his comments about animals breathing in space. Yet it *is* a precarious course that he is navigating. His refusal may have as much to do with fear that the activity will expose his inability to read the chapter book he has chosen. There are other clues in this extract to suggest George can't read the book he chose, such as focusing on length rather than content, unfamiliarity with the title, and the book remaining closed on his desk. Chapter books were often talked of as books children graduated to from picturebooks. Through his choice of book, he could be claiming status as a reader that his fluency level and group position continually denied him.

This practice of pretending to read high-status books rather than be seen reading less socially prestigious ones has been found in other studies of boys' reading (Hempel-Jorgensen et al., 2018; Moss, 2000, 2007). It is a gendered behaviour that can be interpreted as an attempt to 'save face'. *Face* is a concept used by Goffman (1967) to denote mutual respect that is maintained in interactions when the participants behave generally as expected in that context. *Saving face* might then occur as a form of rescue when this mutual respect is threatened by someone not fitting what is expected. In George's case, it could be acting as the proficient reader that is expected and validated among his peers. As Moss (2000, p. 103) emphasises,

> Particularly where proficiency judgements were made highly visible, weaker boy readers, in contrast to weaker girl readers, spent an inordinate amount of time in flight from such judgements. They put a lot of energy into disguising their lower status and escaping from the consequences of that designation.

It is important to again hold an awareness that being positioned in the bottom reading group is only one of the subordinated positions unwillingly inhabited by George and by Puzzle. They were also subject to the teacher's authority, engaged in instructed tasks, and navigating high-stakes literacy. They were coping with the status attached to different types of reading material *and* learning to read under the researcher's gaze. In fact, Puzzle's glare mentioned above, when observed stumbling over a word, continued after ability-grouped reading had been replaced by mixed-attainment reading. This cautions against over-simplistic optimism that elimination of ability groups might eliminate engrained reading hierarchies though it may still disrupt them. Although George and Puzzle may not like being seen as learners, rather than 'knowers', in whatever context, the hierarchical and very public nature of ability-grouped reading surely exacerbates their discomfort and anger.

Conclusion

The stories unfolded in this chapter suggest a re-examination of the deeply engrained and often unquestioned pedagogy of ability-grouped reading, often termed guided reading, has been long overdue. By addressing the first of my research question, the chapter demonstrates that the practice does affect children's identities as readers in distinct ways. Most children were aware of the hierarchical structure of the reading groups and of their place in that hierarchy. How they enacted their reader identities was socially constructed, with and against others, orientated to a significant extent by their group position, and woven into the social fabric of classroom life. Those in the highest positioned group almost universally presented as insiders who occupied a hallowed place in the social world of classroom reading. Although there were tensions in the highest group about who counted as a top 'top' reader, the language used to describe themselves was consistently that of superiority. Nor was it just as readers that they claimed superiority – they distinguished themselves as more intelligent, happy and confident than those in other groups. And they had the social capital to make these self-judgements stick. Conversely, as all marks of distinction are made against the 'other', those in the lowest positioned group were stigmatised not only as struggling readers but as sad and unintelligent, characteristics unrelated to reading print.

Children's insider status was also marked by the way they portrayed reading as the connective tissue in their friendships. Girls spoke explicitly about how reading strengthened the emotionally supportive bonds in their friendships while boys spoke of friendships built around sharing and swapping books. Significantly, these claims to reading friendships appeared available only to those in the higher positioned group. I argue that as hierarchical reading groups marked and separated those in the lowest group, they lacked the social capital and status as readers to forge friendships around reading. This positioned them as outsiders to the apparently thriving community of readers in the study. Research has shown the positive impact that cultivating communities of readers can have on children's reading engagement and on socioeconomic disparity in reading attainment (Clark & Rumbold, 2006; Cremin, 2019; Cremin et al., 2014). To be excluded from this reading community because of visible hierarchies may be a largely unrecognised and injurious consequence of ability-grouped reading.

These are some of the constraints within which children in the lowest positioned reading group lived and learned. They responded with agency but still faced costs. The fact that some believed they would never move groups suggests the system may have already begun to fix their reader identity in restrictive ways. And although others, often girls, believed their group would help them become better readers, and potentially move group, their responses were framed by stillness and whisper. The quietness of these utterances, when contrasted to their talk of family and other pastimes, could still suggest hesitancy in their identity as readers.

This hesitancy, together with their social exclusion from reading friendships, may illuminate the emotional and social cost of being lowly positioned within ability-grouped reading.

Another pattern of responses involved a refusal to occupy the position of struggling reader, particularly by those more strongly invested in appearing knowledgeable. This was a feisty but precarious course. It often involved subterfuge and avoidance of reading to stake a claim as a confident reader, a position that was denied them by those higher up the reading hierarchy. How children were allocated to these high-status and stigmatised groups was not a matter of luck, intelligence or even aptitude for reading print. As the next chapter will make clear, this is a classed, and to an extent racialised, process that begins shortly after children begin formal schooling.

Notes

1 George was a White working-class boy of Scottish heritage.
2 Children's level of fluency was assessed in the study using running reading records. See Appendix 1 for an explanation and example of this process.
3 I first identified Kayla, Alexa and Claudia as White middle-class girls of Scottish heritage who spoke English as a first language but on returning to the data, I realised my knowledge was too sketchy to make a claim about class. All three girls talked about hobbies, like gymnastics and playing with friends, that were as typical of the cultural pursuits of working-class as middle-class children in the study. Alexa's mum was a doctor, a traditionally middle-class occupation, but otherwise their parents' jobs did not define them strongly as working or middle class, e.g., "dad works in a kids' house".
4 Amay was in the 'middle' reading group and I identified her as a White working-class girl of Scottish heritage.
5 I didn't get to know Lily and Jennifer's home context well and I am unsure of the class positioning. Their parents' jobs, like warden, trainee teacher and admin council worker fall into those less defined groups that could be working/lower middle class.
6 Although I assumed both Cain and Kirkby were White and of Scottish heritage, I did not get to know them well and could not begin to situate them in terms of class.
7 A 'made for mums' website suggests the series for children aged 2 and above. https://www.madeformums.com/reviews/best-personalised-books-children/
8 Gary, a White boy of Scottish heritage, was difficult to situate in class terms on the basis of his parents' jobs but when Gary spoke about time spent with his grandad, I imagined his mum had a working-class upbringing similar in some ways to mine, but this may not be accurate.
9 Lewis is a middle-class Child of Colour, of Pakistani heritage. Jake is White, of Scottish heritage but I did not get to know him well enough to situate him in terms of class. Both were in Triangles, the 'top' reading group in Kelvin class, Fairfield.
10 Jeffy is a White working-class boy of Scottish heritage.
11 Lionel-CR7 is a child in the 'top' reading group in Clyde, at St Jude's. He began the study with the pseudonym Lionel, which is the first name of Messi, one of the most successful footballers of all time. Halfway through the study he changed his pseudonym to CR7, the acronym for Cristiano Ronaldo (7 represents the number on his football jersey). Ronaldo is the only footballer of the era to challenge Messi's supremacy. I chose to combine these pseudonyms because, together, they seem to say something interesting about the status Lionel-CR7 assumes in the classroom, that he could claim not one but two iconic footballers' names.

References

Bourdieu, P. (1977). *Outline of a theory of practice*. Cambridge University Press.
Bourdieu, P. (1984). *Distinction: A social critique of the judgement of taste*. Routledge & Kegan Paul.
Bourdieu, P. (1990). *In other words: Essays towards a reflexive sociology*. Stanford University Press.
Clark, C., & Rumbold, K. (2006). *Reading for pleasure: A research overview*. National Literacy Trust.
Cremin, T. (2019). Reading Communities: Why, what and how? *NATE Primary Matters Magazine*, Summer.
Cremin, T., Mottram, M., Collins, F. M., Powell, S., & Safford, K. (2014). *Building communities of engaged readers: Reading for pleasure*. Routledge.
Duckworth, V. (2013). *Learning trajectories, violence and empowerment amongst adult basic skills learners*. Routledge.
Goffman, E. (1967). *Interaction ritual: Essays on face-to-face behavior* (1st ed.). Anchor Books.
Goffman, E. (1990). *The presentation of self in everyday life*. Penguin Books.
Gregory, E. (2008). *Learning to read in a new language: Making sense of words and worlds*. SAGE. https://doi.org/10.4135/9781446214077
Hempel-Jorgensen, A., Cremin, T., Harris, D., & Chamberlain, L. (2018). Pedagogy for reading for pleasure in low socio-economic primary schools: Beyond 'pedagogy of poverty'? *Literacy*, 52(2), 86–94. https://doi.org/10.1111/lit.12157
Learned, J. E. (2016). "Feeling like I'm slow because I'm in this class": Secondary school contexts and the identification and construction of struggling readers. *Reading Research Quarterly*, 51(4), 367–371. https://doi.org/10.1002/rrq.157
McGeown, S., Goodwin, H., Henderson, N., & Wright, P. (2012). Gender differences in reading motivation: Does sex or gender identity provide a better account? *Journal of Research in Reading*, 35(3), 328–336.
Millard, E. (1997). Differently literate: Gender identity and the construction of the developing reader. *Gender and Education*, 9(1), 31–48.
Moss, G. (2000). Raising boys' attainment in reading: Some principles for intervention. *Reading*, 34(3), 101–106.
Moss, G. (2007). *Literacy and gender: Researching texts, contexts and readers*. Routledge.
Nowotny, H. (1981). Women in public life in Austria. In C. F. Epstein & R. L. Coser (Eds.), *Access to power: Cross-national studies of women and elites*. George Allen & Unwin.
Rankine, C. (2020). *Just us: An American conversation*. Graywolf Press.
Reay, D. (2002). Shaun's story: Troubling discourses of white working-class masculinities. *Gender and Education*, 14(3), 221–234.
Reay, D. (2004). Gendering Bourdieu's concept of capitals?: Emotional capital, women and social class. In L. Adkins & B. Skeggs (Eds.), *Feminism after Bourdieu*. Blackwell Publishing.
Reay, D. (2006). 'I'm not seen as one of the clever children': Consulting primary school pupils about the social conditions of learning. *Educational Review*, 58(2), 171–181. https://doi.org/10.1080/00131910600584066
Reay, D. (2017). *Miseducation: Inequality, education and the working classes (pp. 57-74)*. Policy Press.
Reay, D., & Wiliam, D. (1999). 'I'll be a nothing': Structure, agency and the construction of identity through assessment. *British Educational Research Journal*, 25(3), 343–354. https://doi.org/10.1080/0141192990250305

Renold, E. (2004). *Girls, boys and junior sexualities: Exploring children's gender and sexual relations in the primary school.* Routledge.
Williams, B. T. (2017). *Literacy practices and perceptions of agency: Composing identities.* Routledge.

Children's Literature References

Dahl, R. (1988). *Matilda.* Jonathon Cape.
Donaldson, J. (2013). *The paper dolls.* Macmillan Children's Books.
Hargreaves, R. (1971). *Mr Men* series. Thurman Publishing.
Hoy, C. (2016). *Flying Fergus* series. Piccadilly Press.
Hunt, R., & Brychta, A. (2011). *What a bad dog.* OUP Oxford.
Pilkey, D. (1997–2015). *Captain Underpants* series. Scholastic.
Pilkey, D. (2016). *Dog man.* Scholastic Corporation.
Riddell, C. (2015). *Ottoline and the yellow cat.* Macmillan Children's Books.
Rowling, J. K. (2014). *Harry Potter children's collection: The complete collection.* Bloomsbury Children's Books.
Simonson, L. (2016). *Far out fairy tales.* Stone Arch Books.

5
HOW CLASS MATTERS IN CLASSROOM READING HIERARCHIES

Introduction

In the previous chapter I presented ability-grouped reading as a practice that accrues advantage for those in the 'top' group. This chapter will argue that allocation to these reading groups is not happenchance, nor is it dependent on aptitude for reading print. Rather, I interrogate how social class, in particular, influences group allocation and subsequent accrual of advantage and disadvantage. The ethnographic specificity of the study in relation to reading contributes new insights to the wider debate on ability grouping and social inequity. Yet, that situated specificity also makes class more difficult to talk about. Although I use the terms working and middle class to keep power and privilege in view, how class is lived is messier than this binary suggests. Class boundaries are also blurry in post-industrial countries like the UK. Bourdieu's (1984) analogies of class as clouds or forests, discernible but with diffuse edges, are good to keep in mind here. Although I would situate many of the children discussed in this chapter as traditionally working or middle class, there were some I would situate in the hazy middle (Savage, 2015) and others whom I did not get to know well enough to situate in terms of class.

Organising reading instruction into hierarchical groups is neither necessary nor inevitable. There are alternative non-segregated ways of teaching reading that hold possibilities of liberation and fluidity in children's reading experience. As well as education's role in capitalist reproduction, its liberatory potential to disrupt and challenge systems of oppression has long been advocated (Freire, 2000; hooks, 1994; Luttrell, 2020). Teachers can be motivated into the teaching profession by a passionate desire to support working-class pupils (of all ethnicities) and all Children of Colour to succeed

DOI: 10.4324/9781003488514-5

in an education system they know favours White, middle-class children. Reay's (2017) own experience as a teacher is an example of this commitment while also showing how the education system can undermine these liberatory intentions. Herein lies the push and pull between agency and constraint that is central to my study and to this chapter. The chapter begins with the section *Holding Readers in Place*, exploring the reasons why children are more likely to remain in the same hierarchical reading group than to move fluidly between groups. I will discuss issues of positioning, inertia, misallocation, and pedagogy that contribute to this fixity. In *Not Down to Luck*, while mindful of the particular intersections of class with race and ethnicity in ability grouping generally, I suggest that the 'bottom' reading group is largely a destination for working-class children.[1] This section analyses what class is doing, both in the initial allocation and in children's experience of reading groups. The final section, *Family Habits, Economics and Reading Group Placement*, shows how classed habitus does and does not matter in children's experience of reading and in subsequent group placement.

Holding Readers in Place

As Chapter 4 illustrated, children in the 'bottom' reading group were often fixed in the gaze of others as struggling readers, whose struggles would persist into adulthood. There were a small number of children who were experiencing significant difficulties in reading print, and the next chapter is devoted to their experience. However, and this point is crucial, of the 14 children in the lowest positioned reading group, more than half ($N = 9$) showed no signs of struggling to read. In fact, they were successfully doing everything as readers that those in the 'middle' and 'top' reading groups were doing. To illustrate this similarity of aptitude, I will draw on my own practitioner knowledge, infused by literacy scholarship, particularly Hall's (2005) *Listening to Stephen Read*.

Like those in the 'top' group, children in the lowest positioned group knew that, in English orthography, print conventionally flows from left to right and is sectioned into words. They attended to each word, sometimes pointing to the words to keep track and sometimes scanning ahead to anticipate what was coming up. There were words they could recognise on sight. They knew the letters of the alphabet, and matched letter symbols to sounds. They also knew the sounds of some digraphs (2-letter sound units, e.g., ch). When approaching unknown words, they could use their graphophonic knowledge to blend sounds together to make words. Although this kind of 'sounding out' and word recognition were their go-to strategies, their attempts often drew on the context of the sentence or story and made sense. At times they attended to the punctuation of the sentence to help maintain sense of the text. Perhaps most importantly, they were engaged in what they read, connecting events across the narrative and with their own lives, as Lucia Jasmine and Jamie[2] do in the following extracts. Again, the words from their book are written in italics to distinguish them from their talk:

Lucia Jasmine: *Do, you, like, green eggs and ham?* ... I don't think he does!
Jess: I don't think he does.
Lucia Jasmine: No, he's like 'yeuch!'
     Conversation and reading with Lucia Jasmine, Fairfield, Kelvin

Go away! The rocket is going to take off. That's such a mean thing to say to a dug [dog]!
  Jamie, Fairfield, Kelvin, running reading records and conversation

These comments show an engagement in and understanding of what is being read, which was typical of the majority in the 'bottom' reading group. Analysis of reading in the 'top' group revealed very similar patterns of knowledge, skill and engagement. It is true that most in the lower positioned group appeared, much of the time, to be less fluent in applying these skills and knowledge. However, this could be explained simply by having had less practice in reading, or of reading in English, in the case of some children who were learning English as an additional language. Yet even this contrast in print fluency was, to an extent, contextual. In the following scenario, Jeffy, who we met in Chapter 3, had chosen to read with his friend Mario, a White boy of Scottish heritage[3] from the 'top' reading group. In this step-out of the usual ability-grouped routine, I would have found it difficult to tell who was in the 'top' and 'bottom' group, as the following extract illustrates:

> Jeffy takes charge of the reading. He holds the book. He decides how much he reads, when to pass it to Mario, and when to take it back. He bends over it, focussing 100% on the text. When he gets to a word he is unsure of he says, "No wait," holding down the page with his hands. He takes time to work it out. One of those words is peppermint which he gets to "papermint" with a concerted effort at working out the sounds. I say what a good reader he is, and he says, "So is Mario." Fluency-wise they appeared similar today, pretty fluid but pausing momentarily at each word, getting most of the words correct, working some out.
>   *Fieldnotes, St Jude's, Clyde*

I was struck by the assertiveness conveyed by Jeffy's words and actions, taking charge of the book, for example. His acceptance of my compliment was, I interpreted, an agreement that he was a good reader, and that Mario was also good, but not better than him. It is also interesting to note just how different their respective fluency seemed in this context compared to their reading groups. In this scenario Jeffy probably had more authority because he had chosen to invite Mario along to read with me, shifting their usual positions in the hierarchy.

This apparent contextual difference in fluency echoes findings in the Learned (2016) study, previously mentioned, about context and reader identifications in a US high school. Most of the time, however, there was a discernible difference in print fluency between groups in my study. At least some of this could be explained by the relative time they had spent practising reading.

Once allocated to a reading group, often early in children's schooling, the gap in fluency could be widened because of different teaching strategies used with each group. The children in the 'top' reading group, for example, had regular opportunities to clarify and expand their vocabulary, and develop layered comprehension through group discussion. This was rarely the focus of instruction with children in the 'bottom' reading group, perhaps because their books (early levels of the reading scheme) did not lend themselves to deeper comprehension or to expanding vocabulary. These books also contain fewer words so children in the lowest positioned group had less reading practice with the teacher than children reading higher levels of the reading scheme or beyond it. And so, those in the 'top' group received significantly more of what might advance them as readers, which potentially widens any gap in reading fluency (Stanovich, 2009). For one teacher in my study, her key concern about trying mixed-attainment reading was that her 'top' group would miss out on this extra comprehension development. For other teachers, they ameliorated, to some extent, this disproportionate input on comprehension by also reading aloud to the class and doing related comprehension/response activities in mixed-attainment groups.

As well as misrecognition as struggling readers, and more limited reading opportunities, ability-grouped reading also appeared to contain an inertia that held children in place. Fluency-wise, some appeared ready to move on in the reading scheme or, indeed, move to another reading group but instead remained in the 'bottom' reading group. The problematic issue of inertia within ability grouping in general has been noted by many studies (e.g., Macintyre & Ireson, 2002; Hallam & Ireson, 2006, 2007; Dunne et al., 2011). In my study, Angel's experience (White, working class, Scottish; St Jude's, Clyde) presented an obvious example of this inertia. As a relative outsider in the classroom, I perceived Angel to be an avid reader, one of the most engaged and fluent in the class. This was conveyed in her narrative portrait in Chapter 4. When she read aloud to me, she performed it like an actor in full command of her audience. Although her current, and previous, teacher had noted her progress, they had both felt a jump to the middle group was too great, potentially denting her confidence as a reader. And so, Angel remained in the lowest positioned reading group, reading much simpler and shorter books than she could comprehend. Both teachers agreed that if it weren't for ability grouping, she could have moved more quickly through the levels of the reading scheme and potentially garnered greater fluency as she went. Instead, she left the school a few months before the fieldwork ended, still held in the 'bottom' reading group.

The inertia of being held on book levels because of perceived needs of the group was also evident in Jamie's story (White, working class, Scottish; Fairfield, Kelvin). When I read with him, he told me that he had been on Level 2 of the reading scheme for two years. He said he (and the rest of his group) had been re-issued with the same book a year on from the first time, and that he could read all those books. When I completed a running reading record with him (Appendix 1) it was evident that he could read and comprehend books at Level 7 of the scheme. This was the level of book the middle group was reading. He had also apparently mastered the art of reading upside down. One day when I was reading with Lucia Jasmine, he chipped in with the words she was unsure of, despite sitting opposite her.

But for Jamie, the issue of inertia overlaps with another concern, that of misallocation to the 'bottom' reading group based on home circumstances rather than reading fluency. Within the study, it was White working-class boys who experienced this 'downward' misallocation. This experience recalls the many studies that have found Black and White working-class pupils susceptible to low teacher expectations that result in their over-representation in lower groups (e.g., Education Endowment Foundation, 2016; Gillborn et al., 2021; Joseph-Salisbury, 2020). When I asked the teacher why Jamie was in the bottom group, she told me he had missed a lot of school because of his mum's poor mental health, and that despite being clever, he was behind in his reading and writing. Yet as the running reading records had shown, his reading level matched that of most of the class. When I inadvertently gave him a Level 6 book, which he read with ease, I recorded in my fieldnotes that, "he smiled; one of those smiles where he kept his lips tight shut but the smile still tilted his mouth upwards." Nevertheless, when I wondered aloud whether he might skip to Level 7 he was adamant that he wanted to read all the books in the series and to stay with his reading group; he thought he would always be in this group. Only once did I hear Jamie express doubt about his reading, when I said, "You know that word. You've read it before." "I forget things really quickly," he said, sounding defeated. More often Jamie portrayed a positive identity as a reader, largely uncoupled from the stigma, expressed by other pupils, of being in the 'bottom' reading group. He maintained this not because of this pedagogical practice, which constrained his experience, but despite it.

Like Jamie, Mark (White, working class, Scottish; Fairfield, Kelvin) had been placed in the 'bottom' reading group the previous year because of family circumstances. The teacher described this as a "supportive measure" because family breakdown had affected his behaviour. When I invited him to read, he said, even before he sat down, that his younger brother was reading at a higher level than him. Yet, when I assessed his reading level, it was higher than that of his brother's. In fact, it was similar to the most fluent readers in his class.

Despite now being in the middle group, when I commented what a good reader he was, he returned to negative comparisons with his brother. From his words and the tone of those words I suggest Mark's self-view as a reader had not benefited from his "supportive" placement in the regularly stigmatised bottom reading group the year before.

Children in their first two years of learning English as an additional language (EAL) were also placed in the 'bottom' reading group, as the previous chapter indicated, and I suggest this too is a problematic allocation. The level of print fluency of bilingual learners[4] did match their group placement, and there was evidence that they moved group as their English fluency developed. Nevertheless, issues with the practice are highlighted in literature on multilingualism and education. Firstly, it takes between five and seven years for children learning EAL to match the English proficiency of first-language English speakers, according to Cummins (2000). Therefore, if children are placed in ability groups by their English proficiency rather than their aptitude for subjects, they could be in groups for years that do not stretch them intellectually (Earnshaw, 2022). Teachers have also reported challenges in distinguishing between EAL and special educational needs, opening the potential for misrecognition (Gardiner-Hyland, 2021; Gardiner-Hyland & Burke, 2018). This could explain the over-representation of linguistically marginalised children in low positioned groups generally (Scanlan et al., 2012). While ability grouping persists, and education systems are organised around multilingualism as a deficit rather than asset, linguistically minoritised children will continue to be over-represented in stigmatised low positioned groups (Barros et al., 2021; Lucas et al., 2008).

To sum up, this section has argued, ability-grouped reading holds children in place, even as they resist or welcome their group position. It held them in place by labelling them as struggling readers early in their reading lives, as seen in Chapter 4, and by the inertia and misallocation to which ability grouping is prone. Pedagogical action also presented greater opportunities to the 'top' group to read more, develop linguistically and delve deeper into comprehension of text. Any initial gap in fluency therefore was likely to widen rather than close because of ability grouping. Social class was rarely named directly in the field, but it was signalled over and over again in children's experience in reading groups as the next section will show.

Not Down to Luck: Placement and Relationship in Hierarchical Reading Groups

Classed assumptions around reading run deep in education, with damaging material effects; these assumptions show up in ability-grouped reading. This section further explores influences on allocation to reading groups, including the economic, temporal, and educational resources available to middle-class and working-class parents that impact differently the time and space available to support children's reading.

Many of the critiques of ability grouping in general (i.e., not specifically about reading groups) highlight the classed and racialised nature of placement, with working-class pupils and some minoritised ethnic groups significantly over-represented in the lower sets (Gillborn et al., 2021; Francis & Tereshchenko, 2020; Reay 2017). Bourdieu (1999, p. 423, 425) refers to setting and streaming as "… 'gentle' exclusionary practices" creating, "outcasts on the inside". Likewise, in my study, class struggle (while I am mindful of its intersections with race, ethnicity and language) exerted significant influence on children's likely reading group destination. Although there were working-class children in the middle and highest positioned reading groups, there were no middle-class children in the lowest positioned group. One middle-class child was kept out of the 'bottom' reading group by his teachers, despite similar levels of print fluency, because of how his parents might feel about him being there.[5]

These socioeconomic patterns of allocation most likely appear unsurprising because, I suggest, it is common knowledge that middle-class pupils dominate 'top' groups and working-class pupils are over-represented in 'lower' groups. However, what is less understood, and is contested, is how these classed patterns in reading groups come to be produced and reproduced. Some of this patterning I have already ascribed to classed misallocations. That said, there were more children in the study whose level of print fluency seemed to match their reading group, even if this match partly depended on reading context, as illustrated in an earlier section. This compatibility between reading fluency and group placement, for most children, raised a question: what influences children's early reading fluency which then produces classed patterns of group allocation? I didn't want to ask this question because I feared it would lead me into a cul-de-sac of deficit views on working-class child-rearing.

Deficit views on social class are commonplace in literacy research, particularly in psychology-based scholarship. Differences in print fluency are often attributed to inferior child rearing and poor literacy practices of working-class parents. Vellutino et al. (2004), for example, use the term "limited home background" to refer to working-class families in their discussion of dyslexia. In Buckingham et al. (2014, p. 429) "low quality home literacy environments" provide the reason for "poor children becoming poor readers". This classist disparagement of working-class lives is both common and sustained beyond education, and through this disparagement, Tyler (2013, 2020) argues, classed privilege is maintained and reproduced.

Bourdieu's concept of class habitus, combined with the notion of symbolic violence, helped me out of this deficit cul-de-sac. As Chapter 2 introduced, habitus is formed of dispositions engendered from birth that affect (but do not determine) ways of being in the world. Collective histories into which one is born are held and expressed in, and as, habitus. Despite multifarious individual differences, classed patterns of lifestyle, including literacy practices, arise from similar historical conditions of existence. Such conditions of existence include families' economic distance from, or proximity to, necessity. They also include compositions of cultural capital passed down or blocked generationally. Class works relationally within fields, such as education, whereby not all cultural heritage is equally valorised as cultural capital. Cultural capital refers specifically to cultural resources that can accrue advantage to the individual or group in dominant fields (Bourdieu, 1984, 1990). As Tyler (2013, 2020) has argued convincingly, the cultural and communicative ways associated with working-class existence are often stigmatised within powerful fields like education. Bourdieu and Passeron (1990) term this stigmatisation and delegitimisation, symbolic violence. I have interrogated the empirical material from my study using Bourdieu's concepts to explain further the factors contributing to the classed composition of reading groups, as follows.

Middle-class families can experience work-related pressures on family life, yet it was only children in the 'bottom' reading group who expressed awareness of the effect that (low-paid) work and home responsibilities had on parents' availability to read with them. Jeffy (St Jude's, Clyde) told me he couldn't ask his mum or dad to read with him because of the long hours they had to work. His mum, he said, had a job in a superstore and made craft products at home. His dad had become a delivery driver during the pandemic and now got home late each evening and had only one day off per week. In his tone and words, Jeffy expressed the injustice of this. Often on his dad's day off the family drove to the coast for a walk and an ice cream. Jeffy described a loving home that was temporally and economically stretched in ways that limited their capacity to read regularly with him. His experience contrasts starkly to that of Jack, a middle class, White, Scottish boy in Kelvin class at Fairfield. Jack talked about how his mum gave up her studies, supported by his dad's income as a lawyer, to spend more time with him and his brother. This time included regular reading and searching for books he might enjoy.

Mothers predominantly do the work of transmitting familial cultural capital to their children (Reay, 1995, 2004). Millie's stepdad, for example, left the house early for work on a building site and did not feature again in Millie's account of their daily life. Her mum was a care worker as well as fitting in the many home responsibilities described here by Millie[6] in the following extract, constructed from Millie's words about reading at home:

> Well ma mum doesn't really have time (for reading) because she wants to keep the house clean and all that. And I don't have time for it 'cause she starts making the dinner after she's done a wee bit of work and then when I ask her to do ma homework she usually, she's always doing the washing, or dishes, or making the dinner so I don't really have time. But if she does have time, she always does it with me. I still try and do it 'cause I know I'm, eh, I'm supposed to read the books every night. I don't practise every night because ma mum never has the time. I still practise a lot. Sometimes if I don't get it done then the next day my mum does that homework with me.

The capacity to transmit cultural capital, which could include knowledge of books and reading proficiency, depends on the amount of available time for this work and not only on the nature of the capital parents possess (Bourdieu, 1986; Reay, 2004). For Millie's mum, as for Jeffy's parents, there may simply be less time available to read together. In her words, Millie appears caught between the school's expectations of daily home reading ("I still try and do it 'cause I know I'm supposed to read books every night") and defending her mum ("but if she does have time she always does it with me"). The effect of economic pressure on time and emotional space to read with children was highlighted in a survey conducted by the National Literacy Trust (2023) about parents' reading with children during what is often referred to as the cost-of-living crisis. The report found that almost one-quarter of parents and carers experiencing financial hardship felt too stressed to read with their children as they had before because of their financial worries.

But, as well as economic constraint, parents' capacity to transmit literacy capital depends on the cultural capital they possess (Bourdieu, 1986); and this again may affect their child's allocation to a prestigious or stigmatised reading group. For parents who might have substantial legitimated literacy capital, like Lewis's mum,[7] who was doing a doctorate and Emma's mum,[8] a journalist, reading with their children *may* be easy, relaxing and productive. But for some parents, particularly if they have experienced reading difficulties, a very different set of emotions may come into play when sharing books with their children, emotions like stress and feelings of inadequacy (Duckworth, 2013). Some of the children in the lowest positioned reading group spoke of their mother's difficulties with reading. Car, a working class, White boy of Scottish and English heritage at Fairfield whose mum cultivated his love of books, also spoke about the difficulties she had with words:

Car: My dad never reads to me anymore ... he's not living in ma house anymore.
Jess: So, did he used to read to you?
Car: Yeh and even ma mum, 'cause ma dad's a wee bit better ... ma mum doesn't know some of the words ... the hard ones she never knowed ... Ma mum can't read some of *The Owl That Was Afraid of the Dark*.
Conversation with Car, Lewis and Jack, Fairfield, Kelvin

Car seems to appreciate, with "even ma mum", that his mum reads with him, even though she doesn't find reading easy, so that he can do his homework. *The Owl That Was Afraid of the Dark* by Jill Tomlinson was the class novel, which children were required to read at home. Puffy (working class, White, Scottish; Fairfield, Kelvin) also seemed to believe his mum had difficulties with reading when he said and repeated that his mum "can't", when I asked if they had read his library book, issued the day before. Yet she clearly had read the book with him, evident in the small details he recalled, which he wouldn't have been able to read for himself. He didn't articulate what he felt she couldn't do when I asked him, and I fill the space with a guess that he feels she doesn't read like school adults seem to read.

I share these examples for two reasons. Firstly, they emphasise that parents of children in the 'bottom' reading group do read with their children even when they may find it stressful. Secondly, the examples suggest that those efforts may not reap as much value for their children in terms of reading-group placement. As the beginning of the chapter argued, once allocated to a particular group based on parental capital, ability-grouped reading serves to favour the reading development of those in the top spot and hold back those in the 'lower' group. This seems deeply unjust. In the next section I will delve deeper into the influence that children's home life has on their reading group placement.

Family Habits and Reading Group Placement

The value judgement that 'good' parents read with their children sits within a "dominant set of cultural repertoires about how children should be raised," according to Lareau (2011, p. 4). In a review of studies mainly from the US and Europe on shared book reading, Anderson et al. (2003) suggest there is a widespread misassumption in literacy research that "non-mainstream" families do not share books with their children or if they do, they do so in the wrong ways. In a study of Bangladeshi mothers in the UK, for example, mothers spoke of teachers who assumed they were illiterate and advised them on how to share books with their child (Blackledge, 1999). This entrenched view of lack, Anderson et al. argue, appears impervious to the many studies that suggest most families, across cultures, race and class, read with young children. The authors also suggest that there is little homogeneity *within* cultural groups, including the middle classes, who are popularly perceived to have homogeneous book reading habits, held up as the correct way to read books with children.

In an earlier draft of this chapter, I was attempting to create a binary between family reading as described by children in the 'top' and 'bottom' reading groups. This distinction would then be used as further evidence that ability-grouped reading favoured certain home literacy practices and was therefore discriminatory to children with less experience of shared reading at home. However, this binary felt stretched and untrue to the data. On closer examination, I found that these differences were less distinct than I first thought. What follows is, I believe, a messier but 'truer' portrayal of reading and other pastimes in the children's home lives that might affect their group placement.

Although time and resources did affect shared book reading, the children in the lowest positioned reading group also described intimate reading experiences with their parents, often mothers. Puffy, with a smile in his words, spoke of reading at nighttime with his mum, and the popcorn and chocolate that was part of this ritual. His fellow reading-group member, Car, shared his love of *Mr Men* books with his mum, as the following extract from fieldnotes describes:

> Car tells me about his family. His mum works in a breakfast club and nursery. One day it was so windy they had to bring the sand pit inside. I ask if he has any books at home and he says he has loads. They are all in this big cupboard. His favourite books are Christmas books. Mum sometimes reads to him at bedtime. He gets to choose between his iPad and stories. Car and his mum love *Mr Men* books, he says, and they're trying to get all of them.

As I reflected on my conversation with Car, I sensed the closeness he feels to his mum, which seems in part mediated by stories she told him of her work and by a shared love of books. The children in the lowest positioned reading group described family lives that were teeming with such enthusiasms, tender moments, and cultural worth. Books are therefore present, though often decentred by a wealth of other cultural activity. Included in the enthusiasms that children in the lowest positioned group spoke of, echoing Lareau's (2011) study, was hanging out with cousins and playing outside with friends. The pleasure got from computer games was also frequently discussed. When Alf (working class, White, Scottish; Fairfield, Kelvin) told me about his favourite things they included his dog, Daisy, his goldfish, budgies, his mum and dad, and the 15 footballs crammed under his table. He also spoke of reading his Simpsons comic book with his mum when she had time. His mum had multiple cleaning jobs, one of which had to be done in the middle of the night, according to Alf. Tender moments recounted between children and their parents often involved non-print mediums such as oral story telling (as discussed in Chapter 3), television and the internet. Jeffy, for example, described creeping downstairs when he couldn't sleep and curling up on the sofa with his dad to watch World Wrestling Entertainment (WWE). On another occasion he recounted looking up the planetary system with his mum on her phone then going to the window to see if he could see the red planet of Mars.

Conversations with children in the 'top' reading group tended to be less divergent and more focused on their home book reading experience, which was done both with adults and independently. Some talked of favourite places where they could go and read quietly. Most reported having a large accessible collection of books close to hand in bookcases near their beds. This prominence of books echoes Heath's (1983) classic description of middle-class child rearing where bookshelves and book characters were installed "along with the crib". In my study I saw similar patterns in book geography, of where books were and how they were presented. Those in the 'bottom' reading group talked mostly about books being in cupboards, sometimes out of reach, and of objects like soft toys, Lego, electronic devices and footballs being closer to hand. The difference in book geography could reflect different amounts of available space in different homes. Car, for example, talked about his room being very small and the space being dominated by a large inflatable ball. It could also point to the relative importance of different objects in children's lives and identities. The intentional cultivation of a reader identity, symbolised by the prominence and organisation of books, appeared more typical of middle-class homes, which brings me to the concept of *concerted cultivation*.

Lareau (2011) suggests that "concerted cultivation" distinguishes middle-class child rearing from working-class child rearing. In her study, both Black and White middle-class parents saw themselves as developers of their children's talents to serve their future economic, cultural and social gain. Concerted cultivation was apparent in parents' relentless organisation of gallery visits, sports and musical activities for their children, as it had been in Heath's (1983) earlier study. Middle-class children's language use and dispositions, inculcated through imitation and training, also prepared them to assume authority in social and institutional contexts. Although intentionally cultivated, Heath (1983) reminds us how natural these practices may seem to middle-class parents who have gained societal success through similar up-bringing.

Interestingly though, given the extensive time Lareau and her researchers spent with the families, routines of intergenerational reading (of books and other printed material) featured little in her accounts of middle-class family life. Nor did Heath (1983) suggest that competition was a key driver in the way middle-class parents read with their children. Stretching their work, I suggest that cultivation of daily reading and investment in and display of books are core aspects of concerted cultivation. Indeed, studies that have interrogated Lareau's concept suggest that reading habits, more than elite cultural activities, predict educational attainment (De Graaf et al., 2000). Reading may be done to prepare children for getting ahead in education as much as to engage in a nurturing and bonding activity. This is illustrated in the following exchange:

Jack: I used to be in a group on ma own ... and I was way ahead of everyone.
Bella May: See when I told ma mum she was determined to get me over you!
Lola: When I told ma mum she wanted me to get way over Bella May.
Bella May: And so ma mum got ... level four to five Biff, Chip and Kipper books to read to get over Jack [she laughs].
Jack [interjects]: I was just ... really good at reading when I first came to P1, so I just read a book and then it was like perfect.
Jess: ...did you do a lot of practice?

FIGURE 5.1   Self-portraits by Bella May and Jack.

Jack: Yeh, I did quite a lot of practice ... ma mum read a short book for me then I just said the words out. So, it ... was kinda connected to me learning words.
Conversation with Lola, Bella May and Jack, Fairfield, Kelvin

This snippet of conversation happened when I was drawing and chatting with three members of the highest positioned reading group at Fairfield. The audio recorder was on and, prompted by my questions, the conversation meandered through how they felt about their and others' reading groups. Jack (White, middle class, Scottish) describes the sustained, intentional practice of learning to read with his mum before he started formal schooling. As he spoke, Bella May (White, middle class, Scottish) burst into his words to tell him about the competitive spirit his reading skills had sparked in her mum. The upshot of this competition was a concerted effort to catch him up by purchasing and practising two levels of the reading scheme (the Biff, Chip and Kipper books). These actions speak as much to availability of time and money (e.g., to buy the reading scheme) as it does to motivation. The middle-class parents of both Bella May and Jack appear (from their children's comments) to be intentionally preparing them to step confidently into the world of school and societal literacies. And they have succeeded: their children occupy a privileged educational and social position in the class hierarchy as we saw in Chapter 4. Consequently, ability-grouped reading has in this example reproduced middle-class cultural advantage, which Bourdieu and Passeron (1990, p. 11) suggest is characteristic of much pedagogical action in the school system.

> ... because they correspond to the material and symbolic interests of groups and classes differently situated within the power relations, these (pedagogical actions) always tend to reproduce the structure of the distribution of cultural capital among these groups or classes, thereby contributing to the reproduction of the social structure.

The language above conveys *tendencies* rather than *determinacy*, yet social structure may 'always' be reproduced, nonetheless. There is much that seems predictable about the advantage gained through ability-grouped reading because of middle-class cultural reproduction and concerted cultivation of reading. Yet the language of tendency over inevitability is crucial to hold onto because class positioning can also be disrupted, resisted and transformed, even if it bounces back. An example of this disruption arose in the same conversation between Bella May, Lola and Jack. Lola, a White, working-class girl of Scottish heritage, also said her mum wanted her to read better than her friend Bella May but spoke at other points of having taught herself to read. Her mum, she said, was too busy to read with her, as the following narrative portrait, composed from Lola's words, conveys.

How class matters Classroom reading hierarchies **107**

FIGURE 5.2   Self-portrait by Lola.

Lola: A Narrative Portrait

>Nobody actually taught me to read. I just taught maself. Because ma mum was too busy with ma wee brother, and my dad and mum don't live with each other. And ma big sister only plays schools and does her make-up, she won't help me at all. Nope! That's why I don't want a sister. When I'm older I'm going to be a writer so I can help children that can't read. I read lots of books. I read in the library that's across from ma house. I don't really read them with anyone, and I just love it so much. I've got a whole stack at home. It's about to fall! I ask for them at Christmas and at ma birthday. And see at night when ma mum tells us to get to sleep, I hide under ma covers and read ma book with ma torch. *Captain Underpants, Emily Jane,*[9] she is a little doll that's really naughty. She even poured tea down the toy soldiers' trousers!
>
>*Lola, Fairfield, Kelvin*

Lola giggled as she recalled the naughty exploits of Emily Jane. Through her words and the energy of their utterance, I sense her rollicking affective delight in reading. Despite her comment about her mum wanting her to outread Bella May, what she describes is more akin to Lareau's (2011) concept of "natural growth", which Lareau suggests is characteristic of working-class child rearing. The term "natural growth", as Lareau points out, does not deny the often exhausting labour involved in loving children, feeding, clothing, getting them to school and keeping them safe when socioeconomic conditions are harsh. And, according to the school, Lola's mum was indeed navigating hard economic and relational conditions as she worked lovingly to raise her children. Rather, natural growth refers to the autonomy working-class children often have to organise their free time, according to Lareau. If they did engage in organised activities, Lareau suggests, it was generally the child who requested this rather than the result of parental orchestration. In Lola's words, I hear her navigating her own way through the reading world. Her mum supports her love of books by responding to her requests for books as gifts, and perhaps by ignoring the late-night torch reading under the covers, but the impetus seems to come from Lola herself.

And so, Lola's entry to the 'top' group could represent a rupture to the classed allocation to reading groups. She appears to have made it into the 'top' group by her own efforts rather than because of parental cultivation. Close attention to our conversation reveals, however, that her position in the 'top' group is more precarious than those of her middle-class friends:

Jess: Are you all in the same reading group?
Jack: Well no
Bella May: Nnn
Lola: Yeh!
Jack: Well, uh, well
Lola: You've got *Clever Monkey* but I've got *Ella's Umbrella*.[10]
Jack: Yeh (sounding relieved, an audible breath expelled) ...
Bella May: So, we're in the same group but we've not got the same books.
Conversation with Lola, Bella May and Jack, Fairfield, Kelvin

In the extract, Lola needs to claim her membership of the 'top' reading group and for that to be apparently sanctioned by her middle-class friends. She also volunteered that, despite being at the top of Level 9 in Primary 2 (P2), she "went right back" when she began P3:

Lola: I went back to *Green Island* again.
Jess: Ah right. Is that still on Level 9?
Lola: Yeh but,
Jess: But the beginning of Level 9?
Lola: Yup!
Jess: Mmm. Do you know why?
Lola: No!
Jess: How did you feel about that?
Lola: It wasn't really exciting when the same book I've read in P2 ... 'cause I actually knew what happens.

This exchange reminds me of Reay's (2017, p. 77) words, "For working-class children, classrooms are often places of routine everyday humiliations and slights." In the absence of an explanation, it might appear that the ladder Lola climbed to get to the top of Level 9 had randomly met with a snake that had sent her sliding down the board. She refuses the lower position assigned to her by the book levels, and by dint of her agency and love of reading she has established herself as a 'top'-group reader, but her position appears less secure than that of Jack and Bella May. A similar insecurity in holding a top position for Black middle-class children, because of racism, is highlighted by Rollock et al. (2016). In my study, Lewis, the only Child of Colour in the 'top' reading group, appeared to be relatively secure in his position, in that he was frequently described by other children as one of the three top 'top' readers in the class. Nonetheless, he did not appear to form a reading-friendship triad with Jack and Bella May, as might be expected from their shared 'top' status.[11] This may or may not be significant in his social positioning in the 'top' group. A child in the 'middle' group, Oliver, a Slovak speaker who was gaining fluency in English, spoke of really liking reading with Lewis because of his kindness and friendship.[12] I wonder if there was a shared valuable connection between the boys, influenced partly by being positioned as outsiders to the White, Scottish, English-speaking norms of the classroom.

And so, although social class and race were rarely spoken of in the classroom, their effect was signalled in the allocation to, and experience of, ability-grouped reading. Initial allocation to groups was influenced by children's familiarity with books on school entry, which in turn was influenced by classed patterns of concerted cultivation and natural growth (Lareau, 2011). For some middle-class families, a concerted effort was made to arrive at school as one of the 'top' readers. Once in the 'top' and 'bottom' group, the conditions of ability-grouped reading served to consolidate the unfair advantage that comes from securing a place in the 'top' reading group. This unfairness, built into school-based reading, is neither unavoidable nor necessary.

Conclusion

Pedagogical actions and inaction help maintain the social order, which of course is built on the unequal distribution of power, privilege and wealth (Bourdieu & Passeron, 1979, 1990). This chapter shows how, as a relational practice, ability-grouped reading can reproduce classed patterns of exclusion and inclusion in school-based literacies. Literacy capital is a valuable asset, progressively more so perhaps in post-industrial knowledge economies (Olssen & Peters, 2005; Unger, 2022). Feeling at home in this dominant literacy world can be socially, emotionally and economically advantageous (Duckworth, 2013; Williams, 2017).

The chapter illustrates that initial group allocation sets up subsequent inclusions and exclusions in school-based reading. Based largely on reading fluency and familiarity with print, allocation appeared to reflect (through the stories children told) unequal distributions of economic and cultural (literacy/educational) familial capital. Concerted competitive cultivation of reading by some parents, as described by children in the 'top' group, may also have ensured their children gained a top reading spot. The unfairness of ability-grouped reading is masked by the assumption that middle-class children will automatically outperform working-class children (Reay, 2012).

Particular interrelated aspects of ability-grouped reading then serve to maintain this classed allocation by constraining mobility and increasing differences in reading fluency as children move through school. This is not inevitable. The first of those aspects, discussed more in the previous chapter, is the contrasting social status ascribed to, and claimed by, different groups. Such judgements can have profound effects on children's learning, motivation and performance (Reay, 2017). Misallocations to reading groups also had the potential to affect children's self-view, motivation and progress as readers. Middle-class children could be kept out of the 'bottom' reading group because of how their parents might feel. Conversely, working-class children, particularly boys, were misallocated to the 'bottom' group because of their perceived family circumstances when fluency-wise they fitted more into the 'middle' or even 'top' group.

Greater opportunity to develop comprehension, expand vocabulary and read more text in the 'top' group meant those children could advance more quickly, thus widening the gap in reading fluency between groups (Stanovich, 2009). The inertia within ability grouping compounded this trajectory. Individual children could be held back on a lower level of the reading scheme because the group was required to read the same book. When children progressed in reading, they could be held back because the leap to a higher group was deemed too large, and risked denting confidence.

Bourdieu and Wacquant (1992) use the analogy of a game of cards to explain the relationship between structural constraints like those in ability-grouped reading and human agency. The rules of the game and the hand you are dealt are set unless the game changes. How the hand is played means the constraints do not wholly predict how children's experience will unfold. Although classed patterns appeared to reproduce, they did not do so neatly. This chapter, and the previous two, have foregrounded such tensions between agency and constraint. White working-class children claimed a place in the 'top' reading group but found their position there to be more precarious than that of their middle-class peers. One Child of Colour was also in the 'top' reading group when high positioned groups are often characterised by White dominance (Gillborn et al., 2021; Francis & Tereshchenko, 2020). In this instance, his position seemed more secure than that of the working-class White children in the 'top' group. Yet although he was often spoken about as one of the three top 'top' readers, his reading friendships took him outside this elite group of three. This may or may not have had something to do with positioning of minoritised ethnic groups within this White dominant space.

To sum up, this chapter has presented ability-grouped reading as a pedagogical practice that reproduces, for example, classed inequalities.[13] Eliminating ability-grouped reading will not change the composition of resources parents draw on to support children's reading prior to starting school. Nevertheless, the chapter shows that by ranking children in reading groups, and then holding them in place, advantages are unfairly capitalised on, even if this is resisted and sometimes transformed. As Chapter 7 will show there are non-hierarchical ways to organise and support reading development for all children that do not weight advantage towards children who are more versed in print when they begin school.

Notes

1. Because the term *working class* can be misrecognised as only White (Sandhu, 2018), I state here for the avoidance of doubt that by working class I refer to working-class children of all ethnicities.
2. Lucia Jasmine and Jamie, who you met first in Chapter 3, are both White working-class children with Scottish heritage in Kelvin class, Fairfield.
3. Jeffy is a White working-class boy of Scottish heritage. I did not get to know Mario well enough to situate him in terms of class.
4. I understand the term *bilingual* to encompass a continuum that includes children in the early stages of learning an additional language and those who are equally fluent in more than one language.
5. I do not specify school or year group to help maintain anonymity.
6. Millie, who was introduced in Chapter 3, was a White working-class girl with Scottish heritage in Avon class at St Jude's.
7. Lewis, introduced in Chapter 4, was in Kelvin class at Fairfield, was middle class, a Child of Colour and of Pakistani heritage.
8. Emma was in Avon class at St Jude's, was middle class, White and of Scottish heritage.
9. *Captain Underpants* is a series written by Dav Pilkey. I couldn't find reference to a book called *Emily Jane* so I assume she is a character in a book.
10. *Clever Monkey* and *Ella's Umbrella* are titles in the Oxford Reading Tree. Although the children are in the same group, the books reveal they are not on the same level of the reading scheme. *Clever Monkey* is Level 11 and *Ella's Umbrella* is Level 9. My interpretation of Jack's audible relief is that Lola presents a way they can be in the same group and be friends together, when in his mind he might distinguish between children on Levels 11 and 9.
11. See the example shared in the previous chapter where Jack and Bella May were swapping books by post during the pandemic.
12. Oliver was White and of Slovakian heritage. He seemed quiet in class and did not seek me out as many of the White English-speaking children did. I had only one conversation and reading session with him, which did not shed light on how I might situate him in terms of class. Lewis is an English speaker who had never

spoken the first language of his parents, which was Sindhi. He may be positioned as an outsider (by the White, Scottish children) by the colour of his skin and his Pakistani heritage.
13 Ability-grouped reading also negatively positions bilingual learners if children are placed in the 'bottom' reading group.

References

Anderson, J., Anderson, A., Lynch, J., & Shapiro, J. (2003). Storybook reading in a multicultural society: Critical perspectives. In A. v. Kleeck, S. A. Stahl, & U. B. Bauer (Eds.), *On reading books to children* (pp. 203–230). Routledge.

Barros, S., Domke, L. M., Symons, C., & Ponzio, C. (2021). Challenging monolingual ways of looking at multilingualism: Insights for curriculum development in teacher preparation. *Journal of Language, Identity & Education*, 20(4), 239–254. https://doi.org/10.1080/15348458.2020.1753196

Blackledge, A. (1999). Language, literacy and social justice: The experiences of Bangladeshi women in Birmingham, UK. *Journal of Multilingual and Multicultural Development*, 20(3), 179–193. https://doi.org/10.1080/01434639908666375

Bourdieu, P. (1984). *Distinction: A social critique of the judgement of taste*. Routledge & Kegan Paul.

Bourdieu, P. (1986). The forms of capital. In J. Richardson (Ed.) *Handbook for theory and research for the sociology of education* (pp. 241–258). Greenwood Press.

Bourdieu, P. (1990). *The logic of practice*. Stanford University Press.

Bourdieu, P., & Accardo, A. (1999). *The weight of the world: Social suffering in contemporary society*. Stanford University Press.

Bourdieu, P., & Passeron, J. C. (1979). *The inheritors: French students and their relation to culture*. University of Chicago Press.

Bourdieu, P., & Passeron, J. C. (1990). *Reproduction in education, society and culture*. SAGE.

Bourdieu, P., & Wacquant, L. J. D. (1992). *An invitation to reflexive sociology*. University of Chicago Press.

Buckingham, J., Beaman, R., & Wheldall, K. (2014). Why poor children are more likely to become poor readers: The early years. *Educational Review*, 66(4), 428–446.

Cummins, J. (2000). *Language, power, and pedagogy: Bilingual children in the crossfire*. Multilingual Matters.

De Graaf, N. D., De Graaf, P. M., & Kraaykamp, G. (2000). Parental cultural capital and educational attainment in the Netherlands: A refinement of the cultural capital perspective. *Sociology of Education*, 73(2), 92–11.

Duckworth, V. (2013). *Learning trajectories, violence and empowerment amongst adult basic skills learners*. Routledge.

Dunne, M., Humphreys, S., Sebba, J., Dyson, A., Gallannaugh, F., & Muijs, D. (2011). *Effective teaching and learning for pupils in low attaining groups*. University of Sussex. https://dera.ioe.ac.uk/6622/

Earnshaw, J. (2022, January 7). *The placement of learners with EAL in groups, sets and streams*. EMTAS Moodle. https://emtas.hias.hants.gov.uk/blog/index.php?entryid=98

Education Endowment Foundation (EEF). (2016). *Teaching and learning toolkit, within-class attainment grouping*. https://educationendowmentfoundation.org.uk/resources/teaching-learning-toolkit

Francis, B., & Tereshchenko, A. (2020). *Reassessing ability groupings: Improving practice for equity and attainment.* Routledge.

Freire, P. (2000). *Pedagogy of the oppressed* (30th anniversary ed.). Continuum.

Gardiner-Hyland, F. (2021). Don't forget us! Challenges supporting children with EAL in Irish primary schools. *European Journal of Applied Linguistics and TEFL, 10*(2), 177–199.

Gardiner-Hyland, F., & Burke, P. (2018). "It's very hard to know how much is the EAL and how much is the learning difficulty": Challenges in organising support for the EAL learners in Irish primary schools. *Learn Journal, 40,* Chapter 3, 54–64. Irish Support Association.

Gillborn, D., Bhopal, K., Crawford, C., Demack, S., Gholami, R., Kitching, K., Kiwan, D., & Warmington, P. (2021). *Evidence for the commission on race and ethnic disparities.* University of Birmingham CRRE. https://doi.org/10.25500/epapers.bham.00003389

Hall, K., (2005). *Listening to Stephen Read: Multiple perspectives on literacy.* Open University Press.

Hallam, S., & Ireson, J. (2006). Secondary school pupils' preferences for different types of structured grouping practices. *British Educational Research Journal, 32*(4), 583–599.

Hallam, S., & Ireson, J. (2007). Secondary school pupils' satisfaction with their ability grouping placements. *British Educational Research Journal, 33*(1), 27–45.

Heath, S. B. (1983). *Ways with words: Language, life and work in communities and classrooms.* Cambridge University Press.

Hooks, b. (1994). *Teaching to transgress: Education as the practice of freedom.* Routledge.

Joseph-Salisbury, R. (2020). *Race and racism in English secondary schools.* Runnymede Trust. https://assets-global.website-files.com/61488f992b58e687f1108c7c/61bcc0cc2a023368396c03d4_Runnymede%20Secondary%20Schools%20report%20FINAL.pdf

Lareau, A. (2011). *Unequal childhoods: Class, race, and family life.* University of California Press.

Learned, J. E. (2016). "Feeling like I'm slow because I'm in this class": Secondary school contexts and the identification and construction of struggling readers. *Reading Research Quarterly, 51*(4), 367–371. https://doi.org/10.1002/rrq.157

Lucas, T., Villegas, A. M., & Freedson-Gonzalez, M. (2008). Linguistically responsive teacher education: Preparing classroom teachers to teach English language learners. *Journal of Teacher Education, 59*(4), 361–373.

Luttrell, W. (2020). *Children framing childhoods: Working-class kids' vision of care.* Polity Press.

MacIntyre, H., & Ireson, J. (2002). Within-class ability grouping: Placement of pupils in groups and self-concept. *British Educational Research Journal, 28*(2), 249–263. https://doi.org/10.1080/01411920120122176

National Literacy Trust (2023). *Children and young people's access to books and educational devices at home during the cost-of-living-crisis. A survey of over 3000 parents and carers.* National Literacy Trust. https://cdn.literacytrust.org.uk/media/documents/Access_to_books_and_devices_during_cost-of-living_crisis.pdf

Olssen, M., & Peters, M.A. (2005). Neoliberalism, higher education and the knowledge economy: From the free market to knowledge capitalism. *Journal of Education Policy, 20*(3), 313–345.

Reay, D. (1995). A silent majority? Mothers in parental involvement. *Women's Studies International Forum, 18*(3), 337–348.

Reay, D. (2004). Gendering Bourdieu's concept of capitals? Emotional capital, women and social class. In L. Adkins & B. Skeggs (Eds.), *Feminism after Bourdieu* (pp. 57-74). Blackwell Publishing.

Reay, D. (2012). What would a socially just education system look like?: Saving the minnows from the pike. *Journal of Education Policy, 27*(5), 587–599.

Reay, D. (2017). *Miseducation: Inequality, education and the working classes.* Polity Press.

Rollock, N., Gillborn, D., Warmington, P., & Demack, S. (2016). *Race, racism and education: Inequality, resilience and reform in policy.* University of Birmingham.

Sandhu, K. (2018, March 16). Working class in Britain? You must be White. New Internationalist. https://newint.org/features/2018/03/01/working-class-in-britain

Savage, M. (2015). *Social class in the 21st century.* Pelican Books.

Scanlan, M., & López, F. (2012). ¡Vamos! How school leaders promote equity and excellence for bilingual students. *Educational Administration Quarterly, 48*(4), 583–625.

Stanovich, K. E. (2009). Matthew effects in reading: Some consequences of individual differences in the acquisition of literacy. *Journal of Education, 189*(1–2), 23–55.

Tyler, I. (2013). *Revolting subjects: Social abjection and resistance in neoliberal Britain.* Zed Books.

Tyler, I. (2020). *Stigma: The machinery of inequality.* Zed Books.

Unger, R. M. (2022). *The knowledge economy.* Verso Books.

Vellutino, F. R., Fletcher, J. M., Snowling, M. J., & Scanlon, D. M. (2004). Specific reading disability (dyslexia): What have we learned in the past four decades? *Journal of Child Psychology and Psychiatry, 45*(1), 2–40.

Williams, B. T. (2017). *Literacy practices and perceptions of agency: Composing identities.* Routledge.

Children's Literature References

Butterworth, N. (2005). *Percy the badger.* Collins.

Dr Seuss. (1960). *Green eggs and ham.* Random House.

Elboz, S., & Bowman, P. (2016). *Clever monkey.* Oxford University Press.

Groening, M. (1998). *Simpsons on parade.* Titan Books Ltd.

Hargreaves, R. (1971). *Mr Men* series. Thurman Publishing.

Hunt, R., Page, T., & Brychta, A. (2011). Selection of books featuring Biff, Chip and Kipper. For example: *Kipper's Laces.* OUP Oxford.

Hunt, R., Page, T., & Brychta, A. (2008). *Green Island.* OUP Oxford.

Pilkey, D. (1997–2015). *Captain Underpants* series. Scholastic.

Powling, C. (2015). *Ella's umbrella.* OUP Oxford.

Tomlinson, J. (2004). *The owl that was Afraid of the dark.* Egmont.

6
PRINT READING DIFFICULTIES AND ABILITY-GROUPED READING

Introduction

The previous chapter consolidated the core proposition that ability-grouped reading reflects and rewards classed practices, resources and assumptions, rather than necessarily reflecting greater or lesser aptitude for print reading. Yet not all children showed similar aptitude for reading print: a small number ($n = 5$) in the 'bottom' reading group were finding reading extraordinarily difficult and this chapter is devoted to their experience. Reading involves comprehension, connection and emotional engagement with multimodal signals, including image, colour, sound, shape and words (Kress, 2000; Narey, 2017; Pahl & Rowsell, 2020). That said, because print dominates in education and society, the deciphering of words can matter disproportionately in how readers are positioned and in the emotional, social and intellectual experience of readers in low positioned reading groups (Maybin, 2013; Learned, 2016; Scherer, 2016).[1]

This chapter will provide a close-up, situated critique of ability-grouped reading when reading is difficult, linking to broader reproduction of privilege and disadvantage through the reification of print communication in society (Collinson, 2012, 2020). There can be both fixity and fluidity in how readers are recognised and misrecognised when the processing of print is very difficult. Reading difficulties *can* be examined and their effect on identity explored without essentialising those difficulties. That is, they can be examined without assuming those difficulties are unaffected by social, emotional or temporal conditions, and also without allowing difficulties in decoding print to occlude other aspects of children's relationship with reading. To maintain fluidity of perception while recognising how readers can become fixed in their self-view, and in peers' and educators' gaze, is the guiding principle of this chapter.

In offering this critique I will engage critically with psychological interpretations of reading difficulties (e.g., Snowling & Hulme, 2005; Snowling, 2019) by bringing them into conversation with relational perspectives on reading (e.g., Dudley-Marling, 2004; Kirk, 2001; Williams, 2017). Some of the writers I draw on here offer autoethnographic accounts of feeling like outsiders in the world of powerful literacies in childhood (Chapman, 2012; Kirk, 2001; McQueen, 2020; Stuart, 2021). Their stories are included, not as predictors of how children's reading will be in the future, but to point towards the relations of power within which children's reading develops; they also act as cautionary tales against seeing reading difficulties, as they present in childhood, as being fixed. I deliberately attribute as much epistemological authority to these autoethnographic insights as I do to literacy theorists writing in more traditional academic registers. Each are chosen for their thought-provoking challenges to essentialist views on reading difficulties, and for bringing class and race into the frame of discussion.

The first section of the chapter, *A Double Bind? Navigating Print Challenges in the 'Bottom' Reading Group*, explores reader identities and positioning in ability-grouped reading for children having difficulties processing print. The second section, *A Close Encounter with Print Reading Difficulties*, offers a detailed empirical account of the experience of one child, Cash, when engaging with print. This close analysis provides the grounding for subsequent analysis beginning with the third section, *Developmental Dyslexia: Affordances and Limitations*, which interrogates the efficacy of neurolinguistic explanations for enduring reading difficulties. The fourth section, *Affective Shifts, Cultural Resonance and Dissonance in Reader Identities*, suggests that difficulties which appear fixed can *sometimes* prove more fluid when viewed through a prism of temporal, social and affective conditions around reading. The chapter concludes with *Symbolic Violence and the Tyranny of Print Literacy*, which reconceptualises Cash's story within the affective, sociocultural and neurolinguistic landscape of the chapter.

The process of writing this chapter in particular has been hesitant, deliberative and in-progress. Such deliberation has provided the reflexive space to grapple with conceptualisations that challenged my practitioner understanding of reading difficulties and to probe the close empirical material from children's reading. The process has also enabled me to reflect on how different experiences of reading become legitimised and delegitimised within education, work and social life. More than any other chapter, my mind has been changed through the process of writing it. The chapter represents an evolution of my thinking towards psychological perspectives, troubled within sociopolitical and affective interpretations of reading difficulties.

This epistemological decision to make visible how my knowledge has developed may help some readers to think along with me. I have chosen to write often in the present tense when discussing the children, to add immediacy to this evolution of thinking.

A Double Bind? Navigating Print Challenges in the 'Bottom' Reading Group

As Chapter 4 illustrated, children in the 'bottom' reading group were very often viewed by other children as not only less adept at reading, but also less intelligent, less happy and less confident than those in the 'top' reading group. In these perceptions, little distinction was made between those who were making sustained progress and those who were finding reading impossibly difficult. When asked, children speculated that those in the 'bottom' reading group would all struggle to read as adults. Those experiencing difficulties in processing print seemed no more or less likely to be imagined as a future poor adult reader than those who were currently making smoother progress in reading. One exception to the view that less fluent readers would forever remain less fluent, was expressed by Lola (working class, White, Scottish; Fairfield, Kelvin, 'top' reading group). By asserting that anyone could become a skilled reader with practice, she challenged the 'common sense' myth that those in the 'top' group were essentially more intelligent or more naturally gifted at reading, a myth built on ideas of natural superiority of the middle classes. As Reay (2012, p. 593) expands:

> As long as the upper and middle classes remain invested in the belief of their own social and intellectual superiority, they will continue to associate fairness in education with their own children winning what is an extremely unfair educational contest.

Occasionally, children in the lowest positioned group distanced themselves from those perceived to be making very limited progress in processing print. This could be expressed in the claiming of higher status reading material such as chapter books, as Millie appeared to do in Chapter 4, and illustrated in the following conversation:

Millie: I can't really read the chapters …
Jess: So, you chose *Horrid Henry* [a short chapter book] didn't you?
Millie: 'cause it's on telly and then I know some of the stories from it … I'm also quickly look at pages because I like the ones that have pictures in it 'cause then you can know what the words in that maybe,

Jess:	Does everybody choose a chapter book?
Millie and Ellie:	(in unison) No!
Ellie:	Some people in our class are not the *best* (her emphasis).

Conversation with Millie and Ellie, St Jude's, Avon

Millie's choice of chapter books (with pictures), despite finding chapter books difficult, may align her with her friend Ellie from the 'top' reading group[2] and distance her from others in the so-called bottom reading group that Ellie describes as "not the best". George, a working-class, White boy of Scottish heritage and another member of Millie's group, chose quite long chapter books with few pictures. His reading, unlike Millie's, was not progressing along a normative arc and he couldn't yet read the books he chose. He may have to choose between aligning with the chapter-reading majority and the stigma of reading lower status accessible texts. This is an example of the pressure to perform as a confident reader when status judgements are highly visible (as they are in ability-grouped reading), which can affect the text choices that children make.

The reading lives of those who experience difficulties in processing print are richer, however, than this chapter book/picturebook dichotomy introduces. They are also richer than a singular focus on their difficulties would suggest. Through the following narrative portrait of Alf, a working class, White boy of Scottish heritage I hope to convey the joy, agency, uncertainty and constraints that can be present when children find reading difficult. This portrait is composed from fieldnotes and audio-taped conversations.

Alf: A Narrative Portrait

The children gather on the carpet in front of the teacher's chair. A chorus of voices spontaneously call out to each other what reading scheme level they are on. I hear Alf's voice buoyantly proclaim that he is on level 2; this is the lowest level for the class. Later that day, he is reading a graphic novel, *The Simpsons on Parade*. His head is bent over the book and his eyes scan across the comic frames. I ask if he enjoys reading and he says yes, "if it's too easy, if it's too hard, I can still look at the pictures." He asks if I have a favourite Simpson and when I say, "Marge," he says, "Bart, because he does funny things." He reads *The Simpsons* with his mum at home, after homework and dinner, when she gets a moment. His mum has five cleaning jobs, he says, and a big bunch of keys.

Another occasion, reading a *Dr Seuss* book, Alf wonders what a machine in the book is making. I point to the word *donuts*. He stares at the word but says nothing. I cover all but the first letter *d*, inviting him to say the sound. He is silent, still, staring at the page, then turns to me and says, "It's really cold today." I agree, and we leave the book aside. The children

Print reading difficulties and ability-grouped reading   **119**

FIGURE 6.1   Self-portrait by Alf.

use the five-finger rule to choose books. Alf explains, "You start with 5 fingers up and every time you don't know a word you put a finger down and if all five fingers are down the book is too hard for you, so you put it back." He speaks with authority, as a reader in class who uses this system, and I ask if he could show me how it works using a book. He stops, stock still, and after a pause says quietly, "I can't read anything." His words feel like a confession, the stillness contrasts to the movement and glee he expresses when reading a familiar book from the reading scheme. In those moments he frequently rubs his hands together and beams a smile, like when he sees a character's mum bringing hot chocolate. His reading connects, and is interspersed with, stories from home. "Imagine," he says when Chip and Kipper jump out and surprise Biff, "I do that to my brother!"

I return to Alf's comment that he can't read anything. He is an avid reader of images, also an avid and respected online gamer among his peers but these may not be framed as reading in Alf's school world. I wonder about his knowledge of letters and words. I write down and ask him to circle the letters he knows. He circles *a, e, s, k, m, x* and *o*, before saying "I'm looking for the one that goes Z," which he draws with his finger in the air, and I realise I missed out *z*. There are many letters he doesn't know, including *f* which is in his name. He says he doesn't know any words but when I write out *a, is, the, in, on* he says gleefully "if you turn the *o* and the *n* it [*on*] makes *no*!" I ask if he knows *the* and he says he always forgets that one. His teacher is concerned about his memory and has requested that he be assessed by the educational psychologist. Meanwhile when he needs to log into *Roblox* on his iPad he enlists the help of the internet for the letters he doesn't know. He demonstrates, calling across the room, as if to the computer-generated assistant, "Alexa! How d'you spell *two-player tycoon?*" A smile laces his words, as he shares his ingenuity.

Alf, Fairfield, Kelvin

Alf's narrative suggests ways that the position of struggling reader can be ignored, pushed back but also embodied. There seemed a lack of awareness or perhaps a lack of concern about how other children might position him as a level two reader when they boasted of higher reading levels. There was an infectious joy in his engagement with comic books, as he connected them to events in his own life that make him laugh. From other stories he told, like his budgie pooping in his dad's dinner, I imagined a household that laughs easily. There was also what I interpreted as fear or tension as his body froze, his eyes widened and his voice quietened when his inability to decipher print was revealed. In explaining the five-finger rule to me he enacted a reader identity, promoted in the classroom, of readers who could discern for themselves which books were a good level for them. Yet, this rule only works if there is some print knowledge and Alf at this stage could recognise only a few letters and fewer words. I regretted my question that prompted this exposure and the distress I perceived in his response that he couldn't read. He was also denied the identity of reader (when tightly imagined as print reader) that multimodal conceptions of reading would have opened up through his reading of comic books and computer games (Narey, 2017; Kress, 2010; Vasquez, 2014).

When reading difficulties are experienced, the gap between a child's print fluency and that of the majority grows ever wider with the passing of time (Kirk, 2001). Children appear doubly held by emotion around their difficulties, and by messages of fixity that ability-grouped reading conveys whether difficulties are experienced or not. As the two previous chapters have argued, ability-grouped reading encourages a view that some children naturally belong in the 'top' group and others in the 'bottom' group. A particularly unhelpful message for a child who fears their reading is not going according to plan is that positions in the reading hierarchy are already fixed, even into adulthood (Duckworth, 2013; Kirk, 2001). And so, reading differences, perceived as difficulties, exist in social contexts and within relationships with other (real or imagined) readers despite often being individualised as a problem within the child (Dudley-Marling, 2004).

Acknowledging this socially constructed relationality does not ignore the challenges faced by individuals whose reading does not fit societal norms. The following section delves deeper into those challenges when deciphering print is difficult.

A Close Encounter with Print Reading Difficulties

Many studies of children who struggle with reading either focus solely on decontextualised episodes of decoding print (e.g., Leppänen et al., 2012; Velluntino & Fletcher, 2005; Wagner et al., 1999) or only on the social and affective dimensions of reading (e.g., Hempel-Jorgensen et al., 2018; Scherer, 2016). An exception is Kabuto's (2016) study of the social construction of a "reading (dis)ability", which pays close attention to how print is read within the sociocultural dynamics of reading. Following Kabuto, the next section presents a complex portrayal of Cash as a reader that attends equally to the minutia of deciphering print when this is difficult, and to the affective and social contexts of reading. By attending to both, novel perspectives on print reading difficulties can be constructed.

Cash is a working-class, White boy of Scottish heritage in Clyde class at St Jude's, who loves electronic and playground games, his little sister, dinosaurs and his pet tortoise. He is also an astute and engaged lover and interpreter of stories. In the following fieldnote I recorded his response when the teacher was reading to the class *Pugs of the Frozen North* by Reeves & McIntyre, a novel about a race to an imaginary North Pole. At one point the contestants encounter a noodle bar run by yetis. If the contestants eat the noodles, they mysteriously decide to give up the race and stay to eat more noodles.

> Today Cash said that he thought maybe the noodles were like beer. If you drink a lot of beer, it makes you forget things and maybe the noodles were making the characters forget things.

In this example I imagine Cash making sense of the story by interpreting events through the lens of his own experience, where adults may become forgetful around alcohol (Chambers, 2011; Rosenblatt, 1978). He also finds reading print at this point in his life very difficult. Another extract from my fieldnotes reminds me of the emotional and physical tension I perceived in him, each time I observed him read with me or his teacher.

> The teacher is reading a book about the circus with Cash. His body seems very still, upright, almost frozen, except for his hands that wring around each other under the desk. His expression seems anxious, and his eyes flit from the teacher's face to mine, and only momentarily, to the text in the

book. It is the teacher who scans the print, using her finger to point to each word. It is she who leans towards the book, says each word.

In my conversations with Cash, he talked about finding reading difficult. When telling me about reading to his little sister he said, "I don't (know) how to read dead dood [good]. If I don't know a word then I just make it up." But when reading to an adult in class he seems to know that making it up won't serve him. Nor will he be helped in this context by the interpretative sophistication he shows when the teacher reads aloud to the class.

When it comes to reading to the teacher, he is left frozen, with limited options, because he often can't decipher the words and, in this context, this is what he is being asked to do. He seems to have great difficulty in blending individual sounds into words, as the following extract illustrates. The letters and words from the book are italicised to distinguish them from our chat:

Cash: [begins to read] *I* (pause) *n-i-s hiss* (pause)
Jess: Do you know what that is?
Cash: It's like when a cat's like angry they hiss and they do sss. And spit. I know it says *spit* in the page somewhere 'cause I've read it. I think I'm read up to [sound of turning pages]. I think I've read the whole entire book! That's how I know.
Jess: And I think you might find it. Shall we read on and see if we can find it?
Cash: [continues reading] *And s-p-i- ts* (longer pause)
Jess: Have another go.
Cash: *S-p-i- s-t-s-p-i-ts* (pause) *s pis*.
Jess: What about [pointing to a section of the word], do you know that word?
Cash: *It*
Jess: *It*, so you've got '*it*'. So you don't need to do that. You can just go '*it*'. So that's a?
Cash: *it i-s –p*
Jess: *S-p-it*
Cash: *Spit, spit*!
Jess: That's it!

Read and Chat with Cash, St Jude's, Clyde

Cash knows the word *spit* is coming up, remembered from past readings, and it appears almost as the next word. And yet, knowing it is coming up *and* knowing the letters/sounds in the word, are not enough to make the word come together in his mind when he sees it. This strategy of sounding out words is one that he is taught daily in an intervention group for children with reading difficulties. Breaking up words into phonemes (single units of sound) can remind me of breaking up a jigsaw puzzle to see the picture, especially when it proves unhelpful, as it seems to do for Cash. His mispronunciation of *hiss* as "n-i-s", before correctly saying *hiss* is also revealing. It suggests he already knows the word but breaks it up anyway. Perhaps sounding out letters is part of the school reading game he has learned to play, even when unnecessary. However, when children find it exceptionally difficult to remember letter sounds, or bring them together to make a word, it can make reading frustrating and dispiriting. It is far from the only skill readers utilise, but it does play a crucial role in reading, given the alphabetic coding system in English orthography (Hall, 2005).

Another incident, reflected in my fieldnotes, suggests that Cash may not yet have grasped the way words work in English print. When encountering the word *cross* he paused, and I offered the first sound, *c*. He took this and attached it to another word that made sense in the context, by saying "c-angry". In the making of a non-word, *c-angry*, Cash's attempt may again suggest compliance in a school reading game, without being quite sure what that game is. Cash wants to be able to read print and talks about this. However, despite his best efforts, in three successive years each of his teachers told me the same thing, that Cash was beginning to get to grips with reading consonant-vowel-consonant (CVC) words such as 'cat'. From my vantage point, I heard that despite his effort and desire to read, little progress was being made in deciphering print. This inability to progress in print reading has material consequences, and perhaps progressively more so in global economies dominated by knowledge as capital (Olssen & Peters, 2005; Patrick, 2013; Peters, 2001). Negative impacts of print-processing difficulties on education and employment are also felt more acutely the less economic, social and cultural capital one has to exchange (Macdonald & Deacon, 2019).

When Cash spoke, his speech contained non-normative articulation of certain sounds, unrelated to accent or dialect, which I sometimes found difficult to understand. Although *what* he spoke about was complex, knowledgeable and insightful, his speech patterns reminded me of a younger child. He often used soft, in place of hard, consonants. For example, when talking about his gran and his bedroom he pronounced them *dran* and *dedroom*. Milk was pronounced *milt*. These non-normative pronunciations may make sounding out words in reading harder. His speech also seemed to be missing some grammatical connective tissue, like in the following example:

> I can't remember 'cause we're not near the library then can't remember when we be the library 'cause it's been a long time.
> *Conversation with Cash, St Jude's, Clyde*

If, as psycholinguists suggest, readers bring their syntactic knowledge to successfully anticipating what is written, these grammatical partialities in his speech could also limit his success in reading print (Goodman, 1967; see also Hall, 2005). In the next section I begin by thinking about Cash's reading challenges in terms of developmental dyslexia, that is, of enduring phonological processing difficulties. Then, utilising Collinson's (2020, 2012) concept of *lexism* with Bourdieu and Passeron's (1990) concepts of symbolic violence and the cultural arbitrary, I trouble the portrayal of reading differences as an impairment by reflecting on the relations of power always lurking within literacy practices.

Developmental Dyslexia: Affordances and Limitations

My starting position when considering specific reading difficulties, like those described through Cash's reading, was that they do exist, based on the enduring reading difficulties I observed in a small number of children in each year of my teaching career. I have taught children across spectrums of class, race and ethnicity who find deciphering print exceptionally difficult, despite sustained practice, effort and engagement with books. I have also witnessed the emotional effects of these difficulties. Attending closely to Cash's struggles to decipher words, recalling the freeze in his upright body, his wringing hands and panicked eyes, my mind first turns to the phonological challenges framed as dyslexia in the field of developmental psychology. Indeed, Cash was diagnosed as dyslexic in Primary 5, after fieldwork had ended.

Dyslexia is ascribed to neurodevelopmental differences, often believed to be genetically inherited (Vellutino et al., 2004; see also Becker et al., 2017 for a systematic review of research into developmental dyslexia). It is proposed that the cognitive activity involved in processing language includes phonological awareness, memory and production (Wagner et al., 1999). Phonological awareness is defined as the conceptual understanding that, for example, the words we hear are made up of individual sounds (phonemes) and groups of sounds, such as syllables (Velluntino & Fletcher, 2005). Phonological memory and production, the authors suggest, allow us to store, hear, distinguish, recall and manipulate units of sounds. Phonological processing difficulties are believed to be the key factor in developmental dyslexia, according to developmental psychologists (e.g., Snowling, 1998, 2019; Snowling & Hulme, 2005). Cash appeared to have such phonological processing difficulties, illustrated by his struggles over *spit*, his attempt of *c-angry* for *cross*, and the very limited progress he had made in deciphering CVC words over a three-year period. In addition, phonological differences in producing speech sounds beyond the age children begin to read, and contained in Cash's speech, can also be characteristic of developmental dyslexia (Leppänen et al., 2012).

Cash's print and speech processing differences were similar to the other four children who were finding reading difficult in the study. The majority of children in the lowest positioned reading group did not have such difficulty processing print, and they had a conceptual grasp of how print worked that Cash seemed not to have. This conceptual understanding included, for example, that English orthography is organised into words, with spaces in between, and that letters in words are ordered by the sounds they make in those words.

For some people the concept, and diagnosis, of dyslexia is a liberating one that challenges commonplace associations of reading differences with lack of intelligence. See, for example, Robinson's (2017) autoethnography of being a gifted Black male dyslexic in a racialised education system that failed to recognise his potential to succeed academically. Although I question the notion of giftedness upon which his analysis is based, his writing usefully highlights the empowerment, and shift in educational trajectories, that can occur when a dyslexia diagnosis is received. Drawing on critical disability theory (Reaume, 2014), he also suggests it is institutions that dis-able people by pathologising differences.

Collinson (2012, 2020) too suggests that it is society that dis-ables dyslexics but challenges the notion that dyslexics have a learning disability as Robinson suggests. It is by thinking along with Collinson and his concept of *lexism*, that has broken open my thinking about reading difficulties from my psychological starting point described above. It further challenged my own normative elevation of reading print above other mediums of communication. Collinson positions himself as a dyslexic who rejects dominant dyslexia discourses. The following quote is helpful in explaining the crucial distinction he makes between being a dyslexic and the concept of dyslexia as a condition or impairment:

> … dyslexia can be thought of as a concept which is created, required and disguised by another set of concepts surrounding literacy which define the shape and form of the shadow it casts. The object that creates the shadow and defines its shape is what I have termed 'Lexism': the normative practices and assumptions of literacy.
>
> *Collinson, 2012, p. 63*

Collinson does not reject the idea that people experience biologically influenced difficulties in processing written text, a rejection which he suggests some critiques of dyslexia make. Instead, he argues that dyslexics can be described as "those whose aptitude in literacy and short-term/working memory fall below the social norms and practices of literacy; who are thus 'othered' by Lexism" (2012, p. 63). By coining the term *lexism*, Collinson points to the discrimination and pathologising of people who do not conform to the normative practices of literacy in a society and education system that favours, and is mediated by, print literacy.

Lexism could be an expression of the symbolic violence and delegitimisation of non-dominant cultural practices in Bourdieu's (1977; Bourdieu

& Passeron, 1990) notion of the *cultural arbitrary*. By cultural arbitrary, Bourdieu refers to the arbitrariness of what comes to be regarded as culturally superior, as having legitimacy, and therefore exchange value, in the educational, social and economic marketplace. Cultural practices are legitimated through the power relations between groups. Legitimation always expresses the interests of dominant groups (Bourdieu, 1977). The power of symbolic violence is, as suggested by its name, symbolic. Its violence is expressed through the stigmatising of cultural practices of non-dominant groups (Tyler, 2013, 2020).

Thinking about Cash in the light of Collinson's work changes the way I think of his reading. His difficulty in deciphering print does not need to be ignored to recognise that it is normative assessments of reading, such as age-related reading speeds and accuracy, that construct Cash as a struggling reader. This returns to the point made by Dudley-Marling (2004) that no child can have a reading difficulty on their own. It is always relative to the positions of other readers and to the legitimated value ascribed to reading print in education and society. If the norm of communication was, for example, oral and diagrammatical, then having a relatively weak aptitude for print would no more be regarded as an impairment than a limited aptitude for drawing is (Collinson, 2012).

When reading is uncoupled from print and reconceptualised as communication through images, words, situations, colours etc., then Cash's reading begins to look quite different (Hamilton, 2016; Kress, 2000; Pahl & Rowsell, 2020). He presents very differently as a reader, for example, in his insightful interpretations of *Pugs of the Frozen North* when read aloud in class. I am also reminded of an incident when Cash was scanning a book during a group reading session. After struggling to decipher words under the gaze of the teacher he turned to the pictures and, as if hungry, flipped back and forward, devouring them. He then turned to me and recounted exactly what was happening in the story through information he'd gleaned from the illustrations. I am reminded too of Alf's engagement with, and sense of ownership of, *The Simpson's* comic book, where there is much to work out through the interplay of visuals, text and typography.

Affective Shifts, Cultural Resonance and Dissonance in Reader Experiences

Despite my shifts in conceptualisation of reading difficulties through writing this chapter, I still held an assumption that print processing differences, like those of Cash, Alf and others, would persist unchanged into adulthood. It is this notion of permanency I now wish to trouble by reflecting further on the (always) socially and affectively situated nature of reading (Albright & Luke, 2010; Leander & Ehret, 2019; Street, 2013). In this troubling, I do not challenge experience shared by dyslexics (e.g., Collinson, 2020, 2012; Robinson, 2017) that *some* print reading differences endure. Notwithstanding this, I suggest that there *are* differences that may appear fixed or innate in childhood but change with time and circumstance. To explore this temporality within the classed, raced and gendered landscapes in which reading occurs, I will now draw on adult recollections of childhood reading difficulties, conveyed through social stories, academic, political and artistic contemplation.

This variety reflects an epistemological valuing of all knowledge that develops my understanding, whether it hails from the academic canon or not (e.g., McQueen, 2020; Chapman, 2012; Stuart, 2021). The stories act here as cautionary tales against swift judgements that label children as poor readers and allocate them to a reading group from which it is then difficult to get out. I have no intention of mapping these adult stories onto the children in the study. Only time will tell how the children's relationship with print evolves.

Nevertheless, the stories raise affective and sociological issues that are worth considering in the context of the study.

The first thing apparent in the adult stories is the emotional intensities felt when their reading did not develop as quickly as their peers and resulted in negative labelling and segregation. This experience and its effects are described by Chapman (2012) in a personal experience article in *The Guardian Newspaper*. Chapman describes successfully learning to read when she was 60 years old after a lifetime of keeping her print illiteracy secret. Crucially, she points to a dissonance between her (White) working-class home that did not centre reading and the school literacy culture. She recalls being bamboozled by how books worked when first encountered in school and being quickly labelled lazy and stupid rather than inexperienced in the medium of print; such negative labelling, she feels, stymied her progress as a reader. To repeat Reay's (2017) point, the capacity to learn and succeed can be significantly curtailed by perceiving that others expect you to fail. Conversely, Chapman attributes her adult success in reading not only to her own desire and courage but also to the empathetic encouragement of an adult education tutor in the slow and daunting process of learning to read. She now counts 63 things she can do because she can read print including making menu choices in cafés, navigating journeys and reading novels. Her print reading difficulties had, certainly to some extent, been affectively, socially and culturally situated.

Similarly, Kirk (2001, p. 420) describes the affective impact of being positioned as a struggling reader in school:

> My first attempts at reading left me emotionally drained and intimidated. This was a complex responsibility for a young (White) boy from

the Appalachian Mountains ... with very limited experiences outside the home or literacy background within my home culture. Those failed early literacy efforts flattened my self-esteem and acted as a punishment, and left me feeling dumb, stupid, and illiterate.

The feelings he describes and the identities to which they attach, "dumb, stupid, and illiterate", would act as brakes on his efforts to read. His story also illustrates the disorientating and corrosive effect on reading and learning when education makes space only for the dominant culture, and when it assumes a familiarity with school-based reading that not all children bring to school. Compounding these ostracised feelings was his physical segregation, first in the 'bottom' reading group and then in younger classes.

Like Chapman, Kirk cites the redemptive influence of kindness and support in changing his difficult relationship with reading. When he was 10 years old a teacher's appreciation of his artistic talents, and the self-esteem that engendered in him, helped unlock an agency to try again to decipher print. He went on, over many years, to teach himself to read, complete a PhD and become an academic. Again, what may have appeared to him and others, aged 10, as a fixed condition, changed. The effect on reading of segregation and of a culturally dissonant education system are highlighted in his autoethnographic writing. He found strategies that helped, including reading culturally resonant texts, and having the agency to keep trying.

These two stories of transformation in reading experience within shifting emotional and relational landscapes speak to the tenets of sociocultural theories of literacies (e.g., Comber, 2014; Cremin et al., 2015; Street, 2002, 2013) that one's relationship with reading and writing is always socially and culturally mediated. Williams (2017, p. 17) reminds us too that how we feel about and approach reading or writing is emotionally influenced by previous literacy encounters, which in turn affects success:

> If we feel bored, confused, resistant, anxious, intimidated, self-conscious, uncertain, we won't do well. If we are confident, engaged, respected, safe, we will do well.

Williams' words may not account for the influence of neurolinguistic differences on reading outcomes, i.e., we may not "do well" however supportive the emotional conditions. However, it also highlights the debilitating effect that anxiety and feeling unsafe can have on learning. This view is echoed by Douglas Stuart, introduced previously as a Booker prize-winning author, whose childhood anxiety involved coping with his mother's alcoholism, as well as poverty and being queer in a heteronormative world. In a radio interview in 2021 (26:35), he says of reading, "To be able to read takes an awful lot of peace inside yourself and also in your environment." Like Kirk,

Stuart's insights are also useful in pointing to the effects on reading of different classed and geopolitical positionings towards literature. Growing up in a post-industrial White working-class home in Glasgow, he reflects on how reading was situated and perceived:

> We weren't big readers, and you know I don't think that was unusual for the time and the place. And often actually we felt excluded by books. They felt like they were things that were happening for people in the south, in London. Not only were the books not talking to us directly but the culture around books wasn't talking to us.
>
> *Stuart, 2021, 07:41*

This sense of classed cultural exclusion from books and its effect on reading is echoed by McGarvey (2017, p. xxiii) who says, "The realm of print felt so impossibly exclusive that I developed a fear and anxiety around books despite my interest in their main ingredient: words." Reading was regarded by many of his male peers as, "either feminine or the preserve of posh people or freaks" (p. xxiii). He speculates whether reading would have felt as difficult if he'd gone to a school where being good at reading was less socially ostracising. In his words there are echoes of the psychic tension illustrated by Reay (2002) in her article, "Shaun's Story", of navigating the school's academic culture and belonging in his peer group.

Intricate connections between reading difficulties, emotional stress, racism, classism and sociocultural resonance are deftly drawn by film maker and artist, Steve McQueen in his semi-autobiographical film, *Education* (2020). The film charts the traumatic and ultimately redemptive experiences of Kingsley, a Black British working-class boy who dreams of stars and planetary systems and who finds reading impossibly difficult. The film highlights the devastating impact of institutional racism on the young protagonist's reading difficulties. The casual cruelty in the classroom scene where he is forced to 'read' aloud what he can't read is emotionally gruelling to watch. In an interview a few years earlier Steve McQueen described his own harsh experience of reading in school:

> It was a very early stage of my life to see the discrimination against black and working-class people ... I've never said this before, ever. But I was dyslexic. And I've hidden it, because I was so ashamed. I thought it meant I was stupid ... Also, I had a lazy eye. So I had a patch. When you're in front of the chalk board, you still can't fucking see. So it was a terrible start. And people make judgements very quick. So you're put to one side very quickly.
>
> *McQueen, in Aitkenhead, 2014*

The swiftness of classed and racialised judgements that McQueen speaks of, which result in children being marginalised, echo the experiences of

Chapman (2012) and Kirk (2001). McQueen points to the enduring effects of stigmatising conditions around finding reading hard, which have affected his identity into adulthood ("I've hidden it because I was so ashamed") despite phenomenal success in his field. But his story also highlights how the experience of reading can change when reading material and environments resonate rather than dissonate with one's cultural life. McQueen, like Kingsley in *Education*, attended a Black supplementary school[3] in his childhood, which had been inspired by the writings of Coard (1971), the Grenadian educationalist. This experience, he says, instilled pride in his African heritage, opened up his love of art and, consequently, changed the course of his life from that projected in school. Yet as well as the redemptive power of cultural resonance in McQueen's story, he believes, as does Robinson (2017) and Collinson (2020) above, that he is a dyslexic. Aspects of his reading difficulties required specific help that was not given in school, he believes (Aitkenhead, 2014). These views serve as a caution against a singular perspective of print reading difficulties as being always, or wholly, affectively, socially and culturally situated.

The effects of being ostracised and labelled as stupid when reading is difficult is a theme that runs through each of the stories in this section. Particularly, they question the impact on reading when children's home lives do not match the school reading culture, and they ask what role classism and racism might play in reading difficulties that may appear fixed and innate. They also point to the inner emotional states that help and hinder reading. In the next section I will return to Cash and use the themes developed from these stories to complicate my earlier portrayal of neurodevelopmental differences in children's experience as struggling, potentially dyslexic, readers in the so-called bottom reading group. I do this without suggesting that the stories can *predict* how Cash's reading might change if circumstances change.

Symbolic Violence and the Tyranny of Print Literacy

In the first section of this chapter, Cash's difficulties in processing print were illustrated through the tension in his body while reading with the teacher (hands wringing and eyes darting between me, the teacher, and only occasionally, the text) and an extract of dialogue in which he struggled to read *spit* in a book about cats. The difficulties that were evident in these two reading events fit with descriptions of developmental dyslexia; that is, difficulties blending sounds to make words, and grasping how words are constructed in English orthography. His non-normative speech sounds unrelated to accent, such as substituting soft for hard consonants (*dran* for *gran*), are again identified with dyslexia. I then troubled the concept of dyslexia, using Collinson's idea of *lexism*, while assuming the difficulties I perceived

Cash having would endure into adulthood. Influenced by the social, cultural and affective themes arising from the adults' stories in this chapter, I now return to these classroom reading events with greater curiosity about the effects of relations of power affectively enacted through them, and so consider whether his difficulties may be less fixed than they appeared. Cash, for example, described a different affective experience of reading with his little sister ("making it up", as he described it, when unsure of words) to how he appeared when reading to adults in the classroom. In turning attention towards power within reading events I draw on the relational within the affective turn in literacy research:

> Affective intensities are not merely experienced by an individual, as we often describe emotion in the vernacular, but are rather experienced in the warp and woof of movements involving multiple actors – the everyday movements of people and things approaching and pushing against one another, coming up alongside, making a dance-like turn, pulling apart.
> *Leander and Ehret, 2019, p. 6*

Consider the players involved in the reading events introduced in the first section, both embodied and symbolic. These players include Cash, the teacher, myself, other children watching on, the text and the normativity of literacy in society. All are present and now, recalling the scene, I heed more the "warp and woof of movements involving multiple actors" in the reading dance. The teacher and I are leaning in and straining, forcing this scene, forcing Cash, however gently we try do it. Cash wrings his hands, I read fear in his eyes as he looks at us, then down at the words and back to us, the freeze in his body. The teacher, Cash and I are visited by a tension, a panic; Cash's reading is not going according to the normative rules of the school literacy game. Each of us appears to know this, though it is not named.

The "dance" feels stressful, which could significantly increase Cash's difficulties deciphering print, but I also wonder if stress of living filters in and makes it more difficult for Cash to settle into reading. This is just a hunch, influenced by writers who speaks of poverty-related stress and its impact on the emotional headspace needed for reading (McGarvey, 2017; Stuart, 2021). This wondering about emotional stress is also influenced by descriptions of his home life as "chaotic" by the teacher. *Chaotic* is a word I have come to interpret in the school context as a code for 'unrespectable' working-class lives. Not that chaos is contained in one class: middle-class chaos is just easier to hide, being less likely to spill out onto the street and attract attention (McGarvey, 2017). In addition, my wondering is based on small pieces of information that may not add up to my conjecture, like his poor attendance (he missed half the previous school year), the premature loss of all his baby teeth, and his familiarity with the forgetful qualities of drinking beer, perhaps in the adults around him, when he commented on the hypnotising qualities of the yetis' noodles in *Pugs of the Frozen North*. He may also have lost, through school absence, valuable ground in learning to decipher print compared to his peers and this too could increase anxiety.

Cash *may* have neurolinguistic differences that affect his capacity to decode print but so too might his capacity to read be temporally and affectively hampered by emotional stress. It would require longitudinal time to shed light on this, which the study didn't have. The important point, however, is that reading difficulties that present as a neurological condition could also be caused or exacerbated by emotional, positional and environmental factors that can change, as illustrated through the adult stories told in this chapter. This insight could help change the way schools work with children experiencing reading difficulties, without leaving children to struggle in the ways criticised by McQueen (Aitkenhead, 2014).

Bourdieu's (1977) inter-related concepts of the *cultural arbitrary, legitimacy* and *symbolic violence* help to interrogate my, and others', steps in the dance around Cash and his reading. In the following conversation, Cash could be portrayed as internalising the symbolic violence that delegitimises some of the reality of his experience. In particular, his words do not convey the rich source of interest that non-print-based mediums appear to have for him, and instead print (a source of frustration) is elevated above those other mediums:

Jess: ... What do you think about reading?
Cash: Yeh
Jess: Do you think it's easy, do you think it's hard?
Cash: A bit hard for me. Yeh. 'cept like some people say ... you get more things out a book. Yes, like there's more information about it ...
Jess: I think sometimes if it's like, if it's a book you learn more about the characters in a book.
Cash: Yeh and all that ... 'cept a book like tells you what it's all about ... Books are like something else. They only, 'cause you can stop like the thing and like take a little rest, 'cept a movie like you're supposed to pause, if you want a break you're supposed to pause it and all that. Oh yeh, a book you can, don't need to like pause it or something. You can just take a breath and all that.
Jess: That's true and you can put it down and
Cash: But!
Jess: Then pick it up.
Cash: [with urgency] Yeh like 'cept like if 'cept a TV's like you don't like do any words. You don't learn anything from it. A book like you learn things about it too. And you learn how to read a little better and all that.

Jess: Mmm, so do you think it's worth really working hard?
Cash: Yeh
Jess: To get better at it?
Cash: Yeh, (I've an) idea. See when I go home, I think that if something pops up like something I'll try to read it and all that.
Jess: Pops up on?
Cash: Yeh like on a game or something or like TV, might read it or something.

Read and Chat with Cash, St Jude's, Clyde

In this conversation, metanarratives of literacy's symbolic superiority show up in the stories Cash tells of reading. He asserts the importance of reading words, which is said with urgency and rising energy, cutting me off with a "but". You learn nothing from television unlike books he says, despite this apparently running counter to his experience. When, on a visit to the school library, I pointed out a book on dinosaurs that we could read together, he wasn't too interested. He preferred to tell me the (much more extensive) knowledge he had about dinosaurs, learned from the internet and television programmes. Yet in the extract both he *and I* elevate reading above all other ways of finding things out and of learning. He expresses an intention to learn to read by paying attention to the words in his video games and on TV. As the listener and "coaxer" of his stories (Plummer, 1995), I hear neoliberal narratives of self-responsibility, in his expressed belief that if only he tries harder and longer, reading print won't be the hard thing it currently is. Yet he already puts enormous effort into trying to work out words from the sounds they contain.

This social, affective and political reading of the dialogue between myself and Cash also draws on Plummer's (1995) approach of symbolic interactionism in understanding how our stories are historically situated, constructed in dialogue with others, and with dominant narratives. In Plummer's research, the stories told were those of "sexual suffering and survival" in, for example, coming out as lesbian or gay. In Cash's case the stories are of readers, situated within dominant narratives which frame print as a superior medium of communication and creative expression; it is a powerful and enduring narrative (Collinson, 2012, 2020; Stuckey, 1991). When Cash acknowledges that reading is hard for him, he immediately qualifies this, and aligns himself with "some people (who) say … you get more things out a book" than a film.

The initial reason he gives for the superiority of print, that it is more pause-able, sounds unconvincing. I wonder if this is said more to express connection with "some people" than because he experiences reading as more satisfactory, although he may do. The introduction of "some people" prompts speculation about who those people are who promote the superiority of reading. An educated guess would tell me that his teachers may promote this, and perhaps other children who hear similar things. I am here too in this conversation, reinforcing the view that you learn more from reading than from watching a film.

Listening back, with new insights into my own unquestioning narratives of print superiority, reveals the impermanency of perception. Already I would have contributed differently to this conversation with Cash because of thinking along with writers (e.g., Collinson, 2020; Kress, 2010; Bearne, 2009) who challenge the dominant and dominating position of print literacy in print-mediated societies. Yet, the ability and inability to read words have real effects in a society where print-based literacy dominates communication in education and beyond. Considering the social, affective and political landscape in which Cash's print reading takes place, as this section has done, creates space for uncertainty in conceptualising his reading. The possibility that temporal, emotional and social conditions may affect his capacity to settle and make sense of print can be considered without discounting the influence that neurolinguistic differences may have on his phonological processing and word recall.

Conclusion

Identifying children as poor readers, unintelligent and sad, as ability-grouped reading seems to encourage, and also physically segregating them, must surely add social and emotional pressure to children experiencing difficulties in reading. These identifications potentially fix a belief that one is not a good reader and will never be, thus making it more difficult to persevere when reading is hard. Kirk (2001) shows both the grip and push back from these constraining positionings. It would be simplistic, however, to suggest that shifting to non-hierarchical reading would alleviate all the stress of print reading for Cash, Alf or others. Indeed, the stressful reading episode involving Cash, the teacher and the circus book occurred once mixed-attainment reading was established in the class.

This chapter has gone beyond group positioning to develop cross-discipline perspectives on print reading difficulties and reader identity. Phonological-processing challenges are held within conversations about power and within affective, social and cultural influences on reading. I neither suggest that reading differences *are* explainable biologically nor, conversely, that biology plays no part in how people read print. Rather, singular perspectives on reading difficulties are troubled, whether they are based on physiological, affective, sociocultural or political narratives. There are multiple factors that influence how we evolve, and continue to evolve, as readers, including the fixing effects of ability-grouped reading.

Some print reading differences and identities can appear to be fixed and then change over time and context, while others are enduring, according to adults who experience them. The chapter brings attention to the affective movements within reading events, those that tense the engagement, making it difficult to progress, and those that allow curiosity and creativity to flow. This flow can be apparent when reading in a visual or auditory form when print reading is difficult. Influencing these affective movements is the stress that can arise when children are required to read to others. The effect of racism, anxiety and poverty-related stress can also affect one's capacity to settle into reading and sustain engagement.

Influencing these affective movements are multiple actors, including the reader, teacher, researcher, other children and parents. These actors push and are pushed by the demands of school-based literacy and by its legitimated supremacy as a cultural channel of communication. As Collinson (2020, 2012) asserts, differences around reading aptitude only become problematic in the context of a social system that asserts print-based dominance.

Spatial symbols of that dominance, in the form of ability-grouped reading for example, emphasise one's place in the hierarchy but they are not its only source. Dominant literacy has always been a potent form of cultural capital that reproduces advantage for those most versed in it (Bourdieu, 1986). And those most versed are often the middle and upper classes. The domestic transmission of cultural capital, Bourdieu (1986, p. 244) reminds us, is one of the "best hidden and socially most determinant educational investment(s)". This does not mean that middle-class and upper-class children never experience reading difficulties; they do.

The next chapter will introduce ways to disrupt print dominance and other aspects of reading hierarchies in the classroom to help create more egalitarian conditions around reading and communication. It will argue, for example, that if school-based literacies were genuinely reconfigured to teach the reading of images as much as the reading of print it could destigmatise print-reading difficulties. It could also prepare all children more thoroughly for participation in multimodal knowledge-based economies in the future.[4]

Notes

1. For ease of reading, I will sometimes omit the word 'print' from 'print reading' in this chapter but 'reading' will signify 'print reading' unless multimodal conceptions of reading are explicitly indicated.
2. Ellie is White and of Scottish heritage. Class-wise, I would situate her in the hazy middle of lower middle/working class (Savage, 2015). Milllie is White, Scottish and working class.
3. The Black Supplementary School movement in the UK was started by Black parents in the 1960s who were concerned about the impact of racism on their children's education. Classes are held in the evening and weekends to develop children's literacy, maths and science but also to teach children about Black culture and history. See https://www.nabss.org.uk/.
4. Of course, the old hierarchies can reproduce in these 'new' economies. The creative and cultural arts, as well as IT, are not known as great levellers of privilege.

References

Aitkenhead, D. (2014, January 4). Steve McQueen: My hidden shame. *Guardian Newspapers*. https://www.theguardian.com/film/2014/jan/04/steve-mcqueen-my-painful-childhood-shame

Albright, J., & Luke, A. (2010). *Pierre Bourdieu and literacy education*. Routledge.

Bearne, E. (2009). Multimodality, literacy and texts: Developing a discourse. *Journal of Early Childhood Literacy, 9*(2), 156–187.

Becker, N., Vasconcelos, M., Oliveira, V., Santos, F. C. D., Bizarro, L., Almeida, R. M. D., & Carvalho, M. R. S. (2017). Genetic and environmental risk factors for developmental dyslexia in children: Systematic review of the last decade. *Developmental Neuropsychology, 42*(7–8), 423–445.

Bourdieu, P. (1977). *Outline of a theory of practice*. Cambridge University Press.

Bourdieu, P. (1986). The forms of capital. In J. Richardson (Ed.), *Handbook for theory and research for the sociology of education*. Greenwood Press.

Bourdieu, P., & Passeron, J. C. (1990). *Reproduction in education, society and culture*. SAGE.

Chambers, A. (2011). *Tell me: Children reading and talk*. Thimble Press.

Chapman, S. (2012, February 17). Experience: I couldn't read until I was 60. *Guardian Newspaper*. https://www.theguardian.com/lifeandstyle/2012/feb/17/i-couldnt-read-until-i-was-60

Coard, B. (1971). *How the West Indian child is made educationally subnormal in the British school system*. Independently published.

Collinson, C. (2012). Dyslexics in time machines and alternate realities: Thought experiments on the existence of dyslexics, 'dyslexia' and 'Lexism'. *British Journal of Special Education, 39*(2), 63–70. https://doi.org/10.1111/j.1467-8578.2012.00538.x

Collinson, C. (2020). Ordinary language use and the social construction of dyslexia. *Disability & Society, 35*(6), 993–1006. https://doi.org/10.1080/09687599.2019.1669432

Comber, B. (2014). Literacy, poverty and schooling: What matters in young people's education? *Literacy, 48*(3), 115–123.

Cremin, T., Mottram, M., Collins, F. M., Powell, S., & Drury, R. (2015). *Researching literacy lives: Building communities between home and school*. Routledge.

Duckworth, V. (2013). *Learning trajectories, violence and empowerment amongst adult basic skills learners*. Routledge.

Dudley-Marling, C. (2004). The social construction of learning disabilities. *Journal of Learning Disabilities, 37*(6), 482–489. https://doi.org/10.1177/00222194040370060201

Goodman, K. (1967). Reading: A psycholinguistic guessing game. *Journal of the Reading Specialist, 6*(4), 126–135. 10.1080/19388076709556976

Hall, K. (2005). *Listening to Stephen read: Multiple perspectives on literacy*. Open University Press.

Hamilton, D. M. (2016). *Postmodern picturebooks, gender, and reading difficulties: A phenomenological exploration of one boy's experiences*. State University of New York. https://www.proquest.com/docview/1823568727?fromopenview=true&pq-origsite=gscholar

Hempel-Jorgensen, A., Cremin, T., Harris, D., & Chamberlain, L. (2018). Pedagogy for reading for pleasure in low socio-economic primary schools: Beyond 'pedagogy of poverty'? *Literacy, 52*(2), 86–94. https://doi.org/10.1111/lit.12157

Kabuto, B. (2016). The social construction of a reading (dis)ability. *Reading Research Quarterly, 51*(3), 289.

Leppänen, P., Hämäläinen, J., Guttorm, T., Eklund, K., Salminen, H., Tanskanen, A., Torppa, M., Puolakanaho, A., Richardson, U., Pennala, R. & Lyytinen, H. (2012). Infant brain responses associated with reading-related skills before school and at school age. *Neurophysiologie Clinique/Clinical Neurophysiology*, 42(1–2), 35–41.

Kirk, L. R. (2001). Learning to read: Painful mystery or joyful success? *Journal of Adolescent & Adult Literacy*, 44(5), 420.

Kress, G. (2000). Multimodality. In C. Kalantzis (Ed.), *Multiliteracies: Literacy learning and the design of social futures*. Routledge.

Kress, G. (2010). *Multimodality: A social semiotic approach to contemporary communication*. Routledge.

Leander, K. M., & Ehret, C. (2019). *Affect in literacy learning and teaching: Pedagogies, politics and coming to know*. Routledge.

Learned, J. E. (2016). "Feeling like I'm slow because I'm in this class": Secondary school contexts and the identification and construction of struggling readers. *Reading Research Quarterly*, 51(4), 367–371. https://doi.org/10.1002/rrq.157

Macdonald, S. J., & Deacon, L. (2019). Twice upon a time: Examining the effect socio-economic status has on the experience of dyslexia in the United Kingdom. *Dyslexia*, 25(1), 3–19. https://doi.org/10.1002/dys.1606

Maybin, J. (2013). What counts as reading? PIRLS, EastEnders and The Man on the Flying Trapeze. *Literacy*, 47(2), 59–66.

McGarvey, D. (2017). *Poverty safari: Understanding the anger of Britain's underclass*. Picador.

McQueen, S. (2020). *Education*. BBC. https://www.bbc.co.uk/iplayer/episode/m000qfb1/small-axe-series-1-education

Narey, M. J. (2017). "Struggling learner"... or struggling teacher? Questions surrounding teacher development for multimodal language, literacy, and learning. In M. Narey (Ed.), *Multimodal perspectives of language, literacy, and learning in early childhood. Educating the young child* (Vol. 12). Springer. https://doi.org/10.1007/978-3-319-44297-6_15

Olssen, M., & Peters, M. A. (2005). Neoliberalism, higher education and the knowledge economy: From the free market to knowledge capitalism. *Journal of Education Policy*, 20(3), 313–345. https://doi.org/10.1080/02680930500108718

Pahl, K., & Rowsell, J. (2020). *Living literacies: Literacy for social change*. MIT Press.

Patrick, F. (2013). Neoliberalism, the knowledge economy, and the learner: Challenging the inevitability of the commodified self as an outcome of education. *International Scholarly Research Notices*. https://doi.org/10.1155/2013/108705

Peters, M. (2001). National education policy constructions of the 'knowledge economy': Towards a critique. *Journal of Educational Enquiry*, 2(1), 1–22.

Plummer, K. (1995). *Telling sexual stories: Power, change and social worlds*. Routledge. https://doi.org/10.4324/9780203425268

Reaume, G. (2014). Understanding critical disability studies. *CMAJ*, 186(16), 1248–1249. https://doi.org/10.1503/cmaj.141236

Reay, D. (2002). Shaun's story: Troubling discourses of white working-class masculinities. *Gender and Education*, 14(3), 221–234.

Reay, D. (2012). What would a socially just education system look like?: Saving the minnows from the pike. *Journal of Education Policy*. 27(5), 587–599.

Reay, D. (2017). *Miseducation: Inequality, education and the working classes*. Policy Press.

Robinson, S. A. (2017). Phoenix rising: An autoethnographic account of a gifted Black male with dyslexia. *Journal for the Education of the Gifted*, 40(2), 135–151. https://doi.org/10.1177/0162353217701021

Rosenblatt, L. M. (1978). *The reader, the text, the poem: The transactional theory of the literary work*. Southern Illinois University Press.
Savage, M. (2015). *Social Class in the 21st Century*. Pelican Books.
Scherer, L. (2016). 'I am not clever, they are cleverer than us': Children reading in the primary school. *British Journal of Sociology of Education*, 37(3), 389–407. https://doi.org/10.1080/01425692.2014.948989
Snowling, M. (1998). Dyslexia as a phonological deficit: Evidence and implications. *Child Psychology and Psychiatry Review*, 3(1), 4–11.
Snowling, M. J. (2019). *Dyslexia: A very short introduction*. Oxford University Press.
Snowling, M. J., & Hulme, C. (2005). *The science of reading: A handbook*. Blackwell Pub.
Stuart, D. (2021, December 11). *This cultural life* [Radio broadcast]. Radio 4. https://www.bbc.co.uk/programmes/m0012fdp
Street, B. V. (2002). *Literacy and development: Ethnographic perspectives*. Routledge.
Street, B. V. (2013). *Social literacies: Critical approaches to literacy in development, ethnography and education*. Taylor and Francis. https://doi.org/10.4324/9781315844282
Stuckey, J. E. (1991). *The violence of literacy*. Vintage.
Tyler, I. (2013). *Revolting subjects: Social abjection and resistance in neoliberal Britain*. Zed Books.
Tyler, I. (2020). *Stigma: The machinery of inequality*. Zed Books.
Vasquez, V. M. (2014). *Negotiating critical literacies with young children*. Routledge.
Vellutino, F. R., & Fletcher, J. M. (2005). Developmental dyslexia. In M. J. Snowling & C. Hulme (Eds.), *The science of reading, a handbook* (pp. 362–378). Blackwell Publishing.
Vellutino, F. R., Fletcher, J. M., Snowling, M. J., & Scanlon, D. M. (2004). Specific reading disability (dyslexia): What have we learned in the past four decades? *Journal of Child Psychology and Psychiatry*, 45(1), 2–40.
Wagner, R. K., Torgesen, J. K., Rashotte, C. A., & Pearson, N. A. (1999). *Comprehensive test of phonological processing: CTOPP*. Pro-ed Austin.
Williams, B. T. (2017). *Literacy practices and perceptions of agency: Composing identities*. Routledge.

Children's Literature References

Dr Seuss. (2017). *Dr Seuss's ABC*. HarperCollins Children's Books.
Groening, M. (1998). *Simpsons on parade*. Titan Books Ltd.
Simon, F. (2019). *Horrid Henry*. Orion Children's Books.
Reeve, P., & McIntyre, S. (2016). *Pugs of the frozen North*. OUP Oxford.

7
DISRUPTING SCHOOL-BASED READING HIERARCHIES

Introduction

So far this book has largely focused on hierarchies in primary classrooms that constrain reading development for working-class children of all ethnicities. This chapter argues that, far from being inevitable, these reading hierarchies can be challenged and dismantled, even if this requires ongoing commitment by educators, researchers and policymakers rather than singular pedagogical change. The chapter presents and comes to some conclusions on such disruptions to hierarchy that were introduced in the study. The pandemic contributed its own disruptions, however, to this phase of the research. Scottish primary schools closed in March 2020, a month after mixed-attainment reading was introduced at St Jude's and on the week it was scheduled to begin at Fairfield. Because of this, sadly, mixed-attainment reading could not be introduced into the study at Fairfield. By the time schools reopened Kelvin class was no longer with the study teacher.

It was also a bewildering time as teachers, parents and children tried to adapt to online home learning. Educational inequalities were exacerbated in this context, fuelled by uneven access to internet and devices, as well as adult knowledge and time availability. My research role and methods also had to adapt to the online environment, which in turn altered the nature of the research data collected and reported on in this chapter.[1] In particular, the voice of the Avon teacher takes a more prominent place in this chapter as more insights came directly from her. I returned to school in May 2021 and, in a bonus for the research, I was able to observe and have conversations with the children once mixed-attainment reading had been practised for over a year. This allowed for insights to be formed over a longer period of

DOI: 10.4324/9781003488514-7

time than was originally planned. What emerged was a complex and evolving picture and not a straightforward endorsement of any one strategy for disrupting literacy hierarchies. However, although the number of children was reduced and the time through which they had lived was exceptional, there is sufficient cause for optimism to suggest that mixed-attainment reading could open and level the ground upon which children grow as readers in primary school.

This chapter is organised into three sections. In *Mixed-Attainment Reading* the story is told of how ability-grouped reading was replaced by the version of mixed-attainment reading introduced in the study. The promising effects of this change on children's reading experience, learner identities and friendships are explored. Yet switching pedagogies to cultivate greater equity in education belies children's role in perpetuating such hierarchies in the classroom, which often mirror societal privileges and inequalities. The next section, *Wee Books, Chapter Books and Who's Top Reader*, recounts such resistance by children to disruption of reading hierarchies. It also recounts how the teachers and I met this resistance with further efforts to create more equality and space in their reading experience. Yet at the heart of literacy hierarchies is an even more fundamental privileging of print itself as a medium of communication in education and society. The negative effects of this privileging fall disproportionately on children experiencing print-reading difficulties. The final section, *A Radical Decentring of Print*, tackles this privileging head on and suggests what good can come from embracing multimodal concepts of reading. The section offers ways to re-shape the curriculum and decentre print, while paradoxically recognising it as potent cultural capital for children to acquire. This decentring has the potential to broaden and enhance life trajectories, particularly for children with less aptitude for, or experience of, reading and writing words.

Mixed-Attainment Reading

The third research question in the study asked how children's reading and identities might change if an alternative pedagogy, based on mixed-attainment reading, replaced ability-grouped reading. In other words, could the constraining hierarchies seen in ability-grouped reading be disrupted? By introducing an alternative, I hope to loosen practitioners' and policymakers' attachment to ability grouping in general, which has so far proved largely resistant to critiques highlighting its discriminatory qualities (e.g., Francis et al., 2017a; Gillborn, 2008, 2010; Reay, 2017). I reasoned that if teachers and policymakers were presented with a research-informed alternative, perhaps the efficacy of ability-grouped reading would be reconsidered. Although the pandemic left mixed-attainment reading occupying a smaller place in the ethnographic fieldwork than originally intended, its effects still offer scope for optimism.

It is important to stress at this point that mixed-attainment group reading can only ever be one facet of a rich and effective reading pedagogy. Reader response, understanding and engagement need a variety of activities, resources, spaces and relationships, to inspire deep and enduring connections with reading in the children we teach (Cremin et al., 2014). The intention of mixed-attainment group reading is simply to support children in becoming more independent and fluent when reading print and visuals for themselves, and to notice if or when meaning breaks down as they read. It cannot support the collaborative engagement and response to a text's meanings, themes, characters, setting etc., that guided reading might offer (Fountas & Pinnell, 1998; Tennent et al., 2016) since children are reading different books. Because of this, mixed-attainment group reading can only support readers well if collaborative response and understanding are also cultivated through, for example, whole class sharing and exploration of a text which the teacher reads aloud (e.g., Chambers, 2011; O'Sullivan & McGonigle, 2010).

As explained in Chapter 1, the intervention involved children reading with the teacher in fluid mixed-attainment groups. The pedagogy assumes a psycholinguistic perspective on reading, which is that readers draw (more and more automatically and symbiotically) on graphophonic, visual, semantic and syntactic cues when reading. Strategies to decipher words and maintain sense of what is read are shared by the children and teacher before children read aloud to themselves. In contrast to ability-grouped reading, such as guided reading, each child reads a book that matches their particular level of fluency rather than all, in the group, reading the same text. The teacher or child might also suggest an additional response intention such as thinking about what they like about the text as they read, share an interesting fact they discover or what in the story reminds them of people, places or events in their own lives. Following this introduction, the children read aloud to themselves while the teacher moves round, listening in and coaching each child individually. Although at first some children were distracted by others reading aloud next to them, they were soon able to focus on their own reading. Children also jot down words they can't work out or don't know the meaning of. In the plenary they work together with the teacher to decipher these words in the context in which they appeared.

What follows is a narrative portrait (Rodríguez-Dorans & Jacobs, 2020) of a mixed-attainment reading session, composed of a patchwork of observations from various mixed-attainment reading sessions in Avon and Clyde, whose significance will then be discussed. The children's previous group is included in brackets, as it is in the rest of the chapter, e.g., MRG, for 'middle' reading group.

George (BRG) says excitedly when he sees Puzzle's (BRG) book (*Percy the Park Keeper*), "I had this. I really liked this book. This is a different one, *Percy and the Badger*." The teacher begins by asking what they might do if stuck on a word. Responses include looking for a word inside the word, blending letters, reading to the end of the sentence and thinking about what word would make sense.

Puzzle is holding the book with both hands and her eyes follow the text. I hear her say "Percy the p-a-r park k-e-p keeper." George's book is lying flat on the table, and he places one hand on each page.

Puzzle looks over to the teacher and says "Miss, it's just clicking for me." George says, "Miss I don't know that word!" "Write it down," says the teacher. The teacher listens into each child reading then asks the group what words they didn't know. George has *new* written down and says he's worked it out. He noticed the Happy Birthday banner in the picture so thought that the boy would get a *new* kite because you get new things on your birthday. He is commended for his logic.

Kieran (MRG) has written down *mammal*. The teacher suggests splitting the word in two, and he gets mam-mal but doesn't know what a mammal is. Emma (TRG) thinks she knows but she is describing a particular mammal, so the teacher explains it. Kevin (TRG) says, "I found another word I

FIGURE 7.1 Field sketch of Puzzle reading. Sketch by the author.

Disrupting reading hierarchies 143

FIGURE 7.2 Field sketch of George reading. Sketch by the author.

didn't know." Gary (BRG) is listening to these exchanges and says, "Miss I didn't know that word," pointing to his book.

Fieldnote excerpts, St Jude's, Avon & Clyde

These extracts hint at several ways that mixed-attainment reading could disrupt hierarchy that is bound up in ability-grouped reading. When children first sat down together in mixed-attainment reading groups, the impact appeared joyful, in some of the children, and in me and the teachers as witnesses. There was a freedom in the air I had not felt before, particularly from those who had been in the lower positioned groups. This freedom is captured in the narrative portrait when George (working class, White, Scottish), previously so controlled in his movements and speech around reading, called enthusiastically across the table to Puzzle (working class, White, Polish) that he had *Percy and the Badger*. Puzzle, too, who would often scowl when reading in the 'bottom' group turned to her teacher in the first mixed-attainment session and said, exuberantly, "Miss, it's just clicking for me." Both children engage physically with the book, their hands either holding or anchoring it. This suggests more agentic engagement with reading than the hands-off posture I had previously observed. Much of this early freedom appeared to have endured when I returned to the school post-pandemic to observe and elicit children's feelings about mixed-attainment reading. In a series of extended conversations with children from across the old reading groups, their response to this new way of reading was positive, although Horris believed the old way was better for "learning to read" and the new way, "when you could read" (he didn't give a reason for this view, perhaps because I didn't press him to). The following response from Stella[2] (MRG) was echoed by many of the children:

Jess: So the old way or the new way?
Stella: [voice strong and clear] The new way because the old way … I thought that was a bit intimidating because people were looking at you and were seeing if you messed it up. And I like the new way because we can hear other people reading so it makes you feel comfortable, like they're messing up as well as you are.

The collaborative nature of strategy-sharing and working out unfamiliar words in mixed-attainment group reading, which is illustrated in the narrative portrait, meant children could learn from each other, as well as offering comfort that, as Stella put it, we all mess things up. Less fluent readers could pick up strategies from more fluent readers, but there were also examples of them working out words that had baffled a (previous) 'top' group reader. The value of the approach was captured by the teacher when she said,

> None of them are bothered about who's chipping in. And the ones that maybe are less fluent are quite chuffed with themselves 'cause they've managed to give a bit of input to someone who's reading a book that may be a wee bit higher than their ability. (Being less fluent) *they're* probably using strategies more often, whereas the other ones are just reading fluently.

This shifting of positions undermines the idea, expressed by children in Chapter 4, that those from the 'top' group would always be the 'better' readers.

This collaborative working out of unknown words by jotting them down and discussing them in the plenary could hold potential to dissolve fear and concealment that was frequently expressed and observed across all groups when ability-grouped reading was practiced. You may recall, from Chapter 4, Will, from the 'top' group (middle class, White, Scottish, Clyde, St Jude's) describing himself as a "bad reader" because of his lack of confidence reading in front of the class. For some children in the 'bottom' group, particularly those experiencing reading difficulties, the fear of disclosure could result in many hours lost, concealing what they couldn't read, hours that could have been spent enjoying books and growing in confidence as a reader. Talking of George, the teacher said,

> It is really difficult to hear him. His head is down, and he seems scared to say it out loud in case it's wrong. But when I can hear him, much of the time he is saying the words accurately. He seems really frightened to make a mistake.

Given these fears, there could be something transformative about reframing unknown words and 'mistakes' as opportunities to learn and discover. Less fluent readers who resist being positioned as such (Moss, 2000, 2007, 2021) may be more willing to be seen 'not getting words right' if they are not so marked out as struggling by doing so. In the narrative portrait, for example, Gary,[3] who I had often observed disguising words he couldn't read, acknowledges a word he is unsure of in the company of other (more fluent) readers who are doing the same thing. When I had first observed him in the new mixed-attainment context, his finger still slid over the words, pages were turned too quickly, eyes wandered from the text and few words were articulated as he 'read aloud' to himself while the teacher listened into other readers. However, as mixed-attainment reading became more established, and other children shared words *they* were unsure of, the need to be seen 'getting it right' appeared to loosen its grip. I suggest that Gary's risk in acknowledging a word he couldn't work out was sanctioned perhaps by previous 'top' readers who were now sharing unknown words and collaboratively deciphering text.

Mixed-attainment reading gives all children access to the same pedagogical approach. This compares to ability-grouped reading where, it was found, children in the 'top' group received more support in developing understanding and response to what they read;[4] in this way, the rich get richer and the poor poorer (Stanovich, 2009). As well as strategy-sharing and the time spent reading and being coached by the teacher, the session provided opportunities, in small ways, to democratically learn meanings of new words. Through collaborative discussion about words in different children's books, children's vocabulary could expand beyond those that appear in their own texts. In the narrative portrait, for example, everyone participated in the conversation about mammals, an unfamiliar concept that had arisen in one child's book. If, as Krashen (1989, 2004) argues, children learn more new vocabulary from reading than by any other means (which in turn supports reading development), short simple books with predictable words will not expand vocabulary or support reading development as much as more linguistically complex texts. This is, of course, only one minor way that reading can develop language, and expanding vocabulary could be regarded as a minor byproduct of the riches that reading offers children.

As well as democratising the pedagogy by which children's reading was supported, the practice was paradoxically more responsive to individual children's needs and progress than ability-grouped reading had appeared. The teacher put it this way in one of our online conversations:

> You can definitely see the impact that it has because they've got the freedom to go off and read. It's not holding anyone back. But also the ones that aren't quite ready to move on yet are getting to keep working at a level that's suitable for them. Children are reading more at home too. It could be mid-week, and they'll go, 'I'm ready for a new book now. I've finished that book. I've read it a few times. I really enjoyed it. They'll tell me what it's about and then they'll get a new book, so it doesn't always need to be (just) the Monday they get a new book (as it was in ability-grouped reading). They seem to be enjoying it, coming in and showing confidence.

Through the teacher's regular use of running reading records (see Appendix 1) she was able to judge when a child was ready to move to a new level of the reading scheme. Children could also now choose a book that might interest them from a selection of books rather than be allocated a book. These individual decisions were possible because children no longer had to read the same book at the level that best suited their group as they had in ability-group reading. Recall, for example, the story of Angel's reading, told in Chapter 5. Despite consecutive teachers appreciating the greater confidence, engagement and command with which Angel was reading, she remained in the 'bottom' reading group, reading books that offered little interest or challenge because the big leap to the next group could have dented her newfound confidence. Angel's story is a potent reminder of the inertia that holds children in place within ability grouping in general.

While mixed-attainment reading offers greater responsiveness, equality and a reimagining of 'mistakes' as learning moments, it is with respect to reading engagement, relationships and belonging, that mixed-attainment reading appeared to offer the greatest promise to interrupt fixed reading hierarchies. When mixed-attainment reading was first introduced at St Jude's in the month before lock-down it appeared to have an almost instantaneous impact on children's affective relationship with reading and with other readers. Some girls from the 'top' group in Avon at St Jude's were visibly upset when the change was explained. While I assumed they did not want their elite position in the hierarchy disrupted they spoke later of insecurities, that if they couldn't read a word, they wouldn't be able to glean the word from those around them as they could in ability-grouped reading (where everyone in the group reads the same book).

Alternatively, mixed-attainment reading seemed to open up engagement, connection and community around reading to children who had appeared excluded when ability-grouped reading was practiced. This shift could build on the findings of Hempel-Jorgensen et al. (2018) from their influential study of reading for pleasure pedagogy (RfP) in low socio-economic primary schools. When comfortable space and time were created for RfP in the schools but sat within visible hierarchies and pedagogies of performance and proficiency, 'struggling readers' still appeared locked out of the world of reading. In one example, the RfP tent had a hierarchical list of names and reading levels, marking out each child, pinned to the outside. In these circumstances, children continued to appear disengaged and unsatisfied, changing books frequently within the RfP session, flicking pages, yawning, stretching. In contrast, when I returned to St Jude's post-pandemic, when mixed-attainment reading was well established in Avon class, a fundamental shift in reading engagement and connection was apparent. By then Millie (working class, White, Scottish) and Puzzle, both previously in the 'bottom' reading group, were making swift progress in reading (moving through the levels of the reading scheme, according to the teacher), enacting very different reader identities and now appeared part of the reading gang.

When reading had been organised in ability groups, the two girls had professed disinterest in reading, and despite their popularity, reading had not cemented their friendships as it had done for children in the 'top' group, like Kayla, Claudia and Alexa (the "funny girls" from Chapter 4 who liked funny books and for whom books reminded them of how long they had been friends). Now, Puzzle and Millie spoke as avid readers whose friendships were laced through with reading, much like the funny girls. Their talk around reading was agentic and spontaneous, sharing enthusiasms and recommendations. When I spoke to Puzzle, she playfully speculated on her ideal reading group, one that incorporated her best friends and fellow readers.

> I think for the group we should do me and Millie, 'cause best friend, and Kieran and John[5] 'cause they're both like best friends. And I'm Kieran's best friend too. So I think it should be two girls – me and Millie – and Kieran and John. I'd like that a lot. John is like, loves chapter books. Not like comic ones like me but he likes different comic books. Kieran loves comic books too, like he loves *Dog Man* books as well. Me and Kieran are going to start a book about Dog Man. We'll get staples and like staple the pages and then write different things and that. 'cause Kieran and John like made a comic thing so why not I make a comic, like why not? I'm allowed!
>
> *Puzzle, Avon, St Jude's*

FIGURE 7.3 Dog Man themed car built by Puzzle and Stella. Photograph by the author.

Puzzle also talked with gusto about her friendship with Stella (MRG) and *their* shared love of the *Dog Man* series (Dav Pilkey), which they had found together in the class library. For a science experiment, she told me, they had chosen to team up and build a Dog Man themed car.

When I chatted to Puzzle her desire to read me her favourite parts of *Dog Man* was not only self-motivated but was, in fact, bursting out of her. This classic example of "inside-text talk" as described by Cremin et al. (2014) demonstrates a new sociability and reciprocity in her conversations about reading that stimulates volitional reader engagement. This volition had not been discernable when Puzzle occupied the 'bottom' reading group in the ability-grouped hierarchy.

Similarly, in a conversation with Millie and her two friends, Sienna and Emma (TRG; middle class, White, Scottish), there was a shared camaraderie, with all three girls presenting as avid readers. Millie spoke of two particular books as her "favourite chapter books", giving an account of plots, and characters who reminded her of herself and her stepsisters. She reads long into the night, she said. Sometimes she even chose to read rather than be on her phone. In the conversation, Sienna and Emma seemed to vie for the role of Millie's best friend. Millie had always been popular, but this intertwining of reading and friendship was new.

Much of these findings also echo the benefits Cunningham et al. (1991, 1998; Cunningham, 2006) found in their studies of mixed-attainment reading; that is, the effect that democratising the learning experience can have on pupils' motivation as readers. The authors attribute these results in part to maintenance of enthusiasm and self-belief in children who would previously have been placed in the 'bottom' reading group on school entry.

> First graders who come with little print experience but much eagerness to learn maintain that eagerness and their 'I can do anything' attitude. Many of our inexperienced first graders become grade-level or better readers and writers.
>
> *Cunningham et al., 1998, p. 663*

The teachers and literacy researchers in the Cunningham et al. studies had been motivated by concern about the social isolation they witnessed of children in the 'bottom' reading group. Based on a simple survey of naming best friends in the 1998 study, friendships now appeared to cross traditional attainment lines. The authors also found that the shift away from ability-grouped reading had a significant positive effect on the poverty-related attainment gap in the US (Cunningham, 2006).

Other international and UK studies have drawn positive connections between reading engagement, reading attainment and being part of a community of readers (e.g., Cremin et al., 2014; OECD, 2002). In the previously mentioned UKLA study, *Teachers as Readers: Building Communities of Readers*, Cremin et al. (2014) show the positive effect on children's engagement with, attitudes to and attainment in reading when reading in primary schools becomes more reciprocal and sociable, stimulated in that study by teachers developing and sharing their own knowledge and enthusiasm for children's literature. The greater democracy, openness and equality introduced by mixed-attainment reading could be another way to increase the fertility of the ground in which communities of readers can open out and blossom. The new inclusivity, reciprocal book chat and enthusiasm for reading experienced by those previously occupying the 'bottom' reading group is no small change. Although it is important not to make too much of these shifts in reading sociability given the peculiar pandemic times the children had lived through, they still suggest that mixed-attainment reading is worth investigating further in the spirit of educational equity.

Wee Books, Chapter Books and Who's the Top Reader

While the shift to mixed-attainment reading showed potential to make children's reading experience fairer and more inclusive, the story did not, and could never, end there. Hierarchies in school reflect those in society and when they are disrupted, they tend to find new pathways. As educators and researchers we should be mindful of this. It would be counterproductive to view any single pedagogical change as 'job done' in terms of making learning more equitable. Other literacy hierarchies were highlighted in the study that, although strengthened by ability-grouped reading, did not necessarily originate in the practice. When the teachers and I noticed hierarchies that lingered or morphed after mixed-attainment reading was established, the focus of the project shifted to pedagogical change as an ongoing process of disruption rather than a destination. With this shift a new question arose: what might it mean for educational practice if there was an ongoing commitment towards the reflexive noticing and disruption of literacy hierarchies in the interests of social justice, however they presented or reformed?

The first thing apparent was that children actively reinforce literacy hierarchies, and this did not end with the introduction of mixed-attainment reading. Here I stretch Bourdieu's (1984) notion of *distinction making* in adults to that of children in the study. In many societies, to be an accomplished reader and writer of dominant literacies accrues social prestige and, later, economic gain (Albright & Luke, 2010; Bourdieu & Passeron, 1979, 1990). Most children in the study coupled intelligence, happiness and confidence with being a better reader, and believed the advantages of reading superiority in childhood would endure into adulthood. One vehicle for asserting reading prowess once ability-grouped reading was abandoned was to call attention to the books they were reading in mixed-attainment reading. As one mixed-attainment reading session in St Jude's Clyde class was about to get under way, I listened in as children established who was reading at the highest level by comparing the level on the back of their reading scheme books. Higher levels of the reading scheme trumped lower levels and reading scheme chapters books were trumped by non-scheme chapter books. For example, recall the threat described in Chapter 4 to Jake's[6] position as a 'top'-group reader in Kelvin class (Fairfield) when Lewis (middle class, Child of Colour, Pakistani) drew a distinction between himself and two others who were reading 'real' chapter books compared to others in the 'top' group who were still reading (chapter books) within the reading scheme.

The teachers and I met to discuss how we might fracture this hierarchy around book levels within group reading instruction. One of the premises of reading development, introduced in Chapter 1, is the efficacy of children reading texts that they can read with 'easy difficulty', i.e., in which they could accurately read or decipher between 90 and 95% of the words. Below this level, meaning can break down and frustration arise, which can blunt children's enthusiasm for reading (Bodman & Franklin, 2014; Clay, 1993). Although the visibly levelled nature of a reading scheme encourages children to distinguish themselves by making self-flattering comparisons, it also offers a large stock of books that provide suitable levels of challenge to children at different stages of print fluency. As such it was not deemed practical to discard the scheme in favour of non-levelled, non-scheme texts alone; there simply weren't enough non-scheme books available to do this.

With a desire to at least soften the competition and positioning based on book levels, the teachers made two changes to the book stock used in reading instruction. Non-scheme picturebooks that had been banded for text complexity were slotted in with the reading scheme so that children sometimes read a book that was not visibly levelled (Institute of Education Reading Recovery Network, 2000). The children were also, as previously mentioned, offered choice in their reading book from a selection at their current level of fluency. In Millie's words, this meant "a pile of books that we can read so we can choose what ones we would like to listen to 'cause some of the books (were about) stuff that I didn't really like." For Sienna, some of the books the teacher had given them she wouldn't understand and it was a lot better now because, having chosen them, she understood the books she was reading. This decision to offer choice of reading book replaced the practice of giving the same reading book to everyone at the same level of text. The change could not only increase children's engagement with the books as they could choose a subject that interested them, but also avoid the possibility that children mentally reinstate the ability groups, based on who are reading the same book.

We also needed to look honestly and clearly at the influence of mixed-attainment reading on the subset of children experiencing reading difficulties, given the practice was intended to disrupt hierarchy forming around reading fluency. What I observed was not the unequivocal picture of liberation I anticipated, and this felt both disappointing and emotionally difficult to witness. The reading friendships that had opened up for others in the previous 'bottom' reading group, like Puzzle and Millie, had not opened up for those experiencing specific difficulties with print, as described in Chapter 6. There was no inside-text talk, no references to sharing books with friends or text recommendations back and forward when I observed them in class or in our extended conversations post-pandemic.

By breaking up ability groups, children experiencing print difficulties now worked more closely with those whose reading fluency was, by Primary 4 (aged 8–9), far in advance of theirs. In one group situation, observed when mixed-attainment reading was firmly established, George was reading a picturebook, which he had chosen from those at his level of fluency. The book contained a few words per page while two children opposite read weighty novels. The contrast in reading material appeared stark to me, particularly in the context of children stratifying each other by text type as well as level. Despite the liberation George conveyed in an early mixed-attainment session when he called out to Puzzle that he'd enjoyed her book, *Percy the Park Keeper,* George's body now appeared refrozen, as it had often seemed in ability-grouped reading. The book sat open in front of him. His body was motionless, rigid. His head did not tilt towards the page though his eyes gazed downwards. His hands did not touch the book, anchor the pages or follow the print or images; instead, they lay still in his lap. He did not read the book unless prompted by the teacher, and then only in whispers, despite the practice of reading aloud to oneself in mixed-attainment reading.

This scene could, through close-coupled contrasts, heighten the exposure and discomfort of being viewed as a struggling reader. Hierarchy seemed intact and viscerally present in this new context, and I had not anticipated this. Many of the children had said they had found the old way stressful as they feared their mistakes being seen by others. The teacher, however, suggested those with reading difficulties "would be afraid of being seen by those who they considered better than them." Before, they had been reading with children whose fluency was a closer match to their own. My interpretation of the scene was that George did not want to be there, would perhaps have given anything not to be there, surrounded by children whose reading development was following a more normative path. I read shame, embarrassment and anger in his posture and expression. The teacher, having also witnessed this, returned to reading just with him and another boy who experienced similar difficulties in reading. In this context he appeared more relaxed, more willing to engage with the book, his confidence more likely to build. He was, the teacher stresses, someone who wants to do well and is quite competitive.

Watching George that day prompted recollection of an earlier mixed-attainment reading session involving Cash (working class, White, Scottish, Clyde, St Jude's, BRG), before schools closed due to the pandemic. The scene, first described in Chapter 6, centred on Cash, the teacher and a book about the circus. The fieldnote is worth repeating here and remembering that the scene happened in mixed-attainment reading rather than in what I assumed to be the more stressful context of ability-grouped reading.

> The teacher is reading a book about the circus with Cash. His body seems very still, upright, almost frozen, except for his hands that wring around each other under the desk. His expression seems anxious, and his eyes flit from the teacher's face to mine, and only momentarily, to the text in the book. It is the teacher who scans the print, using her finger to point to each word. It is she who leans towards the book, says each word.

And so, these (still performative[7]) reading scenarios involving George, Cash and the teacher suggest that changing to mixed-attainment reading instruction may not have alleviated stress for children experiencing specific difficulties with reading print. Indeed, the shift may have inadvertently added stress due to greater visibility of the difficulties when contrasted, and in closer proximity, to children whose reading was following a more normative trajectory. In the 'bottom' reading group the disparity in fluency had been much less pronounced. This insight reveals the messy and at times contradictory work of disrupting literacy hierarchies. Mixed-attainment reading appears to open the doors of reading communities to many more children while potentially increasing the discomfort of children with reading difficulties. The study found no definitive answers to this tension. Indeed, in the spirit of inquiry, and with an awareness that hierarchies tend to reform when disrupted, perhaps we should not expect definitive answers but rather ongoing provocations, as the next section offers.

A Radical Decentring of Print

The first question that arose on witnessing the discomfort during mixed-attainment reading in children experiencing reading difficulties was as follows: Could children have more choice in the types of reading activities they engage in, based on what they enjoy, and find least stressful and most beneficial? Perhaps, for example, they might choose to receive one-to-one support in reading rather than participate in group reading at all. To an extent, within the study, the Avon teacher initiated this by providing George with the individual reading support he seemed less stressed by. Secondly, because of the discomfort observed around reading material, perhaps mixed-attainment reading, as imagined in this book, is a pedagogy suited more to infant than junior classes. In the earlier years of schooling differences in reading material are less marked between children at different stages of fluency than they become in later years.

If the reading of picturebooks became less stigmatised, however, then it could perhaps be a pedagogy suitable for early junior years too, a supposition that would benefit from further study. Children's negative associations with picturebooks were noted quite early in the study by the ways they chose and described such books. Picturebooks, for example, were associated with struggling readers by children as young as 7 years old. To find out more about these associations, I had introduced a text selection activity to help understand children's motivation for their text choices. The selection contained picturebooks, comics, novels, illustrated and graphic novels, information books, annuals and poetry. Children were invited to browse the texts, then tell me what they might choose if found in their class library and why they might choose it. From this activity, a common association emerged between "small books", including picturebooks, and struggling readers. The desire for distance from this association may have contributed to George's choice of Susan Cooper's *Ghost Hawk,* the longest novel in the selection, and one read more frequently by children in their final year of primary school. His reason for the choice was that he liked big books and he wanted to read it with his dad. According to his teacher, based on George's accounts, his dad would at times chastise him for his poor attempts at reading. In free-choice reading, George also appeared to pretend-read a chapter book rather than read a lower status text he might successfully decipher and enjoy (see Chapter 4).

Witnessing the persistence of hierarchy based on text types, the dominance of print over other mediums of communication, including visual, and the effects this had on less fluent readers' choices, the teachers and I set out to elevate the status of picturebooks in the classroom. The benefits, we figured, could be, at least, two-fold. Firstly, all children could gain from the wealth of wonderful picturebooks available that they might now allow themselves to enjoy. Secondly, and crucially, if picturebooks became cool to read by the most fluent readers, less fluent readers who benefit particularly from their visual cues would be spared the choice between reading accessible material and social inclusion. Such influence of peers on children's text choices is well documented (e.g., Edmunds & Bauserman, 2006; Moje et al., 2008). In Moss and McDonald's (2004) study of primary school library borrowing records they found that when time, space and resources were conducive, child-motivated reading networks thrived and influenced what books children borrowed. In one class there was a distinct preference for longer novels, a pattern which mystified the teacher, who had not promoted the texts. Instead, the preference was traced to a boy whose mum, the school librarian, encouraged him to read such books. Significantly, she felt it was his standing in the classroom, as a leader and footballer, that was the catalyst for children following his text choices. Influenced by this study, the teachers and I created the following conditions to encourage recommendations, connections and shared reading experiences around picturebooks, validated by high status readers.

The teachers at St Jude's introduced picturebooks into their shared text repertoire, which they read and responded to as a whole class. High quality age-appropriate picturebooks were also displayed more prominently in the reading corner. And, perhaps most impactfully, the teacher in Avon class (St Jude's) introduced picturebook-focused reading cafés. Reading cafés were an established and regular event at St Jude's. They consisted of weekly time and space for children to read whatever they wanted with whoever they wanted, while enjoying some juice and biscuits. As well as continuing the tradition to read whatever they chose to, the teacher and I put together a box of new picturebooks that were first available to read in the reading café. Mindful of the opportunity to simultaneously disrupt a different hierarchy, around the dominance of White experience in children's literature, many of the books chosen centred the lives of Children (and families) of Colour (Bishop, 1990; CLPE, 2022) (see Appendix 2). I also organised for two electronic tablets loaded up with interactive visual/word stories to be included but these were lost to the box in the confusions of lockdown. In addition, the children were encouraged to bring in reading material from home for the reading café; we envisioned a second box full of not only picturebooks but also comics, manuals and reading-related games. I hoped that this invitation would also increase classroom hospitality to children's home lives and interests, an action that, in itself, can challenge hierarchies of classed pastimes and reading cultures (Bourdieu, 1984; Thomson, 2002; Tyler; 2020). In the event, the children kept their comics at home, like Sean's[8] wrestling comics and Puzzle's Sponge Bob ones, but what did unexpectedly fill the box were children's own authored books, for which there was a high demand.

In regular online conversations with the teacher, she told me the impact she felt the reading cafés were having on the status of picturebooks in the classroom. What follows is an extended extract from one such conversation:

> The biggest thing about the reading cafés is the shift around picturebooks. In my class last year the girls were really keen to be reading novels. Now when I brought picturebooks to the reading café, sharing them and having them on display, they became so much more appealing for everybody. It was 'oh, I'm going to read that' and yeh it levelled out the playing field. They're reading together a lot of the time so usually they'll buddy up. They'll take a book and look at it, and you can hear them laughing and they'll come up and say 'look at this part', they're wanting to show you. They'll come up at the end and do a wee book sell and tell others what the book was about. Puzzle (BRG) is sitting next to John (TRG) and Kieran (MRG) just now and they have very similar interests so it's as if they're all in a wee team. So anything that one of them picks to read, the other two are jumping on and wanting to read that; then they'll go for another one. This is allowing the less fluent readers to choose picturebooks to read too. The other children have heightened their status.

The teacher's assessment of the shift in status of picturebooks was confirmed in the conversations I had when I returned to school. In one conversation with Millie's friends, Sienna and Emma, from the previous 'top' group, the girls talked about their favourite aspects of the reading café and of how the picturebooks were in high demand. They mentioned the biscuits but also the books. Although Emma's preference for, and avid consumption of, longer novels was legendary in the class (it was frequently mentioned by other children), she was also now actively participating in the increased appreciation for picturebooks. Of one of her favourites, *The True Story of the Three Little Pigs*, by Jon Scieszka, she said, "Whenever I go to the box to get (it) it's never there!" Recommendations, or as they called them in Avon class, "book sells", were also stimulating interest in picturebooks, just as we had hoped they would. Book sells from high status readers carried particular weight, the teacher felt, in shifting the status of picturebook reading in the class. One effect of this shift, according to the teacher, was on those children at earlier stages of fluency, like George, who were no longer selecting novels on the basis of their higher social status and pretending to read them. If there's a book he wants to read now, she said, "you'll usually find him there with a wee group of them sitting reading it. Or he'll come up and ask me 'can you read this book to me' and I'll read that book to him." In the first reading café I observed after returning to school, Charlie (middle class, White, Scottish, MRG) and George were reading *Archie's War,* by Marica Williams, a fictional picturebook designed as a scrap book by a young boy living through the First World War. Both boys had shown an interest in the World Wars, George's older brother was in the army, and responding to this interest the teacher had added *Archie's War* to the reading café box. They were bent over it, pointing to and talking about different sections. At the end of the reading café, Charlie recommended the book to the class. He showed various pages and wanted to find a particular note, which was in an envelope in the book. He passed a lot of other notes to find the one he was looking for.

The shift in hospitality towards picturebooks and elevation of their status could be regarded as a first step in a greater decentring of print in primary classrooms. This shift could in turn create more dignity, self-esteem and equity of experience for children whose aptitude for print does not follow a normative trajectory. Taking George as an example, he showed greater engagement in reading, and more freedom in both his text choices and with whom he chose to read once picturebooks carried a higher status. But again, this should not be considered as a final step in the dismantling of literacy hierarchies. George continued to appear tense and embarrassed, for example, in the context of teacher-led mixed-attainment reading groups. He continued to whisper as the teacher strained to listen to him reading. It was beyond the scope of this study to experiment further with the potential that multimodal conceptions of reading have to create more equitable ground for all children to develop as readers, but this is where the research points and could be taken to.

Multimodal conceptions of reading and other literacies stress their communicative and appreciative aspects and intent in our everyday lives. As such, they encompass mediums of print but also visuals, sound, gesture and other symbols (Jewitt et al., 2016; Kress, 2010). Breaking out from focus on books and print, living literacies are understood and perceived in the multifarious ways people live their lives, including in the realms of music and social media (Pahl & Rowsell, 2020). When multimodality is embraced and centred in the classroom, more of children's diverse ways of communicating can be validated and built upon. In contrast, while the medium of print is legitimated and held above other forms of communication, classroom hierarchies will always form around aptitude for reading print. Within such hierarchies, children with less aptitude for print may always experience the shadow of lexism however reading is organised. Lexism, as described in Chapter 6, can be understood as the "normative practices and assumptions of literacy that might Other and discriminate against dyslexics (and others non-normative readers)" (Collinson, 2022).

There are many ways to develop reading multimodally in the classroom. I hope that as you read this you may have more ideas than are presented here. Hamilton (2016), in her US study of childhood reading difficulties, suggests that engaging with multimodal postmodern picturebooks may help change perception of what it means to be a reader. Postmodern picturebooks are often complex and aimed at older child readers; in them visual information matters just as much, if not more, than words in their nonlinear narratives and self-referential devices. Alternatively, Newfield and Maungedzo (2006) draw on African culture to reconceptualise how poetry is imagined in a Soweto high school. In their study, emphasis in the classroom shifted from analysis to composition, which drew on and was expressed as spoken word, performance, written word and forms of craft, such as embroidered cloth that tells stories. In both cases, children's identity and positioning as readers could change dramatically to the benefit of those with less aptitude for reading and writing print, children who often find themselves in 'bottom' reading groups.

Writers and thinkers who are committed to equality and social justice disagree on the role dominant (print-based) literacy should assume in education (e.g., Albright & Luke, 2010; Bourdieu, 1973; Kramsch, 2010). These differences reflect the paradox of literacy: that it can be at once a source of liberation and a mechanism that maintains inequality (Finn, 1999; Freire, 2000; hooks, 1994). Bourdieu (1973) claims that if schools fail to teach dominant literacy, for example, it allows this valuable capital to remain monopolised by those who inherit it domestically. To this end, Bourdieu argues, it is a mistake to seek social justice through increasing hospitality to non-dominant culture in school. Stuckey (1991) on the other hand strongly argues that (dominant) literacy is always (symbolic) violence visited on diverse communities. It delegitimises ways of talking, reading and writing, and can only be challenged by elevating, and teaching through, diverse literacies across class, race and culture.

It is possible, however, to go beyond such binaries (Albright & Luke, 2010). The consequences of reading differently are acutely felt in a print-based society, both emotionally and materially (Duckworth, 2013). Those consequences fall disproportionately depending on how much cultural, economic and social capital a child inherits (Bourdieu & Passeron, 1979). But if literacy teaching was genuinely reconfigured within multimodal conceptions of reading, which still appreciated the value of print, then it could disrupt hierarchies that stigmatise children whose aptitude for print reading falls below normative levels.

Conclusion

This book has shown some of the pedagogical reasons why odds can be stacked against working class children of all ethnicities thriving as readers in primary school. More specifically it has revealed the privilege unfairly locked in and increased by ability-grouped reading, for children who arrive in school with more familiarity with print. This chapter concludes that there are ways of organising and teaching reading, which can change the rules of this game and the hand that is dealt, which increase the odds of working-class children thriving as readers (Bourdieu & Wacquant, 1992). The study investigated one such pedagogical alternative, mixed-attainment reading, for its potential to offer more egalitarian conditions to develop as readers. There were promising outcomes in this regard despite disruption to the intervention caused by the pandemic. The promise came in the changing relationship that some in the former 'bottom' reading group seemed to have with reading and with other readers when mixed-attainment group reading had become established. They no longer appeared excluded from the reading gang, though this was less true for children experiencing reading difficulties. Mixed-attainment reading also proved more responsive to individual reader's needs while paradoxically offering the same pedagogical approach to all. With this equality of pedagogy, those who had been in the 'bottom' reading group did not lose out on deeper response and comprehension support that had been disproportionately granted those in the 'top' group. Now, all children were supported in this way through sharing and responding to texts as a whole class and in mixed-attainment pairings.

Yet reading hierarchies are complicated, and formed not just by pedagogical practices. Hierarchies can be perpetuated by children within an education system and society that is imbued with inequality and competition, and in which literacy holds a pivotal role. When disrupted, hierarchies often reform. In mixed-attainment reading, children quickly found ways to reassert their superiority, even if the practice itself contains more egalitarian potential. The nature of school-based reading would surely change if researchers, teachers and policymakers were committed to repeatedly spotting and disrupting hierarchy, however it is expressed, in the interest of social justice for all children. Within these disruptions, the social and emotional needs of those who find print reading hardest must be central. It was our commitment to iterative spotting of new or persistent literacy hierarchies within the study that took me and the teachers in the direction of disruption of hierarchy around print itself.

In this regard, we asked, what if the reading of images was elevated to the same level as reading print in classrooms? If reading was understood as a multimodal practice of communication (Kress, 2010; Newfield & Maungedso, 2006; Pahl & Rowsell, 2020) and *all* readers were encouraged to read multimodally, this may disrupt literacy hierarchies grounded strongly in print fluency. This is not to minimise the difficulties and emotional impact that limited aptitude for print evokes in a society still dominated by print nor is it to suggest that readers should be denied access to whatever pedagogy helps them to read print more easily. However, it could be that teaching children to read multimodally could balance their aptitudes, and actually be the best preparation for the world in which they live. As Jewitt (2008) points out, the knowledge economy has reconfigured ways in which information is shared, combining print with sound, and with still and moving images, in multimodal combinations. If mixed-attainment reading was also a context in which reading multimodally was highly valued, it could further disrupt the hierarchy between confident and unconfident print readers that was, to an extent, left intact by its introduction. Although this chapter presents these conclusions from the study, it does so by drawing attention to the inevitable unfinished and untidy nature of pedagogical change in the interests of social equity. In our inequitable society and education system there must always be a call for more action, by educators, researchers and policymakers, towards noticing literacy hierarchies which tend to reform in the wake of their disruption.

Notes

1 Until summer 2020, I maintained communication with the children by reading and posting stories in their online learning communities for them to engage with and comment on. During this period I also had monthly online meetings with the three teachers in the study. Scottish primary schools reopened in August 2020, only to close again in January 2021 and reopen six weeks later. In efforts to limit the spread of the coronavirus, only those adults who were essential to children's education were permitted in school at first. I continued to meet online with the original teacher of Clyde, who was now the teacher of Avon class. This allowed continuity of research participants beyond the original timeframe for the study. Among other topics, we discussed the progress of mixed-attainment reading. I was able to return to school and to ethnographic research methods (of observation, participation and conversation) one month before Scottish schools broke up for the summer holiday in 2021 and before the class moved onto a new teacher in the next school year.
2 Stella is White and of Scottish heritage. I did not get to know her well and I am unsure of how I would identify her in class terms.
3 Gary, from Clyde class, St Jude's, is White and of Scottish heritage. As mentioned in Chapter 4, he is difficult to situate in class terms on the basis of his parents' jobs, but when he spoke about time spent with his grandad, I imagined his mum had a working-class upbringing similar in some ways to mine, but this may not be accurate.

4 The reason why the higher group received more support in understanding and responding to texts was largely down to the books they were reading with the teacher. There was simply more going on, more complexity of language, more to be understood and responded to in their books compared to the early stage books in the reading scheme that those in the 'bottom' reading group were reading.
5 Both Kieran and John had been in the 'top' reading group and were middle class, White and of Scottish heritage.
6 Jake was White and Scottish. I did not get to know him well enough to locate him in terms of class.
7 By performative, I mean that in both scenarios the child is reading at the request of and, in some ways at least, for the teacher. The reading event is not singularly self-motivated. Because of that there may always be more stress incurred in reading to/with the teacher than in reading events that are instigated and motivated by the child.
8 Sean was a working-class, White, Scottish boy who had previously been in the 'middle' reading group.

References

Albright, J., & Luke, A. (2010). *Pierre Bourdieu and literacy education*. Routledge.
Bishop, R. S. (1990, March). Windows and mirrors: Children's books and parallel cultures. In *California State University Reading Conference: 14th Annual Conference Proceedings* (pp. 3–12). California State University.
Bodman, S., & Franklin, G. (2014). *Which book and why*. IOE Press.
Bourdieu, P. (1973). Cultural reproduction and social reproduction. In R. Brown (Ed.), *Knowledge, education, and cultural change* (pp. 56–68). Tavistock Publications.
Bourdieu, P. (1984). *Distinction: A social critique of the judgement of taste*. Routledge & Kegan Paul.
Bourdieu, P., & Passeron, J.-C. (1979). *The inheritors: French students and their relation to culture*. University of Chicago Press.
Bourdieu, P., & Passeron, J. C. (1990). *Reproduction in education, society and culture*. SAGE.
Bourdieu, P., & Wacquant, L. J. D. (1992). *An invitation to reflexive sociology*. University of Chicago press.
Chambers, A. (2011). *Tell me: Children reading and talk*. Thimble Press.
Clay, M. M. (1993). *An observation survey of early literacy achievement*. Heinemann Educational Books.
CLPE (2022). *Reflecting realities: Survey of ethnic Representation within UK children's literature 2017–2021*. https://clpe.org.uk/research/clpe-reflecting-realities-survey-ethnic-representation-within-uk-childrens-literature-2017
Collinson, C. (2022), Dyslexics and othering: An anti-definitional approach to Lexism. *British Journal of Special Education*, 49(1), 24–40. https://doi.org/10.1111/1467-8578.12397
Cremin, T., Mottram, M., Collins, F. M., Powell, S., & Safford, K. (2014). *Building communities of engaged readers: Reading for pleasure*. Routledge.
Cunningham, P. M. (2006). High-poverty schools that beat the odds. *The Reading Teacher*, 60(4), 382–385. https://doi.org/10.1598/RT.60.4.9
Cunningham, P. M., Hall, D. P., & Defee, M. (1991). Non-ability grouped, multilevel instruction: A year in a first-grade classroom. *Reading Teacher*, 44(8), 566–571
Cunningham, P. M., Hall, D. P., & Defee, M. (1998). Nonability-grouped, multilevel instruction: Eight years later. *Reading Teacher*, 51(8), 652–664.

Duckworth, V. (2013). *Learning trajectories, violence and empowerment amongst adult basic skills learners*. Routledge.
Edmunds, K. M., & Bauserman, Kathryn. (2006). What teachers can learn about reading motivation through conversations with children. *The Reading Teacher*, 59(5), 414–424.
Finn, P. J. (1999). *Literacy with an attitude: Educating working-class children in their own self-interest*. State University of New York Press.
Fountas, I. C., & Pinnell, G. S. (1998). *Guided reading: Good first teaching for all children*. Heinemann.
Francis, B., Archer, L., Hodgen, J., Pepper, D., Taylor, B., & Travers M. (2017a). Exploring the relative lack of impact of research on 'ability grouping' in England: A discourse analytic account. *Cambridge Journal of Education*, 47(1), 1–17.
Freire, P. (2000). *Pedagogy of the oppressed* (30th anniversary ed.). Continuum.
Gillborn, D. (2008). *Racism and education: Coincidence or conspiracy?* Routledge.
Gillborn, D. (2010). Reform, racism and the centrality of whiteness: Assessment, ability and the 'new eugenics'. *Irish Educational Studies*, 29(3), 231–252.
Hamilton, D. M. (2016). *Postmodern picturebooks, gender, and reading difficulties: A phenomenological exploration of one boy's experiences*. State University of New York. https://www.proquest.com/docview/1823568727?fromopenview=true&pq-origsite=gscholar
Hempel-Jorgensen, A., Cremin, T., Harris, D., & Chamberlain, L. (2018). Pedagogy for reading for pleasure in low socio-economic primary schools: Beyond 'pedagogy of poverty'? *Literacy*, 52(2), 86–94. https://doi.org/10.1111/lit.12157
hooks, b. (1994). *Teaching to transgress: Education as the practice of freedom*. Routledge.
Institute of Education Reading Recovery Network. (2000). *Book bands for guided reading: Organising key stage one texts for the literacy hour*. Institute of Education Publications.
Jewitt, C. (2008). Multimodality and literacy in school classrooms. *Review of Research in Education*, 32(1), 241–267. https://doi.org/10.3102/0091732x07310586
Jewitt, C., Bezemer, J., & O'Halloran, K. (2016). *Introducing multimodality*. Routledge.
Kramsch, C. (2010). Pierre Bourdieu: A biographical memoir. In J. Albright & A. Luke (Eds.), *Pierre Bourdieu and literacy education* (pp. 31–48). Routledge.
Krashen, S. (1989). We acquire vocabulary and spelling by reading: Additional evidence for the input hypothesis. *The Modern Language Journal*, 73(4), 440–464.
Krashen, S. D. (2004). *The power of reading: Insights from the research*. Heinemann.
Kress, G. (2010). *Multimodality: A social semiotic approach to contemporary communication*. Routledge.
Moje, E. B., Overby, M., Tysvaer, N., & Morris, K. (2008). The complex world of adolescent literacy: Myths, motivations, and mysteries. *Harvard Educational Review*, 78(1), 107–154. https://doi.org/10.17763/haer.78.1.54468j6204x24157
Moss, G. (2000). Raising boys' attainment in reading: Some principles for intervention. *Reading*, 34(3), 101–106.
Moss, G. (2007). *Literacy and gender: Researching texts, contexts and readers*. Routledge.
Moss, G. (2021). Literacies and social practice: Sociological perspectives on reading research. *Education 3–13*, 49(1), 41–51. https://doi.org/10.1080/03004279.2020.1824701
Moss, G., & McDonald, J. W. (2004), The borrowers: Library records as unobtrusive measures of children's reading preferences. *Journal of Research in Reading*, 27(4), 401–412. https://doi.org/10.1111/j.1467-9817.2004.00242.x

Newfield, D., & Maungedzo, R. (2006). Mobilising and modalising poetry in a Soweto classroom. *English Studies in Africa*, 49(1), 71–93. https://doi.org/10.1080/00138390608691344

OECD. (2002). *Reading for change: Performance and engagement across countries: Results from PISA 2002*. Organisation for Economic Co-operation and Development.

O'Sullivan, O. & McGonigle, S. (2010). Transforming readers: Teachers and children in the Centre for Literacy in Primary Education Power of Reading project. *Literacy*, 44(2), 51–59.

Pahl, K., & Rowsell, J. (2020). *Living literacies: Literacy for social change*. MIT press.

Reay, D. (2017). *Miseducation: Inequality, education and the working classes*. Policy Press.

Rodríguez-Dorans, E., & Jacobs, P. (2020). Making narrative portraits: A methodological approach to analysing qualitative data. *International Journal of Social Research Methodology*, 23(6), 611-623. https://doi.org/10.1080/13645579.2020.1719609

Stanovich, K. E. (2009). Matthew effects in reading: Some consequences of individual differences in the acquisition of literacy. *Journal of Education*, 189(1–2), 23–55.

Stuckey, J. E. (1991). *The violence of literacy*. Vintage.

Tennent, W., Reedy, D., Hobsbaum, A., & Gamble, N. (2016). *Guiding readers- layers of meaning: A handbook for teaching reading comprehension to 7–11 year olds*. UCL IoE Press.

Thomson, P. (2002). *Schooling the Rustbelt kids: Making the difference in changing times*. Routledge.

Tyler, I. (2020). *Stigma: The machinery of inequality*. Zed Books.

Children's Literature References

Butterworth, N. (2005). *Percy and the badger*. Collins Big Cat.

Butterworth, N. (2020). *A Percy the park keeper story, one spring day*. Collins Big Cat.

Cooper, S. (2015). *Ghost hawk*. Corgi Childrens.

Pilkey, D. (2016). *Dog man*. Scholastic Corporation.

Scieszka, Jon (1989). *The true story of the 3 little pigs*. Viking Children's Books.

Williams, M. (2009). *Archie's war*. Walker.

8
CONCLUSIONS

Introduction

The book has offered novel elicitations of complex situated realities in ability-grouped reading and its alternatives in primary school. These situated realities are in conversation with pedagogical knowledge and stretched Bourdieusian theories of social reproduction (e.g., Bourdieu & Passeron, 1979, 1990; Bourdieu, 1984; Lareau, 2011; Reay, 2017). What isn't novel is the shared dismay – expressed in the book – over the impact of ability grouping on social inequality. As Ramberg (2016) points out, few topics in education have produced more research than pupil 'ability' segregation. Much of that discussion has focused on how the practice exacerbates social inequality and injustice (e.g., Francis & Tereshchenko, 2020; Gillborn, 2010; Reay, 2017).

However, the affective, social and pedagogical specificities of developing as *readers* within ability groups had been largely absent from this wider debate. It has been particularly scarce since the 1990s when guided reading (organised as ability groups) became commonplace in the UK and US (Department for Education and Employment,1998; Fountas & Pinnell, 1998; Hobsbaum et al., 2006). This scarcity deserved the considered attention the study has given it. The practice of reading within ability groups deserves attention *especially* because of literacy's central role in social positioning and negotiating identities in the UK and beyond (Duckworth, 2013; Williams, 2017). The book has answered the following research questions. Does ability-grouped reading affect children's identities and feelings for reading and, if so, in what ways? How do social inequalities around class, race and gender intersect with the practice of ability grouping for reading development? And what effect does mixed-attainment reading have on children's identity and attitudes to reading? Chapters 4, 5 and 6 answered the first two of these questions. The third was reconceptualised in Chapter 7, as a wider reflection on disrupting literacy hierarchies, still with a focus on mixed-attainment reading.

This chapter is organised in four sections. The first section, *Theoretical and Epistemological Influences*, sets out the key messages I hope the reader will take away, in terms of the usefulness of Bourdieu's conceptual tools and Reay's writing in helping explain educational inequalities. It will also reflect on the epistemological assertions I have made and how helpful they are in telling a story of reading in school. The second section, *The 'Bottom' Reading Group: A Place of Learning, Sanctuary and Stigma*, reaches conclusions on the first research question. It draws out complex perspectives on children as readers from their complicated, sometimes contradictory, experiences in ability-grouped reading. The third section, *Social Inequality and Discrimination Through Ability-Grouped Reading*, answers the second research question. It argues that, despite the situated complexities, grouping readers hierarchically is a deeply unfair practice in terms of social equity. The fourth section, *Disrupting Hierarchy in School-Based Reading*, shows how the third research question expanded to include a meditation on the nature of reading itself. At its heart is the paradox of literacy as a source of liberation and of social reproduction. The section concludes that school-based reading could become more egalitarian if the disruption of hierarchy, including a shift to mixed-attainment reading, became the moral compass of literacy pedagogy. Such disruptions, evident – if embryonic – in the study, hold liberatory promise even as new hierarchies form in their wake to be further challenged.

Theoretical and Epistemological Influences

Bourdieu's writing, and feminist scholars who engage critically with it (e.g., Lareau, 2011; Reay, 2017; Taylor, 2009), provided the core theoretical lens for the study. Bourdieu wrote with insistence that class still mattered amidst socioeconomic change (1996; Bourdieu & Passeron, 1990). I have reorientated his concepts to investigate and explain the *how* of social reproduction in ability-grouped reading, and in doing so, highlight possibilities for greater equity. Understanding how social reproduction continues despite many teachers' dedication to all children's educational advancement has been an underlying theme of the project.

Bourdieu's work has been reorientated in the book in two ways. Firstly, although human agency is integral to Bourdieu's understanding of habitus as generative, social constraint can echo so loudly in his work that reflexivity, creativity and resistance can be difficult to hear. Even in his later work, such as *The Weight of the World* (1999), which is regarded as more orientated towards struggle (e.g., McNay, 2004; Reay, 2004), it is the hopelessness of that struggle, the "anxious submission and powerless revolt" that is conveyed (Bourdieu & Accardo, 1999, p. 425). With a shift of emphasis, I recentred and focused on children's reflexivity, ingenuity and agency within the often constraining conditions of ability-grouped reading. Secondly, Bourdieu speaks of children primarily as inheritors of parental cultural capital, and of distinction-making as an adult activity. I challenged this by bringing Bourdieu's work into conversation with childhood researchers in the 'new sociology of childhood' (e.g., Blaisdell, 2019; Christensen et al., 2008; Punch, 2002) who recognise children as social actors in their own right. The book highlights how children built on inherited capital by actively distinguishing themselves within school reading hierarchies.

Reay's large body of work (e.g., 1995, 2002, 2017) has provided a bright guiding light in the application and reorientation of Bourdieusian principles to this study. Through her example, I have kept the focus on children's agency within literacy practices that can perpetuate social hierarchies. As well as her academic rigour, I appreciate her sensibility and emotional investment in researching social injustice in education. I want to be affected by the scholars I read, and *Miseducation* (2017) swelled my heart and moved me to tears on numerous occasions. More importantly, it called me to action. My anger at the unfairness of ability-grouped reading found many echoes in her work. Through her example, I have been galvanised to write in ways that I hope have had an emotional as well as intellectual effect on those who read this book.

Shaun's Story (2002) was my introduction to Reay's work. Reading it, I understood the emotional and explanatory power of personalised narrative to examine complex realities and develop theoretical perspectives. Influenced by Reay and, later Lareau (2011), I chose to convey the key themes emerging from the research through extended narratives of children occupying different positions in ability-grouped reading. These narratives have illuminated much more of the contextualised, relational and embodied nature of young readers' experience than their disembodied words could alone. If the book comes alive, it comes alive thanks to this complexity; the feistiness, joy, fears and humour of the characters that inhabit the writing. The composition of each narrative portrait was confirmed through a mixture of gut reaction, thematic analysis and writing as a tool of inquiry. I hope the voices stay with you, but also the themes that were developed through them. What follows are the key messages I would like the reader to take from the study.

The 'Bottom' Reading Group: A Place of Learning, Sanctuary and Stigma

As Chapter 5 argued, the lowest positioned group (or set) in a hierarchy of school groups is often portrayed in research literature as *only* a stigmatised place, where pupils feel, accommodate and resist the weight of others' poor opinion of them (e.g., Bourdieu, 1999; Boaler, 2005). Similarly, there can be a singular focus on distress and disaffection in literature about 'struggling readers' (e.g., Hempel-Jorgensen et al., 2018; Scherer, 2016). I intentionally troubled these narratives, and in the close ethnographic work of the study I found messier, more complicated and contradictory realities in the 'bottom' reading group than much of this literature conveys (Chapters 3–6).

My study confirmed the gendered patterns of reading in highly visible hierarchies that Moss had previously found in her work (2000, 2007, 2021). Some girls clearly used the 'bottom' reading group to develop as readers (Chapter 4). Perhaps, they were making "a virtue out of necessity" (Bourdieu, 1984). This was, after all, the place they had been allocated; they did not choose it. But there was something more agentic in their attitude, containing more momentum, than Bourdieu's phrase conjures up for me. The 'bottom' reading group could also be a place of friendship and solace (Chapter 4). For some (not all) children who had joined the school and started learning English as an additional language within the previous two years, this small group could provide ballast to sometimes bewildering and othering classroom experiences. The reading group was a place where you might know and share precious details of family, pastimes and the habits of pets. In those moments the fixed, familiar and predictable nature of the reading group appeared more important than where it sat in a hierarchy of reading groups.

However, while offering learning and sanctuary for some children in some moments, the 'bottom' reading group was also undoubtedly a stigmatised place from the perspective of those positioned further up the reading group hierarchy (Chapter 4). There are other ways to organise the classroom to provide the welcome intimacy of a familiar group without placing children, including bilingual children, in a stigmatised place. As Chapter 4 illustrated, the hierarchical organisation of ability grouping was actively reinforced by children claiming distinction from those in 'lower' groups. The language of the 'top' group was liberally peppered with words that proclaimed their superiority over others. Perceived superiority as readers was melded with non-reading qualities – of greater intelligence, happiness and confidence. Crucially, readers in the 'bottom' group were imagined as likely to struggle as readers in adulthood, suggesting that the stigma of 'struggling reader' could linger for a long time (Duckworth, 2013; Williams, 2017).

These judgements were keenly felt by some in the 'lower' group, in anger and sometimes longing to flee the 'bottom' reading group. Some children, invested in 'doing boy' (Renold, 2004), for example, could fall further behind as readers when judgements about reading proficiency were highly visible, such as in ability-grouped reading. They seemed propelled to perform confident reader identities by pretending to read, and this came at the expense of practising reading. Thus, overt hierarchical positioning could deny children a more comfortable space to develop as readers and to risk getting words wrong. This finding again extends Moss's work on gender and reading (2000, 2007).

The elite and stigmatised positionings described in Chapter 4 suggest social capital is accrued by securing a place in the highest positioned reading group. Social capital is one of Bourdieu's most potent concepts in explaining how social inequality is perpetuated and it has helped explain the social dynamics of reading groups. Through an "alchemy of consecration" (Bourdieu, 1986, p. 250), symbolised by congratulatory clapping when a child was 'promoted' to the 'top' group, social advantage was gained, much like entry to an exclusive club. Likewise, friendships orientated around reading appeared only available to those in 'higher' groups (Chapter 4). Children in the 'bottom' reading group did not or could not participate in this community of readers despite being popular members of the class. Perhaps because of their positioning, they lacked the social capital as readers to cultivate reading friendships. This is a significant finding particularly in the light of research that highlights positive connections between reading communities and reading engagement with the reduction of socioeconomic disparities in reading attainment (Clark & Rumbold, 2006; Cremin et al., 2014; Cunningham et al., 1998). To be excluded from this reading community because of the visible marking of hierarchical reading groups may be an unrecognised and injurious consequence of ability-grouped reading.

Social Inequality and Discrimination through Ability-Grouped Reading

With the second research question in mind and focusing particularly on social class, Chapter 5 examined the mechanisms by which ability-grouped reading reproduces social inequality. The 'bottom' reading group appeared largely a destination for working-class children regardless of their ethnicity, except in the case of children in their first two years of learning English who were placed in the 'bottom' group regardless of class. This reflects patterns of entrenchment found in much of the literature on ability grouping in general (e.g., Bourdieu et al., 1999; Francis & Tereshchenko, 2020). Through situated analysis of how privileging and discrimination operate within ability-grouped reading specifically, the book offers an original disruptive contribution to knowledge that could inform both literacy practice and educational policy.

To understand how class matters in ability-grouped reading, I answered the question: what might prompt the classed allocation to these reading groups? As allocation to hierarchical reading groups often happens soon after starting school, what happens at home, and, more crucially, *how this is received in school*, is significant to the placement. Again, Bourdieu's concepts proved helpful in explaining this pattern of allocation, especially the notion of cultural capital embedded in the habitus. Domestic transmission of cultural knowledge, linguistic skills and literacy practices appeared to influence a child's chances of gaining a spot in the 'top' reading group. Cultural transmission is one of the most valuable forms of capital inheritance precisely because it is not recognised as an inheritance (Bourdieu, 1973). Instead, it masquerades as natural ability when there is a match between a child's literacy habitus and school-based literacy (Bourdieu, 1996). It is this misrecognition as natural ability that gives ability-grouped reading its false legitimacy.

Findings from this research led me to agree with Anderson et al. (2003) that much of the research on home reading misrepresents the intergenerational reading habits of working-class families and families from minoritised ethnic groups. Contrary to assumptions that these groups do not read with their children, Anderson et al. (2003) highlight multiple studies that show the opposite. In fact, most parents in all classes and cultures (that have been studied) read with their children. Likewise in my study, most children from the 'bottom' and 'top' groups spoke of reading with their parents, often their mothers, and sometimes with siblings. The reading episodes they describe ranged from intimate family rituals around sharing books to books read as homework tasks. There were still differences, however, in the space that books and reading seemed to take up in the homes of those in the 'top' and 'bottom' group. In the narratives of children in the 'bottom' group, reading was often decentred by other culturally enriching pastimes (Chapters 3 and 5). In the 'top' group, reading appeared more central, organised and cultivated (Chapter 5). Extending Lareau's (2011) concept of middle-class "concerted cultivation" to reading practices, Chapter 5 showed that regular intergenerational reading was practiced as a means of securing a top spot as a reader, as well as presumably being regarded as an emotionally and culturally enriching pastime.

Class came to matter in other ways too in reading group placement. Children described very different economic conditions and their temporal effects on parents' capacity to read regularly with them (Chapter 5). As well as economic necessities, not all parents had the same educational or literacy resources to support their children's reading. None of this indicates that working-class parents care less about their children's education than middle-class parents (Lawler & Close, 2014). Rather, the study found it is variation in cultural, educational and economic capital that comes to matter in the classed allocation to hierarchical reading groups (Chapter 5).

Most children in the lowest positioned group showed the same aptitude for reading as those in the 'top' group, and this was another crucial finding in the study. Despite similar aptitude, mechanisms within ability-grouped reading restricted, rather than enhanced, children's chances of catching up with the more fluent readers in the 'top' group (Chapters 4 and 5). This holds true even though some children spoke favourably of the smallness of the group, the tailored books and the extra support in framing positive learner identities in the 'bottom' group. A key restriction was their positioning by others as struggling readers with noticeable effects on their identity and self-belief (Chapter 4). Differences in reading pedagogy practised with each group also potentially widened rather than narrowed differences in children's levels of reading fluency.

There was also inertia within ability-grouped reading that constrained children's progress in the 'lower' group. Little movement between groups had occurred since children started school three or four years earlier, despite children making different amounts of progress in reading. There were instances of (White) working-class boys being misallocated 'downwards' because of their perceived family circumstances when, based on fluency, they would have been in a 'higher' group. Conversely there was at least one (White) middle-class child who was kept out of the 'lowest' group because of what their parents might think of them being there (Chapter 5). There were no examples in the study of children from minoritised ethnic groups being misallocated on the basis of reading fluency in English.[1] Notwithstanding this, group inertia and misplacement of Black and other pupils from minoritised ethnic groups to lower sets are dominant themes in the wider literature on race, ethnicity, class and ability grouping (e.g., Francis & Tereshchenko, 2020; Gillborn et al., 2021).

The legitimacy of ability-grouped reading relies on it being misrecognised as fair and beneficial for all children. The study has shown that the opposite is true. Ability-grouped reading is exclusionary and discriminatory, with negative effects. It unfairly compounds the advantage of children who are already advantaged both economically and culturally (in the sense of *legitimated* cultural capital) and reduces the chances of others to progress as readers. As a practice, educators should be mindful of this. By illuminating the mechanisms by which ability-grouped reading reproduces social inequality, I hope the study will encourage policymakers and practitioners to reconsider its appearance of neutrality and explore alternative methods of reading instruction. As I said in the introduction to the book, this project has always had activist intent. My hope is tempered, however, by awareness of the tenacity of ability grouping despite countless studies that expose it as a classed and raced discriminatory practice (Francis, 2017).

Disrupting Hierarchy in School-Based Reading

It was with awareness of the tenacity of ability grouping in the collective educational psyche that an intervention was included in the study design, that of mixed-attainment reading (Chapter 7). By hearing a research-informed alternative, I hope policy makers and practitioners are more likely to reconsider the usefulness of ability-grouped reading in supporting *all* readers. Despite believing in the greater equity of mixed-attainment learning, my own lack of knowledge of alternatives, as a teacher, had perpetuated my practice of ability-grouped reading. Although disrupted by the pandemic, the positive impact of mixed-attainment reading on apparently fixed hierarchies was evident. When children from different ability groups came together there appeared a new vibrancy in the atmosphere, particularly evident in some who had been in the 'bottom' reading group. Pedagogy was democratised, and in the greater collaboration there was a little more risk-taking. Children who had been in the 'top' group shared words they were unsure of, and this may have helped less fluent readers share, rather than hide, words *they* were unsure of, thus aiding progress. Reading friendships expanded to include children who had previously appeared excluded from the community of readers within the class. Again, it is worth pausing on the potential significance of this change for greater social equity in literacy outcomes (Clark & Rumbold, 2006; Cremin, 2019; Cremin et al., 2014).

In addition, a more fundamental question about reading hierarchy arose and was answered from this starting point of mixed-attainment reading. The binary stance of ability-grouped versus mixed-attainment reading belied a complexity to how reading hierarchies are produced and modified, and who are involved in their production (Chapters 6 and 7). Although the pedagogical practice of ability-grouped reading reinforces a hierarchy, it does not do so in isolation. The field of literacy education is a site of struggle, mirroring struggles in wider society. Children live within these struggles and work to distinguish themselves from others, thus challenging, adapting and reinforcing normative reading hierarchies (Bourdieu, 1984; Costa & Murphy, 2015). When mixed-attainment reading was introduced, children actively reproduced the reading hierarchy that had been disrupted by its introduction. During one session, for example, I listened in as children established who was reading at the highest level by comparing their books. There was also much talk about graduating from picturebooks and about the length of chapter books that children were reading. These comparisons appeared to position readers just as much as their place in hierarchical reading groups did.

What might it mean I began to ask, if the iterative disruption of such hierarchies, however they presented, became the moral compass of literacy pedagogy, rather than arriving at a single 'solution'? If taken up, this could mark a significant shift in curriculum development towards social justice, for practitioners and policymakers. It requires a shift, away from imposing change, and towards recursive reflexive listening and nuanced response. Listening must be reflexive because whoever is listening (practitioner, researcher or policymaker) needs to be aware of their own complicity in the perpetuation of reading hierarchies.

The power of reflexive situated inquiry is its ability to engage with the messiness of lived realities and to expose subtleties and contradictions in children's experience that demand further reflection and adjustment. This turn to iterative disruption of hierarchy was prompted by the example of children experiencing reading difficulties (Chapters 5 and 6). Those children did not seem to gain liberation in mixed-attainment reading as others from the 'bottom' reading group had appeared to do. Nor were they any more involved in reading friendships than they had been in ability-grouped reading. Despite an initial period of exhilaration, the freeze in body and gaze for those struggling with print returned and even appeared heightened in mixed-attainment reading. This may be because the gap in reading fluency, represented by their respective texts, was accentuated by their closer proximity. For this reason, mixed-attainment reading may be a pedagogy that is most beneficial in infant classes, perhaps up to the age of 8, when differences of fluency are not so marked by the texts children read. This is a conclusion that could be investigated by teachers who see potential in mixed-attainment reading for social equity.

To disrupt hierarchy between those experiencing reading difficulties and the majority of the class required a more fundamental questioning of the privileging of print in society and education, and curiosity about the emotional impact of finding this highly valued activity difficult (Chapters 6 and 7). Bourdieu's work is again helpful in this questioning as it understands literacy can be both liberatory and conservative, effecting social change as well as social reproduction. The same unequal valuing of home literacy practices that influenced allocation to hierarchical reading groups is mirrored in the forms of reading that are valued and devalued in education and society (Narey, 2017; Pahl & Rowsell, 2020). Through the notion of symbolic violence, Bourdieu and Passeron (1990) name the mechanism by which particular forms of literacy, and of communication more generally, become legitimated and delegitimated. When print is valued above other multimodal forms of communication it disproportionately disadvantages those who find print difficult to decipher, children who would find themselves in the 'bottom' reading group.

Conflicting perspectives exist about the space such dominant literacies should take up in education among academics committed to social justice. Stuckey (1991), for example, writes of literacy as violence, and as uniquely serving the interests of economic capital. By teaching dominant literacies, she suggests, schools are intentionally or inadvertently complicit in perpetuating this violence. Conversely, Bourdieu and Passeron (1979) argue that it would be folly to view dominant culture, which includes print-based literacy, as *only* symbolic violence. Failing to equip students who do not inherit it, with the knowledge and skills required to participate in powerful fields, would serve only to compound their exclusion.

In the interests of disrupting hierarchies that stigmatise children with reading difficulties, I agree with Albright and Luke (2010) that it is possible and essential to move beyond the paradox of literacy as violence, and as inherently valuable and unchanging. No child should be denied acquaintance with, or mastery of, powerful genres, including print-based literacies, but these can be taught critically in ways that invite demystification of the power relations within them. If print-based literacies were taught within a wider conceptualisation of the multimodality of reading, for example, then the shadow of lexism, as coined by Collinson (2012, 2020), would perhaps lose some of its discriminatory power. Lexism, introduced in Chapter 6, is the legitimising of print-based literacies above other mediums, and the resulting discrimination and stigmatisation of those with less than the normative aptitude for deciphering print.

To teach reading as multimodal, where images, words, sounds and gestures can be read, emphasises the worth of different forms of communication (Narey, 2017; Pahl & Rowsell, 2020). This is in fact more representative of how meanings are conveyed in both everyday life and in the knowledge economy, through speech, sound, image, film and print (Jewitt, 2018). Reorientating reading in this way could help reposition children who struggle with print by valorising the power of image, for example, to convey meaning (Chapters 6 and 7). This practice could in turn make mixed-attainment reading a more egalitarian space by equalising the kudos of different text types. A start was made on this multimodal project when a hierarchy around picturebooks and novels became evident (Chapter 7). I worked with the teachers to successfully increase the social currency of picturebooks on the basis that their higher status may allow those who particularly benefitted from the combination of image and text to choose them without risking social exclusion by reading them (Hamilton, 2016). One of the criteria used for picturebook selection was the diversity of ethnic, cultural and social representations in the books so that all children would find positive reflections of their identities and lives in their reading. This required intentional effort given the dominance of White middle-class representations in most children's literature (CLPE, 2022).

The elevation of picturebooks is not, however, proposed as a destination but as an example of an ongoing reflexive commitment to disrupting literacy hierarchies wherever and however they manifest. What began as an inquiry into children's experience of ability-grouped reading has opened out into a meditation on reading itself and the relationships of power entangled within it. This happened without losing sight of how ability-grouped reading operates within these relationships of power. This is egalitarian work, in which teachers could be supported by literacy scholars and researchers in replacing restrictive practices with more equitable conditions for human development (Albright & Luke, 2010). This book is part of this liberatory aspiration by asking what it might mean for literacy pedagogy if, rather being led by particular techniques, it is guided by the recognition and willingness to disrupt social hierarchies, like those seen in ability-grouped reading. Awareness is needed, however, that when hierarchies are disrupted, they often mutate and require further disruption. Undertaking this work requires an ongoing commitment to inquiry, reflection and listening deeply to children.

Final Thoughts: Limits, Dissemination and Further Work

Both the limitation and the strength of this project have lain in my assumptions. The study took place during a period of global and personal consciousness–raising around the many manifestations of racialised oppression and the enduring privileging of Whiteness. If I had been more aware of how this privileging operates in me while collecting data, I might have noted more intersections between race, ethnicity, class and experiences of ability-grouped reading. Furthermore, unexamined classed, and to an extent raced, beliefs around the value of reading books sometimes constrained conversations with children. This potentially left unvoiced other pastimes the children engaged in. In addition, it has been the reflexive work of challenging and partially dismantling my assumptions that has deepened an understanding of symbolic violence and how it operates in the field of literacy education. This has been critical in the analysis of how ability-grouped reading reproduces social inequity and systematically privileges and disadvantages children in the 'top' and 'bottom' groups. I still love reading (books etc.) but my mind has been changed about the superiority it commands in the middle-class imagination.

There were other limitations to the study that were a consequence of unforeseen circumstances, most significantly that of the global pandemic of COVID-19. School closures necessitated a readjustment to the equal balance between interrogating ability-grouped and mixed-attainment reading that was planned. Since schools closed four weeks after mixed-attainment reading was introduced at St Jude's and the week it was due to be introduced at Fairfield, the nature of inquiry into mixed-attainment reading had to change. There were fewer children involved in mixed-attainment reading because of the school closures, and this limits the conclusions that can be drawn from its introduction. In addition, research methods had to change since I was unable to longitudinally immerse myself in the mixed-attainment context as I had for ability-grouped reading. This reduced the volume of multisensory data on children's experience of mixed-attainment reading.

Despite these limitations, the study produced an original contribution to understanding how reading hierarchies, particularly around ability-grouped reading, expand and constrain children's experience, and what might disrupt these hierarchies in the interests of social equity. I advocate taking a reflexive stance towards literacy pedagogy that involves noticing when a pedagogical action exacerbates inequality. This turn to noticing rather than 'implementing' could be powerful in heralding equitable pedagogical changes. Although the study made an original contribution to scholarly knowledge, its usefulness will, I believe, be measured more in the field of practice and policy. My hope is that practitioners, teacher educators and policymakers use this book to inspire a turn towards reflexivity in noticing and disrupting conditions that constrain children's reading lives. Part of this disruption could be experimentation with mixed-attainment reading and a turn towards multimodality in children's reading experience.

I must return to the children in these final, final thoughts. Without doubt they have been the most enlightening of teachers in my attempts to answers questions about reading pedagogy and its effects on social equity and children's identity as readers. The empirical originality of the study has produced unique insights into the ways children are agentic in accommodating, resisting and at times transforming the various constraints on their reading lives. The positioning of children as struggling readers has been troubled throughout by close attention to the minutia of their experience, which stressed mobility, even if within constraining conditions. The children have lit up this book with their individual personalities and collective agency, and my last words are words of thanks to them.

Note

1 Although I highlighted the stigmatising issues with placing children in their first two years of learning English in the so-called bottom reading group, their *reading fluency* in English, and that of others who spoke English in addition to other languages, *did* match that of their group placement, either in the 'top', 'middle' or 'bottom' group.

References

Albright, J. (2010). Problematics and generative possibilities. In J. Albright & A. Luke (Eds.), *Pierre Bourdieu and literacy education*. Routledge.

Anderson, J., Anderson, A., Lynch, J., & Shapiro, J. (2003). Storybook reading in a multicultural society: Critical perspectives. In A. V. Kleeck, S. A. Stahl, & U. B. Bauer (Eds.), *On reading books to children*. Routledge.

Blaisdell, C. (2019). Participatory work with young children: The trouble and transformation of age-based hierarchies. *Children's Geographies*, 17(3), 278–290. https://doi.org/10.1080/14733285.2018.1492703

Boaler, J. (2005). The 'psychological prisons' from which they never escaped: The role of ability grouping in reproducing social class inequalities. *Forum*, 47(2), 125–134. Symposium Journals.

Bourdieu, P. (1973). Cultural reproduction and social reproduction. In R. Brown (Ed.), *Knowledge, education, and cultural change* (pp. 56–68). Tavistock Publications.

Bourdieu, P. (1984). *Distinction: A social critique of the judgement of taste*. Routledge & Kegan Paul.

Bourdieu, P. (1986). The forms of capital. In J. Richardson (Ed.), *Handbook for theory and research for the sociology of education*. Greenwood Press.

Bourdieu, P. (1996). *The state nobility*. Polity Press.

Bourdieu, P., & Accardo, A. (1999). *The weight of the world: Social suffering in contemporary society*. Stanford University Press.
Bourdieu, P., & Passeron, J.-C. (1979). *The inheritors: French students and their relation to culture*. University of Chicago Press.
Bourdieu, P., & Passeron, J. C. (1990). *Reproduction in education, society and culture*. SAGE.
Christensen, P. M., James, A., & Dawsonera. (2008). *Research with children: Perspectives and practices* (2nd ed.). Routledge.
Clark, C., & Rumbold, K. (2006). *Reading for pleasure: A research overview*. National Literacy Trust.
CLPE. (2022). *Reflecting realities: Survey of ethnic representation within UK children's literature 2017–2021*. https://clpe.org.uk/research/clpe-reflecting-realities-survey-ethnic-representation-within-uk-childrens-literature-2017
Collinson, C. (2012). Dyslexics in time machines and alternate realities: thought experiments on the existence of dyslexics, 'dyslexia' and 'Lexism'. *British Journal of Special Education*, 39(2), 63–70. https://doi.org/10.1111/j.1467-8578.2012.00538.x
Collinson, C. (2020). Ordinary language use and the social construction of dyslexia. *Disability & Society*, 35(6), 993–1006. https://doi.org/10.1080/09687599.2019.1669432
Costa, C., & Murphy, M. (2015). *Bourdieu, Habitus and social research: The art of application*. Palgrave Macmillan.
Cunningham, P. M., Hall, D. P., & Defee, M. (1998). Nonability-grouped, multilevel instruction: Eight years later. *Reading Teacher*, 51(8), 652–664.
Cremin, T. (2019). Reading communities: Why, what and how? *NATE Primary Matters Magazine, Summer*.
Cremin, T., Mottram, M., Collins, F. M., Powell, S., & Safford, K. (2014). *Building communities of engaged readers: Reading for pleasure*. Routledge
Department for Education and Employment. (1998). *The National Literacy Strategy: Framework for teaching*. DfEE.
Duckworth, V. (2013). *Learning trajectories, violence and empowerment amongst adult basic skills learners*. Routledge.
Fountas, I.C., & Pinnell, G. S. (1998). *Guided reading: Good first teaching for all children*. Heinemann.
Francis, B., Archer, L., Hodgen, J., Pepper, D., Taylor, B. & Travers M. (2017). Exploring the relative lack of impact of research on 'ability grouping' in England: A discourse analytic account. *Cambridge Journal of Education*, 47(1), 1–17.
Francis, B., & Tereshchenko, A. (2020). *Reassessing ability grouping: Improving practice for equity and attainment*. Routledge.
Gillborn, D. (2010). Reform, racism and the centrality of whiteness: Assessment, ability and the 'new eugenics'. *Irish Educational Studies*, 29(3), 231–252.
Gillborn, D., Bhopal, K., Crawford, C., Demack, S., Gholami, R., Kitching, K., Kiwan, D., & Warmington, P. (2021). *Evidence for the commission on race and ethnic disparities*. University of Birmingham CRRE. https://doi.org/10.25500/epapers.bham.00003389
Hamilton, D. M. (2016). *Postmodern picturebooks, gender, and reading difficulties: A phenomenological exploration of one boy's experiences*. State University of New York at Alabama. https://www.proquest.com/docview/1823568727?fromopenview=true&pq-origsite=gscholar
Hempel-Jorgensen, A., Cremin, T., Harris, D., & Chamberlain, L. (2018). Pedagogy for reading for pleasure in low socio-economic primary schools: Beyond 'pedagogy of poverty'? *Literacy*, 52(2), 86–94. https://doi.org/10.1111/lit.12157

Hobsbaum, A., Gamble, N., & Reedy, D. (2006). *Guiding reading: A handbook for teaching guided reading at key stage 2*. Institute of Education, University of London.

Jewitt, C. (2008). Multimodality and literacy in school classrooms. *Review of Research in Education*, 32(1), 241–267. https://doi.org/10.3102/0091732x07310586

Lareau, A. (2011). *Unequal childhoods: Class, race, and family life*. University of California Press.

Lawler, S., & Close, J. (2014). Blaming working-class parents for inequality lets our rampantly unequal society off the hook. The Conversation. http://theconversation.com/blaming-working-class-parents-for-inequality-lets-our-rampantly-unequal-society-off-the-hook-29674

McNay, L. (2004). Agency and experience: Gender as a lived relation. In L. Adkins & B. Skeggs (Eds.), *Feminism after Bourdieu*. Blackwell Publishing.

Moss, G. (2000). Raising boys' attainment in reading: Some principles for intervention. *Reading*, 34(3), 101–106.

Moss, G. (2007). *Literacy and gender: Researching texts, contexts and readers*. Routledge.

Moss, G. (2021). Literacies and social practice: Sociological perspectives on reading research. *Education 3–13*, 49(1), 41–51. https://doi.org/10.1080/03004279.2020.1824701

Narey, M. J. (2017). "Struggling learner"… or struggling teacher?: Questions surrounding teacher development for multimodal language, literacy, and learning. In M. Narey (Ed.), *Multimodal perspectives of language, literacy, and learning in early childhood: The creative and critical "art" of making meaning* (pp. 291–314). Springer.

Pahl, K., & Rowsell, J. (2020). *Living literacies: Literacy for social change*. MIT press.

Punch, S. (2002). Research with children: The same or different from research with adults? *Childhood*, 9(3), 321–341. https://doi.org/10.1177/0907568202009003005

Ramberg, J. (2016). The extent of ability grouping in Swedish upper secondary schools: A national survey. *International Journal of Inclusive Education*, 20(7), 685–710. https://doi.org/10.1080/13603116.2014.929187

Reay, D. (1995). 'They employ cleaners to do that': Habitus in the primary classroom. *British Journal of Sociology of Education*, 16(3), 353–371. https://doi.org/10.1080/0142569950160305

Reay, D. (2002). Shaun's story: Troubling discourses of white working-class masculinities. *Gender and Education*, 14(3), 221–234.

Reay, D. (2004). Gendering Bourdieu's concept of capitals?: Emotional capital, women and social class. In L. Adkins & B. Skeggs (Eds.), *Feminism after Bourdieu*. Blackwell Publishing.

Reay, D. (2017). *Miseducation: Inequality, education and the working classes*. Policy Press.

Renold, E. (2004). *Girls, boys and junior sexualities: Exploring children's gender and sexual relations in the primary school*. Routledge.

Scherer, L. (2016). 'I am not clever, they are cleverer than us': Children reading in the primary school. *British Journal of Sociology of Education*, 37(3), 389–407. https://doi.org/10.1080/01425692.2014.948989

Stuckey, J. E. (1991). *The violence of literacy*. Vintage.

Taylor, Y. (2009). *Lesbian and gay parenting: Securing social and educational capital*. Palgrave Macmillan.

Williams, B. T. (2017). *Literacy practices and perceptions of agency: Composing identities*. Routledge.

APPENDIX 1

Explanation and Example of a Running Reading Record

The running reading record, also termed 'running record', was devised as a diagnostic and assessment tool for reading by Marie Clay (e.g., 1993), the founder of the Reading Recovery Programme in New Zealand. It is still used extensively, including in the UK, particularly by practitioners who believe that readers use (and should be taught) a combination of semantic, syntactic and graphophonic cues to decipher words and maintain sense of what they read (Bodman & Franklin, 2014).

One of the uses of the running record is to locate which level of text a child can read at between 90 and 95% accuracy. This level of word accuracy is considered to be the optimum level for children to maintain sense of what they read and still be challenged in terms of developing their reading. To ascertain the level of accuracy, the child reads an extract and the adult ticks every time they read a word accurately, as in the example below. If a word is read inaccurately the word from the book is entered and the child's attempt (called a 'miscue') is written above. The percentage accuracy is worked by doing a calculation from the number of miscues in relation to the overall words read. Miscues can also give insight into the cues that a child is using and underusing, e.g., if a miscue makes sense but does not resemble the word, e.g., reading 'car' when the word is 'volvo', this could indicate that the child is using semantic and syntactic cues but underusing graphophonic cues when reading.

I used running records at Fairfield, but not St Jude's, because I perceived a mismatch between some children's level of fluency, book level and group position that I wanted to explore (on reflection I should also have conducted

178 Appendix 1

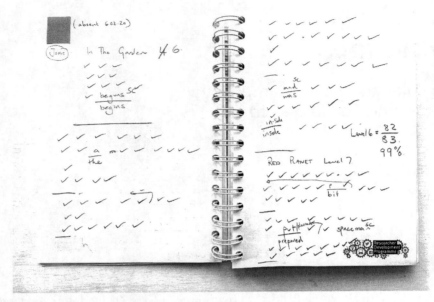

FIGURE 9.1 Running reading record conducted with Jamie, Fairfield, Kelvin, 1 of 3. Image by the author.

running records at St Jude's). Such a mismatch was evident when I conducted a running record with Jamie (working class, White, Scottish, P3, Fairfield), who was in the 'bottom' reading group (see Figures 9.1, 9.2 and 9.3). He told me that he had been reading Level 2 books for two years and was still on Level 2. When I did the running records, it was evident that he could in fact read Level 7 books with 97% accuracy and Level 8 books with 90% accuracy. From his miscues, and his comments while reading, it was clear that he was engaged and able to maintain sense of what he read at Level 8. This suggests he could have confidently read with the 'middle' reading group and was therefore misallocated to the 'bottom' group on the basis of fluency. His example was atypical of the running records conducted with the class, which for most pupils showed a good match between their level of fluency, their reading book and group.

Appendix 1 **179**

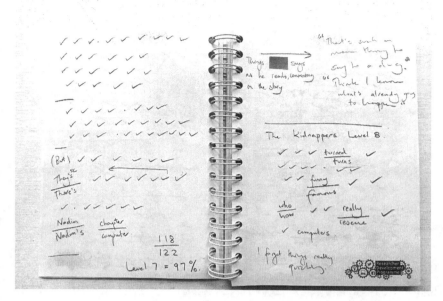

FIGURE 9.2 Running reading record conducted with Jamie, Fairfield, Kelvin, 2 of 3. Image by the author.

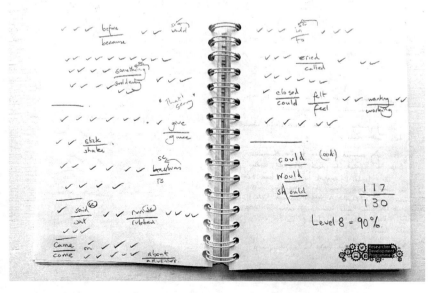

FIGURE 9.3 Running reading record conducted with Jamie, Fairfield, Kelvin, 3 of 3. Image by the author.

APPENDIX 2

Reading café picturebook selection centring and celebrating the lives of Children and Families of Colour

Fiction:

Beaty, A. & Roberts, D. (2016). *Ada Twist, Scientist*. Abrams Books for Young Readers.
Becker, H. & Phumiruk, D. (2021). *Counting on Katherine: How Katherine Johnson Put Astronauts on the Moon*. Macmillan Children's Books.
Byron, N. & Adeola, D. (2019). *Look Up*. Puffin.
Cooke, T. & Oxenbury, H. (2019) *So Much*. Walker Books.
de la Peña, M. & Robinson, C. (2015) *Last Stop on Market Street*. Puffin.
de la Peña, M. & Robinson , C. (2022). *Milo Imagines the World* Two Hoots.
Love, J. (2019). *Julian is a Mermaid*. Walker Books.
Mistry, R. & Mistry, N. (2002) *The Swirling Hijaab*. Mantra Lingua.
Morris, J. & Abdollahi, E. (2019). *The Secret of the Tattered Shoes*. Tiny Owl Publishing.
Muhammad, I., Ali, S,K. & Aly, H. (2020) *The Proudest Blue: A Story of Hijab and Family*. Walker Books.
Shireen, N. (2018). *Billy and the Beast*. Jonathan Cape.
Steptoe, J. (1997). *Mufaro's Beautiful Daughters*. Puffin.
Yousafzai, M. & Kerascoët (2019). *Malala's Magic Pencil*. Puffin.

Non-fiction:

Adeola, D. (2021). *Hey You*. Puffin.
Alexander, K. & Nelson, K. (2020). *The Undefeated*. Andersen Press.
Robert, N.b. & Mayo, D. (2005). *Journey through Islamic Art*. Mantra Lingua.
Steptoe, J. (2016). *Radiant Child: the story of young artist Jean-Michel-Basquiat*. Little Brown and Company.

INDEX

ability-grouped reading 102; appreciation for 69–75; and class habitus 39; different teaching strategies used 96; and economically poor children 30; elite positioning in the 'top' reading group 75–79; emotional dispositions attached to different reading groups 77–78; inertia within 96–97; intelligence and membership of the 'top' reading group, association 77; misallocation to 97–98; reproduces social inequality 167; rupture to classed allocation 108; social inequality reproduced in 31; stigmatised positioning in 84, 85
ability grouping 30, 32–35; and achievement 34–35; and challenging social inequity 29; classed and racialised nature of placement 99; form of class labelling 39; inertia 96, 110, 169; and linguistically minoritised children; practitioners' and policy makers' attachment to 140; stigmatisation 82
affect/ive 63, 131; and ethnography 5; and gendered identities 82; and mixed-attainment reading 146; and reading 32, 47, 55, 58, 64, 74, 107; and working-class feminist academics 8; *see also* emotion
affective turn 14, 36–37

Ahmed, S. 36
Anderson, J. 168
Archie's War 156

Black supplementary schools 130
Blyton, E. 7
book blethers 50
'bottom' reading group *see* ability-grouped reading
Bourdieu, P. 25, 39, 164; class still matters 164; conceptual tools 24–26; 'the cultural arbitrary', concept of 13, 57–58, 126, 132; cultural capital, concept of 26; *distinction*, concept of 12, 68, 76; and dominant literacy 157, 171; "doxa" 75; powerful fields 100; school system reproducing middle-class cultural advantage 106; social capital, concept of 81; stretching his notion of *distinction making* 150; on symbolic violence 26, 58, 100, 126, 132, 171; *see also* cultural capital; habitus; legitimacy; social capital
Bourdieusian conceptualisation of class 4

Chambers, A. 50
Chapman, S. 127
class 23–24; in ability-grouped reading 167; and ability groups 29, 99; classed advantage and disadvantage

17; classed cultural exclusion from books 129; classed outcomes in reading attainment 31; classed patterns of lifestyle 100; classed, raced and gendered stereotypes 32, 35; class habitus 25, 39; as lived experience 13; operates relationally 26; objective markers of 27; and Scots language 40n4
Clay, M. 177
Colby, G. T. 34
Collinson, C. 124–126, 130, 135, 172; *see also* lexism
communities of readers/reading communities 89, 149, 167
computer games 3, 6, 50, 53, 55, 72, 84, 103; Minecraft 71; online gamer 119; *two-player tycoon* 120
concerted cultivation 16–17, 104–106, 109, 110, 168
COVID 19 6–8, 18n6, 173
Cremin, T. 50, 148, 149
critical disability theory 125
cultural capital 37, 77, 100, 101, 135, 140, 168
"cultures of communication", children's 5
Cunningham, P. M. 31–32; and mixed-attainment reading 39, 149
Curriculum for Excellence 30

Davis, S. A. 30, 31
DiAngelo, R. 8
Dog Man 52, 86, 147–148
Duckworth, V. 38, 79
Duntro, E. 37

Eddo-Lodge, R. 8
Education Endowment Foundation (EEF) 34, 41n16
Ehret, C. 39, 64, 131
Eliot, G. 11
emotion: and affect 36, 131; in children's relationship with reading 58; emotionally supportive friendship and reading 80, 89; emotional work in the face of stigmatised positioning 84–86; and literacy 37, 38, 79; parents' emotions and reading 101; and reading difficulties 120, 129, 132; reading and emotional engagement 115; and reading groups 63, 77, 82; social and personal elements of 61
emotional capital 80, 81
English as an additional language 28, 72, 85, 95, 98; *see also* Polish ; Slovak; Urdu
ethnicity 99, 124; *see also* race
ethnography 5, 9, 47

Four Block Framework *see* Cunningham, P. M.
Francis, B. 32
friendship 6, 149, 166; and outsiders to White, Scottish, English-speaking norms of the classroom 109; and reading 79–81, 89, 111, 147, 148, 151, 167, 171

gender 3–5; ability grouping and gendered stereotypes 32; and bonding through reading 79–80; boys and reading 36, 57, 63, 88; enacting hegemonic masculinities 88; gendered identities 82; masculinised enactments 84–85; and reactions to being positioned by reading groups 82; reading regarded as feminine 129; *see also* Moss
Goffman, E. 85, 88
Grant, L. 31
guided reading 15, 16, 29, 30, 32, 88, 141, 163

habitus 25, 38, 39, 100
Haller, E. J 30, 31
Hamilton, D. M. 157
Hamilton, L. 30
Hardy, T. 7
Heath, S. B. 14, 38, 104–105
Hempel-Jorgensen, A. 85, 147
Hermelin 49–50

inside-text talk 148

Joseph-Salisbury, R. 33

Kabuto, B. 121
Kirk, L. 127–128, 134
Kisuule, V. 10
knowledge economy 16, 28–29, 109, 159, 172; and knowledge-based economies 135

Kulik, C.-L. C. 34–35
Kulik, J. A. 34–35

Lareau, A. 28, 33, 102–105, 107, 108; see also concerted cultivation
Leander, K. M. 39, 58, 131
Learned, J. E. 53, 86, 96
legitimacy 39, 57; and reading 77, 126, 168
lexism 124–126, 130, 157, 172
literacy: and the affective turn 14, 37, 131; and attainment in high-poverty contexts 32; classed patterns 100; dominating position of print literacy 134; literacy capital 101, 109; moral panics 29; multimodal 159; role in social positioning 163; and stigmatisation 36
Little Mouse's Big Book of Fears 59, 61, 62
living literacies 14
Lou, Y. 34

Mantel, H. 7
Marx, K. 26
Maungedzo, R. 157
McDonald, J. W. 154
McGarvey, D. 129
McKenzie, L. 25
McNay, L. 25
McQueen, S. 129–130, 132
middle class: assumptions 5; Black middle-class parents 26, 34, 109; book reading 64, 103, 105; in higher groups, children 30, 99; ideas of natural superiority 117; literacy habits 13; parents influencing school policy 33–34, 36; and reading difficulties 135; White middle-class representation in children's literature 172; see also concerted cultivation
mixed-attainment: settings 33, 34; teaching 29; see also mixed-attainment reading
mixed-attainment reading 3, 4, 6–8, 31–32, 140–151
Moss, G. 36, 57, 63, 82, 85, 88, 154, 166, 167
Mr Men books 80, 103
multimodal/ity 120, 135, 156–157, 159, 171, 172

narrative portraits, concept of 9, 47–48; A Narrative Portrait 48–49, 51–56, 58–60, 70–71, 83–84, 107, 118–120; a narrative portrait of mixed-attainment reading 141–143; and thematic analysis 10, 165
National Literacy Strategy 29
National Literacy Trust 101
neoliberalism/neoliberal 11, 16, 24, 25, 29, 40, 133
Newfield, D. 157

Oakes, J. 35
O'Hara, P. 30
orthography 94, 123, 125, 130; standard and non-standard 10

Pahl, K. 14, 38
pandemic 57, 80, 100, 139–141, 149, 158, 170, 173; and post-pandemic 144, 147, 151; and pre-pandemic 57; see also COVID 19
parents 4; and ability grouping (influencing) 30, 33, 35, 36; availability to read with (child) 100; Black Caribbean middle-class parents 26, 34; children as inheritors of parental capital 68, 77, 102, 165; and "concerted cultivation" 104, 110; deficit views of working-class parents 99; and natural growth 108; and seeking advantage 16
Penney, D. 33
picturebooks see reading material
Plummer, K. 133
Polish 4, 51, 65, 85
poverty-related attainment gap 35, 40n1; and literacy 53, 149
Power of Reading Project 48
print, medium of 29, 32, 58, 59, 104, 171
pseudonyms 1, 3, 90
Pugs of the Frozen North 55, 121, 126, 132
Pupil Equity Fund 27, 40n1
Puzio, K. 34

race 11; and (ability) groups 29, 35; capitalisation (of terms) 18n4; and capitals 26, 37; and class 10, 116; class/ed, race/d, gender/ed, intersections 22, 32, 35, 94, 99; and diverse literacies 157; inequalities around class, race and gender 47; and misplacement of Black and other pupils from minoritised ethic

groups to lower sets 169; negative stereotyping of Black pupils 33; and privileging of Whiteness 173; race and religion 71; and reading groups 99, 109; read(ing) with young children 103; in reading encounters 5; recollections of childhood reading difficulties 127; social construction of 25
Rankine, C. 71
reading café 5, 52, 154–156
reading communities *see* communities of readers
reading development, theoretical understandings 14–15; and motivation 15, 30, 110, 149; and notions of intelligence 38; and vocabulary 96, 110, 145, 146; *see also living literacies* ; multimodality
reading difficulties 120; autoethnographic accounts 116, 128; developmental dyslexia 124–126; and emotional stress 129, 132; interpretive sophistication 122; in mixed-attainment reading 151–153; and poverty-related stress 131; socially and affectively situated 126–130
reading for pleasure (pedagogy) 85, 147
reading groups, hierarchical *see* ability-grouped reading
reading helpers, Pixies 2, 87; and hierarchy 2–3
reading material: annuals 153; book geography 104; chapter books/novels 74, 76, 81–82, 117–118, 148, 150, 154; children-authored books 155; comic books 104, 118, 120, 126, 147; comics 15, 64, 153, 155; culturally resonant texts 128; embroidered cloth that tells stories 157; graphic novel 118, 153; information books 153; manuals 155; picturebooks 76, 151, 153–156, 172; poetry 153, 157; postmodern picturebooks 157; reading-related games 155
reading scheme 60, 69, 82, 96, 97, 106, 110, 118, 119, 146, 147, 150
reads/reading aloud, teacher 48, 96, 122, 141
Reay, D. 9, 11, 33–34, 94, 109, 165; bottom sets 38; emotional capital 81; habitus 39; researching with children and young people 35–36; "Shaun's Story" 129
Renold, E. 87; and "doing boy" or "doing girl" 82, 166
research project 4–10; research questions 40; *see also* COVID 19
Rosen, H. 8
Rothenberg, J. 31
Rowsell, J. 14, 38
running reading records 6, 90n2, 97, 146, 177–179

Savage, M. 4, 22, 27
Scherer, L. 38
Scots (language) 10, 28, 40n4, 40n6
self-portraits 9
Skeggs, B. 12–13, 26, 27
Slavin, R. E. 33, 34
Slovak 4, 109
social capital 79–81, 84, 89, 167
Social Mobility Commission 33
Steedman, C. 38
Stuart, D. 37, 41n18, 128
Stuckey, J. E. 157, 171

Taylor, Y. 33, 38
Ten Things I Can Do to help My World 59
Tereshchenko, A. 32
'top' reading group *see* ability-grouped reading
transcription 10
The True Story of the Three Little Pigs 155
Tyler, I. 100

Urdu 4, 65, 70–71

Wilkinson, S. D. 33
Williams, B. 37–38
working-class: and 'bottom' reading group 94, 97, 110, 167; celebration of 11; deficit views/portrayals of 13, 53, 55, 57–58, 99–100; ingenuity and humour 25; feminist academics 8; in lower positioned groups 35; "natural growth" (in child-rearing) 107–109; parents more likely to defer to teachers 33; personal reflection 11–14; and reading 99, 129, 168; and Scots 40n4; susceptible to low teacher expectations 97